NORTHUS SHETLAND CLASSICS

‡

Northus Shetland Classics is a series of reprints of some of the keystones of Shetland's literature. The series has been established under the guiding eye of noted poet and novelist Robert Alan Jamieson, and operates with the assistance of an advisory group of local academics and writers. Each volume has an introduction by an expert. Works in Shetlandic and English, and those which combine the two, will be included. The series is divided into four streams:

Poyims / Poetry

Alting / Non-Fiction

Myndins / Memoir

Yarns / Fiction

SUBSCRIBERS

This series could not have been published without the invaluable assistance of those who subscribed via a crowdfunding platform. The series editor and publisher would like to acknowledge their help with their heartfelt thanks, and, in time-honoured tradition, with public salutation in the following list:

Hazel Anderson; Helen Bowell; Eileen Brooke-Freeman; Wilma Cluness; Eleanor Coghill; Laura Dalgarno-Platt; Christine de Luca; Linda Grains; Alistair Hamilton; John Hunter; Kareen Hunter; Nancy Hunter; Joanne Jamieson; Karen Jamieson; Catherine Jeromson; Angus Johnson; Ingri Johnson; June Johnson; Magnus Laurenson; Morag McGill; Duncan McLean; Paul Manson; Graham March; Tim Morrison; Jim & Rosabel Nicolson; Elizabeth Park; Catherine Post; Neil Ritch; Margaret Roberts; Sheila Robertson; Carla Sassi; Magnus Shearer; Jane Shouesmith-Black; Marina Sinclair; Beryl Smith; Dale Smith; Ingrid Smith; Janet Smith; Jen Stout; Marsali Taylor; Ann & Ian Thomson; Margaret Tong; Kenny Watt; Elizabeth Williamson.

Robert Alan Jamieson & Mike Walmer, November 2021

LETTERS ON SHETLAND

‡

Northus Shetland Classics

Alting

TITLES IN THIS SERIES

already published

Tang J. J. Haldane Burgess

Broken Lights Basil Ramsay Anderson

Foula: Island West of the Sun Sheila Gear

Letters on Shetland Peter Jamieson

forthcoming

Rock-Bound Jessie Saxby

CLIFF: WATNESS   *J. Peterson*

Frontispiece

LETTERS ON SHETLAND

by

PETER JAMIESON

‡

introduced by

Brian Smith

NORTHUS
SHETLAND
CLASSICS

Letters on Shetland first published 1949 by The Moray Press, Edinburgh

© Peter Jamieson 1949

Introduction first published in this edition

Introduction © Brian Smith 2021

This edition published 2021 by

Michael Walmer

North House

Melby

Sandness

Shetland, ZE2 9PL

ISBN 978-0-6452440-1-4 paperback

> aald style of reckoning, so it was still da
> munt a Merch with them.

and:

> At about eight o'clock on Saturday night
> it was showery, but not too cold. One of
> the neighbour women was 'only
> gjaa'nta'stack, ida sooth hill!' The crofter
> laughed, and shook his head: 'Yah, her!
> Diss is juist her time a night!'

For a superb example of Peter's style it is
worth looking at his short story 'A Spring Day
on the Hill', published in *Penguin New Writing 18*
in 1944 (reprinted in the *New Shetlander* in
2016). It too was based around that stay in
Collafirth.

Despite his early departure from school,
Peter was a fine writer. For almost all his life he
depended on his pen to make a living. He
wrote a stream of articles for journals far and
wide, and he encouraged other Shetlanders to
do the same. The Second World War didn't
interfere with his literary activities: it brought
new scenes and faces to Lerwick to

contemplate and write about. There is a vivid account of the first months of the war in chapter III.

During the war years he edited a handwritten circulating journal, passed around from writer to writer. Stella Smith, later Sutherland, and Tom Henderson, were contributors. Peter wanted hard thinking about Shetland and its culture, and in 1947 he founded the *New Shetlander*, a literary and political journal where such thinking might be featured. He edited it until 1956.

If we want to understand the *New Shetlander*, and *Letters on Shetland*, we must study Peter Jamieson's political formation. His brother Robert had been a member of the British Socialist Party before the First World War. There were dozens of activists in Lerwick at that time. They thought that the socialist commonwealth was just round the corner. They and their ideas inspired Peter for the rest of his life.

Then war and eventually depression came. Robert died in France in 1918. For decades the

INTRODUCTION

"In your letter you ask to be told 'all about Shetland!'"

So Peter Jamieson addressed the fictitious* recipient of his *Letters on Shetland*, published by The Moray Press in 1949. It was Peter's second book. His first, *The Viking Isles* (1933), overwritten and sentimental, had got a ferocious reception locally. 'Letters' is a far more mature work. His friend John Stewart said that it portrayed the 'spirit' of the islands better than any other book.

Peter Andrew Jamieson was born at 21 St Magnus Street, Lerwick, in September 1898. He lived at that address for the rest of his life. He was the fifth child and third son of Barbara Ann Williamson, a native of Lunnasting, and James Jamieson, a seaman from Papa Stour.

Peter left school when he was 15, and went to stay for a while with relatives of his mother at the isolated district of Collafirth in Delting.

at the isolated district of Collafirth in Delting. He was a town boy, through and through, but he got a taste for rural life. During the Second World War, planning a novel, he stayed at Collafirth again. There is an account of that sojourn in chapters XII and XIV of 'Letters'. They are a good example of Peter's impressionistic writing: the sentimentality of *The Viking Isles* has disappeared.

> On the top of the hill, [he says,] the wind pressed hard against the car … There seemed no sign of life in the place. The few sheep by the roadside looked weak and poor-amos … after the lang hard winter.

His use of the word 'poor-amos' illustrates another aspect of Peter's writing: his habit, unique at that date, of combining English and Shetland dialect, often in a single sentence. He wasn't afflicted with the idea, common at the time, that no-one outside the islands could understand Shetland speech.

Thus:

> It was the first week of Aaprile, but here in the outlying hills the folk held by da

world looked far more sombre. Peter dabbled in new socialist currents. Like many others he welcomed the Soviet revolution, while playing an active part in the Labour Party in Lerwick from 1924 onwards. On the eve of the Second World War he and others formed a branch of the Communist Party in Lerwick, which didn't last. Then in 1945 he threw himself into Prophet Smith's campaign to become a Labour member of parliament for Orkney and Shetland. Chapter XVI of 'Letters' is an account of all these events, from the heyday of the British Socialist Party up to the post-war activities of the Labour Party. Chapter XVIII is based on the Shetland Labour Party's plan in 1944 to transform the local economy and create - the last words of the book —"a Shetland People's Co-operative Society".

Peter Jamieson was one of Shetland's great autodidacts. In chapter VII of 'Letters' he writes about Shetland's 'crofter-scholars', men like Laurence Williamson of Mid Yell, "the tall, grey-blue eyed, rosy-cheeked man who tilled the rigs of the 'toon a Gairdie'". His portrait of

Williamson, based on original manuscripts and letters, is very vivid.

Throughout his life Peter carried on an extensive correspondence with Shetlanders and scholars all over the world. He used material acquired in that way to make his own work more lively and informative. A highlight of 'Letters', in chapter IX, are two lengthy accounts of life at sea, sent to him by Prophet Smith and Tom Henderson. Peter didn't name them or apparently ask their permission. Prophet forgave him, and went on to be a co-founder of the *New Shetlander*, but Tom was furious. Laughton Johnston has discussed the unfortunate event, and the relationship between Peter and Tom, in his recent work *Tom Henderson: The Seaman who Founded a Museum* (2021).

I knew Peter well during the last ten years of his life. He was shy, and by all accounts had always been shy. He lived with his brothers Willie and Jeemsie; when they died, in 1970 and 1975, he stayed at 21 St Magnus Street on his own. During his whole life Peter lived in poverty. The house was crammed with socialist journals and newspapers and books: that was where the money went.

Peter Jamieson died suddenly in May 1976. His *Letters on Shetland*, his *New Shetlander*, and his extensive manuscripts and letters (now in the Shetland Archives) are full of treasure.

BRIAN SMITH

Weisdale, October 2021.

*PUBLISHER'S NOTE - Strict probity requires mention of the fact that this contention regarding the fictional nature of the recipient of these 'letters' is a conclusion based upon absence of evidence, rather than its presence. The postulation arises from the introducer's examination of the Peter Jamieson archive at the Shetland Museum and Archives. He found no evidence of the correspondence there, and came to the interpretation that is outlined here. This opinion was augmented by personal knowledge of the author. Jamieson asserts to the contrary in his Author's Note, which follows — the introducer sees this as a literary device. Perhaps further scholarly research on Jamieson will in future confirm the truth of this thesis, or indeed otherwise. MW.

AUTHOR'S NOTE

These letters were written from time to time as opportunity arose. Addressed to a friend outside Shetland they may prove of interest to other readers.

Mr. L. G. Johnson of Setter, Mid Yell, Shetland, is thanked for his kind permission to transcribe and publish material from the manuscripts of the late Laurence Williamson of Gairdie, Mid Yell.

PETER JAMIESON.

Lerwick,
  Shetland.
    August 1948.

LIST OF ILLUSTRATIONS

CHAPTER I

In your letter you ask to be told "all about Shetland!"
Well, this is a pretty big order, since it would be difficult
for anyone to tell "all about" the northern British Isles.
Since, however, you seem desirous of knowing something
about the islands and their people, perhaps what is
written here may be of interest.

Yes, as you say, the group is sometimes called "the
hundred isles." You would, however, probably find well
over two hundred "isles," if small rocks and stacks and
bare skerries can be called isles. They stretch from the
"out-stacks" at Flugga in the north to Fair Isle in the
south. To round off the description from "east to west,"
one can say "from Skerries in the east to Foula in the
west."

The Skerries are low-lying isles with very little soil and
few crofts. Their men are among Shetland's finest fishermen, so that "everything that goes in their mouths," and
everything that "goes on their backs," is the result of a
never-ending struggle on the unkind sea. Life in Shetland
for most folk is a constant struggle with adverse natural,
social and economic conditions, but it is probably hardest
in the Skerries and similar out-lying isles.

The Skerries share with Fetlar, a large fertile isle
farther to the north, the distinction of being the islands
of Shetland lying nearest to Norway. There is a tradition
in Fetlar that it was the first place in Shetland to be
settled from the Scandinavian countries, probably by
peasant folk from western and south-western Norway.
This is said by scholars to have been about the seventh
or eighth centuries. Finnie, or Funzie, in Fetlar, is said
to have been the place where "the first Danish ship
came. . . ."

Out of this "hundred isles" barely twenty are inhabited.
The extreme north and south stretch of the archipelago is

about 70 miles, the largest isle, the Mainland, being 54 miles from north to south. It is roughly 21 miles at its widest from east to west.

Fair Isle, one of the "oot-isles," is the first Shetland isle the traveller from the "south" sees as the mail-boat steams north. It is termed "the Isle," and lies roughly mid-way between Orkney and Shetland. Lying in the track of the great spring and autumn migrations the isle is a noted resting-place for birds. Like the rest of Shetland, its rocky coast and heathery hills make homes for many resident birds.

The Mainland has the greater part of the population. Lerwick, the only town, is on the eastern central part of the Mainland, with a population of about 6000.

The North Isles are the next in importance, called Yell, Unst and Fetlar. They lie roughly north-east of the Mainland, with Unst the most northerly.

Yell Sound separates Yell from the Mainland, Bluemull Sound, Unst from Yell, and Colgrave Sound, Fetlar from Yell. Yell and Bluemull Sounds are "never at peace," as very rapid tides run through them. There are several isles in Yell Sound, including Samphrey, whose little kirkyard is said to have few men buried in it, as, according to the tradition, "Samphrey men are taken by the sea." It used to be peopled by fishermen and their families but gradually became depopulated, being used now for grazing sheep. In 1832 six Samphrey men managed to reach Norway when the great gale arose that overtook the sixerns fishing on the haaf. Another Shetland boat reached Norway. The men were very hospitably treated and arrived back home the following spring. The force of the wind was said to have been such that in many places turf dykes were blown over. The sky turned a lurid red. A boat's crew from Whalsay had a remarkable experience. Just when they were thinking their last moments had come a large sailing vessel came in sight. After some difficulty five of the fishermen were got on board, the sixth man meeting his death as he was jumping for the ship. The men were carried to America; being landed at Philadelphia, where they stayed for some months. They at last managed to get a passage in a homeward-bound vessel, reaching Whalsay the following Christmas to find their folk wearing blacks for them. In "the July gale" of 1832 seventeen boats and one hundred and five men were lost.

Bigga is another of the Yell Sound isles, until lately inhabited, but now another "sheep isle." Indeed, under present conditions there seems something like a competition between the sheep and people as to which will claim the greater number of isles. As things are going it would seem as if the sheep are winning.

At Christmas not long ago Bigga came into the news. Headlines in the papers gave prominence to a story that told something of the Shetlander's love of home. Two young seamen from Yell, home on leave, were anxious to reach home in time for Yule. Arriving at Mossbank, they found the ferry-men unwilling to risk the trip across the Sound owing to the stormy weather. It was a Saturday, not far from Yule-day, and the seamen could see the snow-covered hills and dark coast-line of their island home through the haze from the driving sea-spume. It looked a pretty tough crossing, right enough, but used all their lives to handling boats they resolved to risk it in a small open boat.

They got off the Mossbank coast, on the north Mainland, and into the tide-racing, wind-whipped open Sound. They kept on for a bit, but soon found it hard to make any headway. They had got near Bigga, and succeeded in getting ashore just in time, for the wind was rising, bearing icy snow in its teeth. It was bitterly cold, but they came upon the shepherd's hut, with peats ready on the hearth and some paraffin in a lamp. They soon had a fire kindled, and as one of the men had some rations with him they were not troubled by hunger. The bitterness of the cold, for it was hard frost with driving snow, kept them from sleeping. One of them had a fiddle, so to the lively strains of Shetland reels the two seamen whiled away their eventful night on Bigga. Next day a drifter sent to look for them got them off, and Yell was reached that night.

Linga is another of the Sound isles. Its name means "the heather isle." The South Yell folk have names for some of the worst tides that break in the Sound. Some are very fierce with bad weather, the people resembling them to "bitin' grices" or swine. Only seamen with lifelong knowledge of these tides, as well as the tides in other Shetland sounds—as Papa Sound at the west Mainland—can be trusted to handle small craft. Those wanting to "live dangerously," however, need wish for nothing better than sailing an open boat in Yell Sound on a stormy day. A regular ferry service by motor launch is kept up between Yell and the Mainland, the boat often making wide detours to avoid the worst of the tides.

Most folk interested in the north have heard something of Scalloway. This is a village clustered in the shelter of hills at the west side about seven miles from Lerwick. It is the "ancient capital" of Shetland and snuggles at the foot of a long fertile valley, the dale of Tingwall, where near the loch the Norsemen used to hold the Thing, or Shetland parliament. The valley is probably the most fertile in the Mainland, the whole place from the head of the valley at Gott to the water's edge at Scalloway forming one of the "show-places" of the north. During fine summer and autumn weather Tingwall and Scalloway, with the isles in the voe of Scalloway, are ideal holiday places; Scalloway's numerous hotels and boarding-houses, and its fleet of cars, buses and launches, being within easy reach of trout lochs and burns, swimming beaches, bird isles and historic churches, as at Papil in Burra, where recently an ancient carved Celtic stone was discovered. The voe and channel "out-by" are fine boating and fishing places, the wide stretch of water on the west side noted for its haddock grounds being named the Burra Haaf. Tramping or motoring from Lerwick there is

Gestapo. The landings in Norway were mostly all dangerous, and they took toll of many brave Norwegian lives. On two or three occasions some of the smacks came into Shetland voes badly knocked about by Nazi bombs, with men dead and wounded on board. Once, in December 1941, a 55-foot boat had to heave-to off the north of Shetland, and lie there for six days during a severe storm. She pooped a heavy sea off Flugga, and the engine-room was flooded. The storm drove the boat many miles from Shetland, and not till it abated did she reach a Shetland firth. It was a Norwegian boat operating from Scalloway that first sighted the battleship *Bismarck* making for Bergen before going out to the Atlantic. Her movements were thereafter spotted by British aircraft. Scores of thrilling sagas of the underground movement were heard, told in Scalloway homes as the people welcomed the sailors after their hazardous voyages. Verses were written by the Scalloway poet, John J. Hunter, commemorating the defiance of some hunted patriots, and songs of the Motherland "with thy thousand homes" were sung and whistled in the narrow winding streets of "Scalloway Banks."

The "Scalloway Navy" left the port for home for the last time in August 1945, bound for the land they had helped to set free. The wind that fluttered the bright flags on the corvettes and boats as they steamed past Burra soughed and whistled among the gaunt walls of the great castle. Scalloway folk waved a farewell to the men happy to know of Norway's deliverance, yet a little saddened to lose such sterling friends.

The waters beyond Scalloway, with low islands lying one behind the other, entice one's eyes to the sun-glinting sea. Over a dip in the western hills above the village the outline of the "oot-isle" of Foula is seen far on the blue-hazed horizon. It used to be said "see Naples and die," but to stand on Scalloway's Skoard on a sunny day, looking away to Foula and the Atlantic, is a fine experience.

The village of Scalloway was a centre of the Faroe

nothing very out-of-the-ordinary in the way of scenery, although at the "Free Hill" and the Ladies' Drive a mile or two from the town scenes of bustling activity greet one in summer, as here are situated the main peat-banks of the townsfolk. Hundreds of long banks of moor are cut, the peats dried in dykes and heaps, then transported to the town in lorries. The moorland is inclined to be dreary looking, although on days of brilliant sunshine even a Shetland moorland takes on something of beauty. The road between the town and "the aald toon" of Scalloway is well kept, the brig at Fitch having been recently enlarged and capable of sustaining the heaviest traffic. Here in wet weather the Fitch burn roars and rumbles to the sea at Dales Voe, on whose western shore may still be seen some half-score heaps of stones, almost grass-grown. These heaps are all that remain of crofting houses. The crofts were cleared of their tenants during last century, and black-faced sheep put to graze on the ley rigs. Dale is not unattractive, having a very fiord-like appearance, with the long voe creeping in through the land, and high hills on either side. At the top of the western hill the road branches off in two directions at the Windy Grinnd. The north road and west road separate at this spot, its name being well earned, as it always seems to be windy up there. The road to Scalloway runs westward from the Fitch brig, through moorlands where the Scalloway peats are cut, seemingly closed in on both sides by hills, until the ground begins to rise and the Skoard comes in sight. On this height the full beauty of Scalloway and "the Isles" comes into view, lying far down in the fertile green land. The place is sheltered from the north and east winds, and the sun seems to linger longer over the "ancient capital" than elsewhere. Add to this the peculiar fertility of Tingwall and Scalloway soil, and it is not surprising that many rare flowers and shrubs grow there, every house in the village seemingly having a fine garden.

The Skoard is about 200 feet high. The view is entrancing on a fine day. The narrow East Voe lies right below, with the old fishing boat *Silver King* rotting on its western shore. Beyond rises the ruins of Scalloway Castle, standing back from the point of Blackness.

The rugged walls of this castle seem to dominate the whole village. It was put up in the first years of the seventeenth century by order of Earl Patrick Stewart, the Scottish ruler of Shetland at that time. The Earl got his fine mansion built by forced labour, and by levying tribute on the islanders. Patrick was a tyrant, as had been his father, Lord Robert Stewart. Patrick was called to account after the islanders managed to get the story of his oppression to the ears of the Court at Edinburgh. The Earl was executed at the Market Cross, Edinburgh, on 6th February 1615.

Inside the castle there are still to be seen secret passages and cells, in one of which the Earl hid when he was called to give himself up. It is said he might have evaded the officers sent to seize him if he had not been too fond of his pipe, the smoke from which revealed his hiding-place. The iron ring at the top of the square chimney stack, tradition says, was for hanging any of the Shetland udallers (peasant owners) who had tried to rebel against the Earl's harsh decrees.

During the time of the Commonwealth some of Cromwell's soldiers garrisoned Shetland, and some were stationed in the castle. After they left the roof fell in, and the birds began nesting in the walls. The last to live in the tyrant's castle was an old woman, Osla Williamson, about 1810–20. Osla lived in a little room close to the door at the south-east corner.

In April 1940 Hitler's armies invaded Norway. Only 170 miles of sea separated Shetland from the Nazi troops, ready to invade the islands and "restore" them to their ancient Motherland. In the same week some small sea-battered fishing vessels, with torn Norwegian flags at their peaks and exhausted refugees aboard, sailed quietly into Shetland voes. One day in May of that year over a dozen smacks came to Lerwick. At first they made for Catfirth

on the east coast, making this their base, but soon afterwards Scalloway, on the west, was found more convenient.

Some months later Burra folk waiting on Blackness
pier for boats from the isle could not help opening their
eyes in astonishment as they saw small parties of Norske
marines and soldiers carrying long cases from the castle.

Gradually the story leaked out that something like a
measure of poetic justice was being enacted in the quiet
village. The castle of the dreaded Stewart had been turned
into a storehouse for arms and munitions destined for
the Norwegian underground movement. Scalloway folk,
as the war dragged on, had plenty to speak about, but
nothing of the great venture ever leaked out. Ponies
drew carts of goods and weapons down the road from the
Skoard from stores in Lerwick and elsewhere, and sometimes sailors were seen riding bareback on the little ponies
as if they thought they were back in Norway.

With heavy snowfalls the Skoard and other braes
attracted the sailors with their skis, to the wonderment
of the village bairns as they watched the men practising.
More and more Norwegian vessels came to the port;
Norske marines were seen in the streets and around the
castle walls in hundreds. Cars came and went with
important-looking men; and one never-to-be-forgotten
day in October 1943 Crown Prince Olaf came to open
a new slipway at Westshore and decorate sailors for
gallantry.

Corvettes, boats and M.T.B.'s slipped silently from the
Bay on mysterious errands; troops manned the great
batteries of guns at strategic points; Nazi raiders flew over
the place, and the air raid alarm became as familiar a
sound as the crying of the gulls near the herring kilns at
Westshore and Port Arthur. The Scalloway folk soon
became fast friends with the sailors and others engaged
in the task of gun-running to Norway. Young Norske
marines became attracted to the Scalloway lasses, and a
number got married. Some men, at great risk, managed
to get their families from Norway to live in the village.

The Norwegian and Scalloway bairns commingled in happy comradeship in the school playground. Houses sported Norwegian flags in windows and doors, villagers got copies of Hugo's *Norwegian Self-Taught*, and with the aid of their friends, the "Marines," began the study of the language. This in most cases was not very difficult, on account of the Norn basis of the Shetland dialect. One man said, "The Norwegians förstaa me far better whan I spaek da aald wye." ("The Norwegians understand me much better when I speak to them in the old speech.")

This smuggling of arms and other goods, such as provisions and medical requirements, was most intense during the darkest and stormiest time of the year. Small ships had to be used, and in winter and spring scores of these lay moored off Port Arthur, to the west. In the winter of 1941–2 small fishing boats made about sixty voyages to various points between the Lofoten Islands in the north to the southern nesslands of Norway. This meant a round trip of almost 1200 miles.

At first the Germans did not suspect the small vessels to be other than fishing smacks. They often lay near the coast for four or five days on end. The air patrol became severe outside the fishing area. Many vessels had narrow escapes, and after a time they rigged up "Q-ship" armament skilfully disguised as fishing gear. The smacks landed hundreds of tons of stores and numerous agents and instructors for the underground fighters. The air attacks were intensified, however, as the Germans began to suspect something was wrong somewhere. After a time larger vessels, known as submarine chasers, were used in the work, and they carried out one hundred and twenty separate operations on the Norwegian coast. The underground army was organised to help an Allied invasion, and from Scalloway over 500 tons of arms and equipment were sent to them, along with many trained instructors.

Over four hundred people were taken back to Shetland, most being the families of men on the run from the fishing industry in the second half of the nineteenth century when Shetland men went in smacks to the cod grounds at Faroe and Iceland, returning a number of times to ports in Shetland with their catches. These were chiefly cod and ling, which were salted and laid out on beaches for the sun and wind to dry. After the fish were dry they were built up in piles, and then spread out again before being despatched to the markets in Spain and Portugal. Much the same methods of fish-catching and curing obtain in Faroe to-day, Shetland fishermen having instructed the Faroe men in the arts of line-catching fish and Shetland methods of beach-curing. The Shetland industry came to an end in the early years of this century, its place being taken by the herring fishing. The noted Shetlander, Arthur Anderson, who became one of the founders of the P. and O. Steamship Company, started life as a beach boy in Bressay. His employer, Thomas Bolt, used to impress on him the necessity of "doing weel and persevering." Anderson seemingly did both to the best of his ability, as, after some years in the Navy following on his leaving Shetland, he fell in with people prominent in the shipping world, and, mindful of "old Boltie's" advice set about "doing weel," until before long the firm of Wilcox and Anderson had extensive connections. Anderson, for all that, did not forget his home place and the ig-norance and poverty his fellow countrymen were in. He did much to foster education in Shetland by starting the first Shetland paper, endowing a school in Lerwick, and challenging the landed and monied interests in many ways. Without doubt Anderson's name is that of one of the most distinguished Shetlanders of modern times.

The name of the village is derived from the Norse *Skallivaagr*, the "voe of the skallis," or booths of the Thingmen. Its proper pronunciation is Skallawa. The hill rising north-west of the village is the Hill of Berrie, but is more often known as the Gallow Hill. Offenders con-demned to death by the chief court at "Skallawabankis" were executed on this hill. "Skallawabankis" was the

SCALLOWAY

J. Peterson

To face page 16

LANDING AND GUTTING HERRING AT SCALLOWAY

J. Peterson

To face page 17

sloping green banks running north from the castle to near the "Old Ha'." What is called New Street runs from the castle the length of these banks, the base of which is washed by the sea. Witches were also hanged or burned on the Gallow Hill. The last burning of witches on record are those of Barbara Tulloch and her daughter Ellen King. They were both burned in the beginning of the eighteenth century. It is not long since an old man died in the village who could relate traditionary stories of Scalloway and the Gallow Hill, stories of witch-burning he had heard from folk whose forebears had heard them from the lips of people who had actually stood on the hill slopes of Berrie, or on the "bankis," witnessing the dreadful sight.

In 1644 the Court condemned to death Marion Peebles, alias Pardone, "spouse to Swene in Hildiswick," on account of her grievous witchcraft. The full indictment is set out in Hibbert's *A Description of the Shetland Islands.* It begins: "In the first, you the said Marion Peebles, alias Pardone, is Indytit and accusit for the sinful and damnable renouncing of God, your Faith and Baptism, giving and casting of yourself, body and soul, in the hands of the Devil, following, exercising, using and practising of the fearful and damnable craft of Witchcraft, Sorcerie, and Charming, in manner following, viz. In the first, you are Indytit and accusit for coming in the month of [no date given in the source quoted by Hibbert, P. J.] Jmvjc, and thirty years, to the house of John Banks in Turvisetter, and Janet Robertson, his spouse, with a wicked, devilish and malicious intention to cast Witchcraft and Sickness upon them; and missing the said Janet there, for going to Sursetter, where she then was, and after cursing and scolding her, telling her that she should repent what she had done to your daughter and good-son. And for that immediately with the word, ye, by your devilish art of witchcraft, did cast sickness upon the said Janet, who, immediately upon your departure, fell in an extraordinary and unkindly sickness, and lay eight weeks, taking her shours and pains

B

by fits, at midday and midnight, and so continued most
terribly tormented; her said sickness being castin upon her
by your said devilish witchcraft, during the said space,
until the said John Banks came to you and threatened you,
at which time ye gaif him a gullion of silver (2s. *value*)
to hold his peace and conceal the same, promising to him
that nothing should ail his wife. And thereafter, for that
ye sent her ane cheese of the breadth of one loof, composed
by your said devilish art of witchcraft, with ane jinke-
roll, and desiring her the said Janet to eat the same, when
(whereof the said Janet refused to eat), yet immediately
she grew well, but two of her kine died, the said sickness
being casten upon them by your said wicked and devilish
art of witchcraft. . . ."

The indictment ends: "The Assyze being recavit,
sworn and admittit; and, after reading the dittay, and
examination of the panneles thereupon, and having
recavit the depositiunes of divers famous witnesses,
quhilk wer sworne tutching the dittays, proving them, as
lykwayes in consideration of their confessions, and instances markit and set downe in and upon the said
dittayis. They passing out of judgment, and reconsider-
ing the saidis dittayis, togidder with the saidis depositiones
of witnesses, having namit Olla Mansone of Ilesburgh
chancellar; and after examining the hail poyntis and
consultation of the delusions and confessiones of the said
Marion, fyllis hir, that the hail poyntis of ditty are agens
her, boith general and special, except theft of Thomas of
Urabister not provin, and anent Edward Halcro's malt,
quherein they rest clauseure, and

They all in one voice ffylls her of the haill poyntis of
dittay producit, and remittis sentens to the Judges, and
dome to the dempster. In witnes qrof subscribit be the
chancellar. (Signed) Ollaw Magnassone.

Continuis sentence to the morrow xxij Martii 1644.

The Judges adjudges and decerns the pannells to be
taken brought hence to the place of execution to the Hill
of Berrie, and there wyryt at ane stak, and brunt in ashes,

betwix . . . . and 2 afteirnoone, qlk Andro of Offir, dempster, gave for dome."

The site of execution is reputed to have been on a flat grassy space just back from the brow of the steep height. Some years ago a lot of reddish-yellow earth very like peat ash was found underneath the turf on another height about two hundred yards farther back from the grassy level.

The village was the place where William Johnson of Quarff used to live. He was a monumental sculptor with a scientific turn of mind. He worked out some rather original theories and published them in a book called *The Law of Universal Balance: Discovery of the Motive Power in the Heavens: A New Philosophy for the New Century*. In his preface Johnson writes: "It hath been said that authorship would be a fortunate business were it not for the competition of the Dead. At that rate this little effort would be a fortunate one, for as far as I am aware the subject of Balance has never before been treated of. But I had no idea of ever writing anything either on Astronomy or anything else; and, but for some unhappy experiences which will be gathered from the verses appended nothing of the kind would ever have been attempted by me. In order to divert the mind, I began to study inventions, but the man will have better luck than I if his unhappiness is not increased rather than diminished by contact with patent agents and manufacturers of patent inventions. In order to keep clear of these and at the same time to have some elevating study I took up this subject; but by this time I had got to such a state of sleeplessness that I was forced during the night to get up and write down my thoughts, else no more sleep. . . . But here I will state decidedly and distinctly that I do not put forward these theories regarding the creation of the earth and of the solar system as truths. Far from it: it is only a possible theory thought out according to Balance; very much of it can never be ascertained facts. All that I put forward as a fact, is that the planets circle round the Sun according to

Balance. Galileo said 'they move,' and my contention is that the motive power is Balance. If this be so—

> 'When I have dreamed life's mystic dream,
> And shared the common lot;
> This little book may tell a tale,
> That ne'er can be forgot.'"

In his introduction he writes: "Now about the sun's motion and speed through space. Some believe that speed to be about 100,000 miles per hour; others that he travels as fast as light, viz. 691,200,000 miles per hour. Others that 'such a solar motion must necessarily produce a solar aberration, in consequence of which we do not see the stars disposed as they really are, but too much crowded in the region the sun is leaving—too open in that he is approaching,' etc. Now all this theorising about the sun's motion must end in aberration and confusion. But it proves that the modern mind is not satisfied with the Newtonian theory and is feeling after something it finds to be wanting, and that something is, as we believe, a law of Balance. For my contention is that neither sun nor fixed stars (which are just other suns) move at all. They will sway and perhaps circle a little, balancing their own systems, but nothing more. I read somewhere, about a comet going at a tremendous rate of speed as it rounded the sun—the rate of speed was given, but I forget it now —and then when the comet got away back into space again 'it travels no faster than an old tramway horse.' Yet they tell when such a comet will appear again. Then the next paper you take up, you see them seriously discussing the probability of our sun going through space as fast as light. Now, how could they see a comet coming, and measure his rate of speed? It is only by him throwing his light on before him at the speed that light travels, that he can be observed at all before he is upon us; and if he takes it as leisurely as an old tramway horse when he gets back into space, when is he to overtake the sun again, even should he—the sun—travel no faster than 100,000 miles per hour . . .?" And, writing in the section "Balance," he goes on: ". . . But to return to the orbits and motions of the planets. It is a curious thing that the planet Eros just came as if I had sent for it, when I was studying this subject. As I have already noticed, Eros' mean distance is inside that of Mars, but its orbit is so eccentric that part of it is inside and part of it outside the orbit of Mars. Now we are told that 'any two portions of matter in the universe attract each other with a force in direct proportion to the product of the numbers representing their masses.' But if this were so Mars would make a prisoner of Eros; for as soon as they came to that distance apart where the attraction of gravitation and the centrifugal force equally oppose each other, Eros would be caught and carried away with Mars and forced to revolve round him like a satellite. But there is no difficulty when their orbits are considered according to balance, for when they pass each other Eros will be forced in past its natural course and when clear of each other it will swing like a pendulum as far out past its natural orbit. Balance also accounts for the planets and satellites swinging up and down in their orbits in the same way." After another three sections, on "Gravitation," "Attraction," and "Notes," the writer treats of "Submarine and Aerial Navigation," two subjects in which he did a lot of experimenting.

He writes: ". . . It is because the science of Balance has been neglected that man is unable as yet to navigate the air and through the water. I have given the subject of the Aerial Ship a good deal of consideration, as well as the sub-marine Boat. Regarding the latter I had made a working model according to my theory of Balance, and when the dark days of the African war was upon us, in the first of the last year, 1900, I was enthused by the spirit of patriotism that was sweeping over the empire and started to do my best in order to defend my country, and when I was casting about to ascertain the readiest way to get before the proper authority, my idea of submergeable boats in order to defend our ports, or ships when blockading, I learned that a noble Lord was urging patriotism and calling on every man to do his duty in the defence of his country . . . and I sent off my model with all speed. I got the model returned but no reply to my letter. Next I took the model to a representative of H.M.'s Navy, but he laughed heartily at the idea of submergeable boats for war purposes. He said this had been often tried but was not practicable, and he stood with his feet on the floor about two feet apart and showed me how taking his weight off one foot and putting it on the other unbalanced a pretty large vessel under the water but I tried in vain to point out that my boat would be as steady under the water as on its surface, but all of no use; . . . I got the model returned along with a code of regulations, which if I agreed to, then I had to send on the model again to the Admiralty to be examined and tested; but between H.M.'s Post Office, Mail Carriers and Admiralty, my model got lost, and although I sent a registered letter asking if it had still not arrived, and enquiring that if so, if I should make another, I have not yet got a reply. Not many months after this I saw it stated in the papers that the British Government were not only building submarine boats, but were also building submarine boat destroyers. It will be interesting to me at all events, when it is published, how these vessels have been 'balanced' so smartly, that it has become possible to carry on the war underneath the water. 'Balanced' forsooth! I venture to predict that before the century is half run, people will be taking submarine passages on account of the extra steadiness. A passage boat need not go entirely beneath the surface, only through the waves instead of tossing on the top of them. . . . The Aerial ship should be constructed very much on the lines of the submarine boat. There is not so much difference between the flying bird and the diving bird. The bottom of the Aerial ship should be much the same as that of a boat or sea-going vessel, with inclined planes or wings at the sides, forward at the shoulders, and the aerial propellers should be at the shoulders in the base of the wings—that is according to Balance—but experience may show that they would do better farther aft, as then the wind off the propellers would have a forwarding effect on the diminution part of the vessel— with little water propellers down aft, while experimenting —and a large flat horizontal rudder or tail. . . ." There follows diagrams of both the submarine, the "Diver," as it was called, and his "Aerial Ship." A chapter on "Prophetic Dreams" follows, then the book ends with eight of his poems: the first, "Accidental Glimpses concerning the Writer," and the last, "Cliff Sound," being the best of the lot. "The Snowstorm" is also very good, while "The Columbine" is interesting.

The book shows William Johnson to have been a remarkable thinker, and with ability as a writer and poet. In view of what we now know of submarines and aircraft his ideas and diagrams have been remarkably sound.

He was responsible for some useful inventions, including a grate stove, for the design of which he is said to have been presented with six of the stoves. Like other men of genius he was not wary enough in his dealings with "big business." Johnson was also a boat-builder, with original ideas, as is seen from his book; one of his boats, the *Norseman*, still sailing in the Scalloway regatta, one of the sporting and social events of this enterprising village. He was interested in Astronomy, and built a small observatory on the flat roof of his house. This house had some fine carvings on it, but little of this can be seen now. Johnson's grave at Quarff is marked by a heart-shaped stone, on which he inscribed some lines about his mother and himself. This stone was shaped in the form of a heart when he found it lying on the East shore at Scalloway, and he kept it, saying it was to be laid on his last resting place. For long some half dozen copies of his book lay in a Scalloway smithy, but now the volume is very hard to come upon.

Scalloway is also the home place of the poet, John J. Hunter, some of whose work appeared a few years ago in the book *Trums an' Truss.* His latest work is a long historical poem, in dialect, entitled *Taen be da Trows*, and is awaiting a publisher.

The chief isles in the Bay of Scalloway are Burra, Trondra, Havera and Papa. Burra is an important centre of the fishing, the stretch of sea off the south-west part of Shetland, as far as Foula being known as the Burra Haaf. Haaf is the old northern word meaning sea. Hamnavoe in Burra is a go-ahead village, with numerous houses near the shore, and a pier where a small steamer can discharge cargo. A steamer with coal comes to Hamnavoe a number of times each year. All the Hamnavoe men, and at times most of the women and children, come to the pier to discharge the coal, which is purchased and disposed of on a co-operative basis. Burra has hardly any peat moor. What peat is used is obtained from the hills on the nearby Mainland. The Burra men own over a score of motor-driven boats for working the haddock grounds in spring and winter, and the herring grounds in summer and early autumn. Crofting in the sense as known on the Mainland is on a relatively small scale, the Burra folk, like their Skerries kinsfolk, getting mostly everything from line and net. In the course of grave-digging recently in Papil kirkyard, Burra, a sculptured slab was unearthed with other interesting stones thought to date back for more than a thousand years. The stone was near the foundation of the kirk of St. Lawrence, one of the oldest in Shetland. It was near this same kirk that a stone cross was found with part of a skeleton in a half-sitting position, said to have been that of a priest. In 1877 in the same kirkyard the Burra stone was discovered by Gilbert Goudie, a Shetland authority on the antiquities of the north. The Burra stone was sculptured, showing priestly figures carrying croziers. It was at once seen to be an important find. Its designs contributed greatly to a knowledge of a vague period in northern archæology, the time between the builders of the round stone brochs and the coming of the men from Norway.

The Burra Stone is now preserved in the Museum at Edinburgh. The new discovery is thought to be even more important than the celebrated Goudie stone and a similar stone found at Bressay. The Papil slab is about three feet long by one foot in depth. From a rubbing it is possible to give an idea of the figures shown. They are horizontally arranged, depicting five persons in a procession from right to left towards a cross that fills the left-hand end of the slab. Four of the figures carry croziers, and the fifth is riding a horse. He is placed second from the right, so that priests seem to be both leading and following him. The horse seems to be walking, its long tail being well represented. The four figures are walking above a series of designs in the space defined at its left-hand end by the base of the cross. It is significant that a number of ancient stones, showing sculpturing, are being turned up in the same part of the kirkyard. The Papil kirkyard is probably one of the oldest in Shetland. The name Papil is derived from the Papæ, or priests, the followers of St. Ninian, the great missionary to Pictland. From the finds of rare sculptured stones there it seems likely that the place has been a priestly burial-ground.

It has been thought that the Papil Stone, as it has been named, may be about 1000 to 1400 years old. The earlier Papil, or Burra, Stone is said to be of Irish type, a type whose figuring and interlacing are found in the *Book of Durrow*, a chronicle written by monks in a Columban monastery in 670.

A lion on the Burra Stone is similar to one shown in the monks' book, the Bressay stone having an animal more naturalistic in style. The temptation of Anthony appears on the Burra Stone, two women in the form of birds whisper in the Saint's ear, while the Bressay slab has a representation of the monster swallowing and spewing out Jonah. Most ancient horizontal stones have been found in Perthshire. They are said to date from the early eighth century. Much interest is being taken in Shetland in the unearthing of those relics of ancient Celtic culture, the opinion being widely held that all such valuable finds should be retained inside the islands and not removed from their places of origin.

Trondra and Havera are smaller isles and mostly depend on the fishing. Havera was inhabited by two families until quite recently. Trondra is an old northern name, probably from the man's name Trond, hence Trond's ey, or isle.

As you say, Shetland is exposed, with the sea always within sight, always capable of "showing its teeth." It is the case that even in the most "inland" part of the largest isle the sea can still be seen. This is owing to the ragged coastline, with its numerous voes and firths eating into the land, as the great fiords eat into Norway's land. Shetland is indeed a "Norway in little," although without such an extensive "skerryguard" along its coasts. The climate is slightly different too. Trees do not grow in the islands, whereas in Norway, many miles north of Shetland, trees grow in profusion. In Northmavine at the north part of the Mainland, Rønies Voe and Collafirth wind away in through the high rugged land giving to the countryside a very Norway-like touch.

This fiord-like feature makes for one of the delights of travelling in the isles. Inland among the hills it seems dreary. On a dull day in the north the heights take on a drab dark grey-umber colouring, with here and there a patch of dismal green telling of some lonely croft. It conjures up the idea of being in "the wilderness" right enough, the traveller even getting to the stage when he would not be much surprised if some folk in sheep-skins were to appear. A roadman's quarry here and there seems the only sign of "civilisation." The visitor resigns himself to this seemingly never-ending succession of barren hills. Boredom may afflict him, for it looks as if sheep are everywhere. There are white sheep, grey, black, moorit sheep, shaila ones and a few known as "blissit" and "catmuggit." There may even be a few of a colour neither moorit nor brown. It almost seems as if the land were bare of life, but for the nibbling sheep and an occasional seagull or crow flying past.

The traveller keeps on, however, fighting down a desire to turn and get out of this sheep-haunted cluster of hills, back to the town to catch the first boat for Aberdeen. After all he had come to Shetland, the land of the "hundred isles" and the "two hundred firths," and it is only natural he should want to get his money's worth with a sight of "Thule's bays and isles" instead of having to be the centre of interest to hundreds of sheep.

He will not be disappointed in his striving. As he goes along, the bored feeling seems to slip from him as first one, then another, sign of "civilisation" comes in sight. A motor-van, perhaps, hurries by, followed by a youth on a motor-cycle, then he catches sight of a trim-looking croft-house with wireless aerials between the chimneys, and a small windmill affair at the gable, generating electricity for lighting and power. All at once the traveller turns a bend in the road to find himself confronted by a fine sight. Before him lies a number of silvery-blue firths, dotted with pleasant green isles. White-sailed Shetland model boats head out through the nearest firth, while afar off a steamer noses her way to the land, and some trawlers steam past. The sky clears, the sun shines again, and a rare beauty is over the land and sea. The sun-sparkling waters run far into the land between stretches of green and umber shades as the various types of croft rigs, meadows and hill enclosures merge with one another. With the breeze rippling the corn rigs and meadows the different scents of plants and flowers mingle into a strong sweet smell. On each "toon" of croftland he sees what looks like a doll's house gleaming white in the sunshine, with neat felt or thatch roof, and lazy blue peat-smoke spiralling from the chimneys. The voes lie like glass, the hills and crofts reflected in the still water. Some boats are out by the nesslands where the tides run, favourite places for fisher-men with rod or net. Closer inshore one or two bigger boats are lying at anchor, their decks white with gull droppings, for the slump of pre-war days made it impossible for the men to carry on, and the boats were found unsuitable for "Government work."

Rønies Hill is "Shetland's mountain." It is about 1400 feet high, a bluff, round-topped mass of red granite. The ruins of an old watch-house are still at the top of Rønies Hill. This used to be kept in order by the haaf fishermen sailing from Fedaland as a "mead" or guide to the boats when at sea. The deep water mead was "a' da laand doon an' Rønies laek a kumbled kettle." ("All the land down, or out of sight, and Rønies Hill like an upturned kettle.") Other meads used by Fedaland men were: "Da Hill o Ulsta an da Hill o Soond"; "Da Stacks an Da Björgs ower da Isle"; "Eshaness an da Skerrie ower da Blue Hill"; and "Da Toougs an da face o da Isle open."

Rønies Voe was the place where the ill-fated Hull whaler, *Diana*, ended her long drift from the Arctic sea in 1864 with over a dozen of her crew, including her master, Captain Graville, dead on board.

Shetland is at times swept by strong gales. Flimsily built houses are of little use in the northern climate, with its predominance of rain and wind. Wooden huts are lifted bodily and smashed to pieces. Loose crops are thrown "on the sea." In February 1943 a gale reaching 95 miles an hour was registered, and in December 1945 equally violent gales were experienced. When such gales are accompanied by snow or hail, Arctic conditions prevail. Great faans, or drifts, of snow block the roads. Traffic is held up until men with shovels, or trucks with snow-ploughs, come to the rescue. Low-walled crofting houses get practically snowed under, the people remaining isolated from neighbours for days. Sheep are often buried in the drifts for many days. When this happens the sheep eat the wool off one another's backs. Heavy snowfalls are not frequent in the islands, but older people speak of there being plenty of snaa lying for weeks on end in their young days, with lochs and parts of some voes frozen over. Skating and curling were carried on for weeks when the snaa and frost lay over the land. Rainy weather is the most frequently experienced in the north. Some days, with easterly wind, it generally rains the clock round. The Shetland climate, on the whole, is equable, with no extremes of heat or cold, rain or snow. Sometimes long spells of warm weather, with days of bright sunshine, are experienced in spring, summer and autumn. Owing to the prevailing southerly winds some winters are fairly mild. These spells of fine weather turn the dreary and barren isles into places of beauty, places well worth visiting by those in search of rest and quiet.

CHAPTER II

IT is good to know you have found something of interest
in the first letter, and that it has whetted your appetite
for more.

As regards the point you make about the population.
At the last census, in 1931, it was found Shetland had a
population of roughly 21,000. The number of voters in
Shetland in 1939–40 stood at 14,828. Inhabited houses
in the Shetland Valuation Roll for the same period
were 5699.

You are correct in saying the population is dwindling.
This is due to various factors, chiefly economic and social.
Only one island, Whalsay, has shown an increase. In 1931
its population was about 1000. In Whalsay and Skerries
there are 258 inhabited houses. Whalsay is one of the
main fishing centres of the isles, and as it is not unfertile
it has numerous crofts. It is known as "the Bonnie Isle,"
and in summer it does not belie this title. In winter, too,
with the white spume flying over the rocks, there is a
touch of wild beauty in the scene.

Whalsay has a fair depth of peat moor in various parts
of the hills and nesslands. The Skerries folk cut their fuel
at Whalsay, transporting the dried peats in boats across
the sea to the rocks about seven miles to the eastward.
One of the largest Shetland lighthouses stands on one of the
Out Skerries, its warning light visible some twenty miles
off the coast. The lighthouse was attacked on two occasions by Nazi bombers, two women being killed. A fine
song, the *Skerries Boat Song* has been composed by Mr. Neil
Matheson, postmaster at Lerwick during the recent war.

Mr. Matheson has done a lot to revive interest in Shetland
folk-music and songs. Concerts, organised mainly under
his direction, in December 1944 and again in 1945 took
the form of "all-Shetland nights," and were very popular.

At one time when the Skerries people were going across

to "da muckle isle" to work in the peats, the women in the boats kept account of the time and the distance sailed by the number of "loops" or stitches they had knitted on their wires.

It is said some of the fishermen working the Skerries haaf ground in the sixerns, or six-oared boats, recited impromptu rhymes, in a certain measured way, to help them gauge their position and distance off the land. This custom was observed more especially during hazy weather when the boats were approaching the land, and the men were "feeling their way along."

A ballad of eighty or so verses, called *Jeemie an' Nancy*,* formed part of the fishermen's rhyming vocabulary, each man in the boat having a certain number of verses to recite for as long as the boat was on the course requiring the aid of such "navigational" methods. There was a man known as "Clever Lowrie" in one of the boats. He could "tell" every one of the verses of this ballad, forbye other rhymes. It is said he once warned his mates they were going on a wrong course. It was coming down a "shokk a mist," and Lowrie, having taken notice of the dim land before it was blotted out, began reciting the rhymes. The others only laughed, saying, "Yah, Lowrie!" They did not laugh, however, but felt grateful to their mate and his "rhyme-telling" ever after, as his action had saved them from going on a dangerous reef.

On one of the MS., fragments left by Laurence

* Regarding the ballad of *Jeemie an' Nancy* a friend writes: "About 'Jeemie and Nancy.' We tried to get the words in Muness, but beyond the fact that we were told that So-and-so had heard it many a time we got no further. . . . My father was a fisherman in the sixærn days (he was out in 1881), and he says the old men loved to recite and sing, but the younger men took little notice. He does not think they measured distances by song. Many of them had a marked sense of direction, but in fog even the best sometimes went far astray. With long experience they had acquired an evenness and rhythm in rowing which kept the boat at least on a straight course, and thus they had a better chance of 'turning up somewhere' than less experienced men. He remembers roughly that the theme of 'Jeemie and Nancy' was the murder of Jeemie at sea at the instigation of a wealthy father who objected to the attachment of his daughter Nancy to the sailor Jeemie—the return of the murdered man's ghost, and the death of Nancy."

Williamson of Gairdie, Yell, some verses of a ballad similar to the haafmen's one are jotted down, and have been transcribed as follows:

> "When he heard the S. was safe returning,
>   He wrote a letter to the bosun, his friend,
> Saying a handsome reward I will give you
>   If you the life of yung Jamie will end.
>
> "Then void of all fear & love of the money,
>   The cruel b. the same did complete,
> . . . in the ocean he instantly plunged
>   Him into the deep.
>
> "When Jamie was flotting upon the wide ocean,
>   & her cruel parents were plotting the while,
> How that the life of their beautiful daughter
>   With cursed gold they should strive to beguile.
>
> "What is that that is under my window,
>   Surely it is the voice of my dear;
> Then lifting her head from the soft downy pillow
>   Straight to the casement she then did repair,
>
> "Close in her arms the spirit enfolds her. . . ."

Nowadays fishermen have scientific instruments to help them in their navigation; not to speak of the wireless with its "herring fishing bulletin"; but if greater safety and accuracy has thereby been attained, some of the romance has gone with the disappearance of the sea rhymes, words and customs. Up to recent years fishermen had a speech and a body of beliefs and customs of their own. They used many Norse words when at sea, in place of the words they used ashore. This applied to certain things and persons, and was a "taboo language," the words, as they thought, having the power of "sainin," or absolving them, their boats, lines and catches from evil. Certain things could never be mentioned at sea by their ordinary names, among them being ministers, churches, kirkyards, cattle, dogs and the like. Whistling and singing and undue levity were never tolerated at sea. These were among the things

C. J. Williamson

PAPIL STONE

To face page 32

A SHETLAND VOE

C. J. Williamson

To face page 33

strictly "taboo!" To whistle or sing was sure to bring a gale of wind and disaster. When a "taboo" rite was broken by some young fishermen, out of forgetfulness or devilment, things were immediately "sained" by the other men touching the nearest bit of iron or steel and saying "Caald iron."

The men believed the sea-spirits who ruled the deep did not care too much for the Christian faith and its ministers and kirks, so to get around this dislike resort was had to the speech of their ancestors of Norse times. The men referred to the minister as *da upstaander*; the kirk, *da bennihoose*; the sea, *da farr*; a cow, *da dronger*; mice, *wa'-cattle*; the fire-tongs, *anklovan*; a cat, *da foodin*; a horse, *da gengir*; the mast, *da steng*; a rope's end, *dampi*; and so on.

The Whalsay people have a love for their own "bonnie isle," and are not unnaturally proud of its leading position as one of the most progressive places in the north. They recently set up a Development Council, to develop the fisheries, press for a new pier and other needful things. The branch of the Scottish Co-operative Wholesale Society recently opened is going ahead at a good pace. Most of the old insanitary thatch-roofed houses have been replaced by new or repaired buildings, with felt or slate roofs and modern conveniences.

Whalsay can boast the largest and most up-to-date public hall in the Shetland country places. At the same time, in Symbister House, it possesses perhaps the largest "Ha' hoose" or "mansion" in the isles.

Loving as you do, poetry and literature, it will be interesting to you to know that at Sudheim in Whalsay, the author of the *Hymn to Lenin* and other poems, the distinguished Scottish poet, Hugh MacDiarmid, had his home for a large part of the past ten or twelve years.

The isle was long famous for its fiddlers, many of whose "springs" were composed in the place. Isbister, "the east setter," was the home of at least four well-known fiddlers; one of whom, Thomas Arthur, used to go over

C

to the Skerries for a period of about three weeks about Yule time for a number of years in order to play, as there was no fiddler in Skerries at the time. Gilbert Gilbertson of Sandwick was said to have been one of the finest fiddlers in Shetland, rivalling even the Unst men who were indeed "mighty fiddlers before the Lord!" Scores of springs, or reel-tunes, were known in the isle, some of Shetland origin, others again probably Scottish or Irish tunes adapted by native composers.

It may interest you to learn the names of some springs, even if, for the moment, you cannot see the music, or hear them played in the hearty fashion of the ear-trained school of fiddlers. Among tunes known in Whalsay are: *Jeck's Alive*, or *Jeck dat brook da Prison Door; Shaalds a Foola; Dis is no' me nain Hoose; Soople Saandy; Betty an Naanie; Saandy ower da Lee; Smash da Windlass; Da Mirry Boys o' Greenland; Da Aald Wife ahint da Fire; Bressa' Crackers; Boannie Isle a Whaalsa; Turn under Lee; Jeemie at da Helm; Da Weemen's Breest K'nots; Gold fur da Boannie Lasses;* and *Murra's Rant* or *Lowrie Tarl.*

The spring of *Jeck's Alive* is said to have had its origin in the following way: "Jeck," a Whalsay man, had been imprisoned somewhere "south," and his folk had given him up for dead. Jeck, however, was "alive" and biding his time; he one day smashed down the prison door and got clear. He came home to Whalsay, arriving at his "nain hoose" in the dead of the night. Jeck came silently into the house, saw his old fiddle still hanging on the wall at the back of his bed, just as he had left it ere going away to sail, and taking down the fiddle he began playing. This tune was thereafter known as *Jeck's Alive*, or *Jeck dat Brook da Prison Door.*

On lists made up quite recently the names of about three hundred and sixty "springs" appear, many being native to Shetland.

Fredmann Stickle (or Von Steigle) was said to have been a shipwrecked German sailor, or a sailor who ran away from his ship. Stickle came ashore in North Unst and made his home there. A fiddle was about all he had with

him, unless for the clothes he wore. Fredmann, or
"Freddie da Fiddler," as he became known, composed
many tunes. One of these tunes became known as
Stumpie's Reel, or *Stumpie*. It was first printed in one of
Neil Gow's collections of Scots music. In a footnote in
that book the compiler, Neil Gow, says he got the tune
from Mrs. Bruce of Sumburgh.

Discussing old music and songs, a man in Eshaness, in a
letter to the writer, says: ". . . about thirty years back I
can remember no lonely winters; it is now that you will
have loneliness. Why, in my school days I can remember
more laughter in one week than you will hear now in a
year. In those days the winter was looked forward to as
a period of rest and enjoyment; and every week would
witness a social gathering of some kind where the amount
of fun and amusement made the time pass very fast. . . .

"Part of those gatherings were made up of dancings
when two or more Violins would supply the Music. This
district had whole families of fiddlers; but I am afraid the
old springs are now dead out. One of our best fiddlers
died some years back; and never again have I heard anyone who could bring out the melody which he could
bring from the fiddle. He was a natural player from ear,
and I observed him being able to copy from gramophone
records the tunes played by J. Scott Skinner. Although a
great player this man was a very modest, quiet and good-
natured soul, who preferred to live an obscure life rather
than show what he could do on the Violin."

A note in one of the Note-Books of Laurence Williamson,
the scholar of Gairdie, Mid Yell, gives an interesting
account of the traditionary origin of a Shetland spring.
The transcription reads:
"W. A.'s narrative. . . .
"Da Tivs Knw lies i da hill atwin Del in Bre. Hits a
Trowi Know. Da Tivs livd in Know in cam up upo da
niyt in stol da sheep in da yung bes. De wir ferd fir dim,
de taut it de wir supirnatirl. De wr a ald Delting man a

fidler, abut 100 year ago. He ws bin som wy at a wedin ir abut a Xmas time. He ws on is rd him. Som o dem tuk im in in fan somebody der it he kent, in de warnd him it he wisna ta et ir drink in der. He playd t some gud wimen dn de oferd im drink. He refused it. Da (one that) offered was highly offended in he showd it too. De kad im Mansie Kupir. (Magnus Cooper.) Hits within da memory o folk livn whan da man died. He notisd da man spekn ta idrs in gi'n dem instructions in he herd mention med o his blak ku. (Skilladil. Skellaster hes a trowi hill tu. Da trows hed ald Jon Herklson it bed a Flamaster Ng. he ws a famous fidler.) Mansie gt out whan de wir don wi im. Whan he cam hom i da morning dan da wife ws kindlin da fire. In he sd ws sju bin i da byre i da mornin —in sju sed na. In he said sju wid betr ljuke ta da kye. Sju gud i da byre in sju kam in in sju sed da best ku i da byre ws lyin dead on da bisi. Da trows ws shot it. Yon ws da errint it da man ws sent his . . ."

Put into English, this would read:

"W. A.'s narrative. . . .

"The Thieves Knoll lies in the hill between Dale and Brae. It's a Troll Knoll. The Thieves lived in (the) Knoll and came up upon the night and stole the sheep and the young beasts. They were afraid of them, they thought that they were supernatural. There was an old Delting man, a fiddler, about 100 years ago. He (had) been some-(where) at a wedding, or about a Christmas time. He was on his road home. Some of them took him in, and found somebody there that he knew, and they warned him that he wasn't to eat or drink in there. He played to some good women, then they offered him drink. He refused it. The (one that) offered was highly offended, and he showed it too. They called him Mansie Kupir. (Magnus Cooper.) It's in the memory of folk living, when the man died. He noticed the man speaking to others and giving them instructions, and he heard mention made of his black cow. (Skelladale. Skellaster has a troll hill too. The trolls had old Jon Herklson that stayed in

Flamaster Nesting. He was a famous fiddler.) Magnus got out when they had done with him. When he came home in the morning then the wife was kindling the fire. And he said (had) she been in the byre that morning— and she said no. And he said she (had) better look to the cattle. She went in the byre, and she came in and she said the best cow in the byre was lying dead on the floor. The trolls had shot her. That was the errand that the man had sent his . . .''

This man who met ''da tievs'' or da trows in Skeladale, and who learned their spring, was the maternal grand-father of Barron Robertson of Kruegan, Dale, Delting, who was a fiddler of great renown in the first part of this century.

Shetland folk-music largely consists of these fiddle tunes, played at dances and other social gatherings. They were widespread all over Shetland, with the possible exception of Fair Isle, which seems not to have pro-duced many fiddlers. Almost all the island fiddlers were ordinary working people—crofters, seamen, fishermen. Many families seem to have the gift of fiddle-playing, the art of music-making, in their blood. Generation after generation produced fiddlers in the same house, and a great number of ''springs'' owe their composition to men from certain musical families. There are the Stickles, Sutherlands and Smiths of Unst, Sutherlands of Lunna-sting, Arthurs and Hughsons of Whalsay, Coopers and Clarks of Delting, the noted fiddlers of Muckle Rø, Stoves of Lerwick, Duncans of Sandwick, Hunters of Weisdale and Nesting, Johnsons and Andersons of Eshaness, Andersons of Hillswick, Frasers of Waas, and many others. Then there were the Flamister men. There was a man in Flamister, South Nesting. He was a fiddler, ''da Fiddler o' Flamister,'' but his title was soon disputed, and by his own sons. He had seven sons, every one a fiddler. Thomas Jakobson of Brough and James Linklater, Nest-ing, were both noted fiddlers, as were some of the Cogles of Delting. The folk-lore of the "springs" is interesting, as a large part of it seems "trow"-inspired. A "Pechts'" tune from Fetlar, *Wenyadepla*, was heard played by "da Pechts" by a Laurenson man. The sea and ships and names of countries far from Shetland also colour the Shetland folk-music, some of the springs probably being native adaptations of Irish, Scottish and other tunes brought back to the north by seamen. It is said there is even "Yakki" influence in the Shetland fiddle-music. This is the Shetland name for Esquimo, and this is highly probable as many hundreds of seamen from the isles met in with "da Yakks" at Greenland and "da Straits" when on the whaling voyages to the north. Some old Peterhead men, veterans of the whaling days, held a "Foy" at Peterhead on 7th December 1936. This was broadcast in the Scottish programme, and proved a very interesting item. The men sang old whaling songs and yarned "back an' fore" about their experiences in the north. One man mentioned the year 1867 in his yarn. Another kept speaking of "smelling the whale," and the "whaals had a green smell." A third veteran said he "shot two bears." They spoke of superstitions, and of a man on board who had a twist in his "stropps," and he would not put this right the whole time he was on the voyage, in case it brought on "bad luck." A sing-song and feast on board ship were mentioned, and a fiddler "Thomas Manson" played at this sing-song. This may have been a Shetland man, as most Shetlanders with the gift of fiddling used to carry their fiddles wherever they went, to Greenland or "aroond da Horn."

Most of the tunes have very homely names. It is thought that many of the melodies are old, having been the tunes of Norn songs, the words of which have been forgotten. Gradually fiddlers adapted the melodies into reel and other dance tunes. One of the oldest tunes is the *Day Dawn*, which was played at Yule in "da gentry's Haa's." One man played some tunes every Yule morning at his laird's Haa', in this way paying his rent "in kind."

Looking to the popularity of fiddle-playing here in Shetland, it is peculiar that few of the tunes have been written down on paper. This probably arose from the fact that few of the fiddlers were in a position to get instruction in music, unless by "ear," and the folk who knew written music, mostly of the middle and upper classes, thought the "springs" too "common" for their attention. And, of course, the influence of the kirk, as in so many instances, tended against encouraging anything of working-class culture, styling the tunes and songs as relics of "Norn paganism." The "springs" have, therefore, survived in working-class families, having been handed down "by ear" from father to son. There seems reason to believe the revived interest in folk-music may remedy this neglect of a vast field, and we may yet see many native tunes set down on paper. In this way they will be saved, and young fiddlers, now able to learn music, will be in a better position than were their fathers. It is doubtful, however, if they will be better able than the old-time school of ear-trained players to "gie'r sheet" as they "plinnk apo da posh." The "old-timers" generally put "everything they had," as it were, into their playing, "rivin' at" till "da swaet haild frae dem!"

Crofting and fishing are the two mainstays of Shetland's economy. The greater part of the population is employed in agriculture on the three thousand or over holdings in the islands. Some crofters are also fishermen, following the herring fishing in summer, returning to their holdings when the boats are laid up. Many crofters are in the Merchant Service, their holdings kept going during their absence by the women, old and very young folk. The women have a big say in the running of the crofts. Shetland women are hardly ever "haand-idle." They are active all the time in the general "skutterin'" about the croft, carrying, or wheeling manure, delving, harrowing, weeding, curing and carrying peats, carrying hay, shearing, "hentin'" and binding corn, "hirdin-in" da hairst, "biggin" the hay and corn in the hame-yards, harvesting the taattie and neep crops, "rooin" the wool off the sheep, knitting, tending cattle and poultry, helping in the sheep-driving, and dipping, on top of their own household duties. Soon after the war began, a widow, staying on a croft of about one acre of arable land near Lerwick, responded to the appeal for more cultivation by delving an additional six hundred and seventy running yards, mostly rigs which had been ley for ten years. She also broke out some new land, delving it all herself. She sowed the seed and harrowed it. The additional crops were of neeps (turnips) and corn, and good crops were obtained. As some of the rigs were on steep ground, the harrowing by hand was no easy task. Other women, working their crofts without help, did wonders in increasing cultivation, thereby adding to the nation's food supply. These are typical instances of the industrious ways of Shetland's women. Every spell of favourable weather must be taken advantage of to get the rigs wrought and the animals attended. On top of all this outdoor work they wield their knitting wires whenever a spare moment comes their way. The peat-curing, as raisin and roogin, and often carrying, is also largely done by women, the men having flaa'n and kassen the banks in late spring and early summer.

Crofting in Shetland is hampered by poor soil and frequent spells of wet and stormy weather. A struggle against bad natural conditions has to be carried on before even a subsistence living can be won. Social and economic conditions also keep people back. Landlords and merchants were wont to batten on the people, hampering progress. As a crofter once said: "Man, we mite pit up wi' da wadder, in a manner a spaekin, as dat's da will a da Loard's, bit hits yun damned rogues ye hae ta contend wi' it maks things harder!" The truck system still lingers in the islands, crofters going to some shop or other with produce—as potatoes, milk, eggs, mutton, cabbage, wool, hosiery and fish—and getting groceries and other goods in exchange.

Merchants naturally try to beat down prices of croft produce as well as any live-stock the folk come with, while in the course of trade his own prices become fairly high, so often enough the "man behind the counter" with the "huckstering instinct" well developed gets the best of the bargain. Of course, some crofters are shrewd and good at bargain-driving, and generally are able to hold their own, but on the whole the "big man" at the shop tends to score. It sometimes happens that people often find themselves in debt in the merchant's books, strive as they will about croft or on the sea. In a few cases crofters with few animals of their own will be asked by a merchant or cattle-dealer to graze a cow or two, or some sheep, on their land. As things are it is hard to refuse this request, as what little is got for grazing may help to pay the rent or other charges. Again, the merchant's place with its various enterprises—as knitting, weaving and carding machines, bakeshop, garage, pier, boats, etc.—is generally the only centre of any great "industrial" activity near a crofting toonship. If there's anything in the nature of "an outside job" (as distinct from the work on the croft) to be had, it is to be found at "da shop." Folk are "blyde" (glad) of a job "near hame." In this way the merchant (who is often a landlord as well) gets most of his jobs about the place done by people who are also his customers (the next shop may be many miles distant), and in some cases may even be his tenants. Being unorganised, the crofters who work for the "big man" at the commercial centre have no alternative but to take the wages offered and to work "a' hours!" After all, it is a job near home, "aye better than going away to sail," or "having to go to the toon a Lerrook where ye have to pay boardings!" A kind of "Lord of the Manor" atmosphere still lingers in some parts, although the upheaval of the war and the spread of political enlightenment is fortunately breaking this down. Some crofters living at a distance from a centre will agree to sell their sheep, lambs and other stock and produce to the nearest merchant or stock-buyer. This, of course, "saves the crofter a lot of time and bother," as very often outlying crofts have no roads linking them to the main centres, but naturally a somewhat lower price has to be taken than would be the case if the crofter "could get at to sell" his animals or produce direct in an open market. The legend "To rent crop . . ." on the rent receipt from the estate agent (some lairds never see Shetland) is all too familiar in many homes, a reminder that the scriptural truth "the earth is the Lord's and the fullness thereof" should not be taken too literally.

An editorial in the *Shetland Times* for 17th December 1943, headed "No Intimidation," is of interest as throwing a glaring light on the conditions that have helped to keep Shetland working people poor and backward.

"The members just crept up here in ones and twos after dark, saying that it was better to join privately; they were so frightened a merchant might see them going here!

These words were written, not during the Sheffield riots of the middle 'eighties when employers hired gunmen to shoot potential trade unionists, but only a few weeks ago in Shetland itself.

We have had many complaints, anonymous and otherwise, regarding relations between merchants and knitters which, in the absence of authentication, we have refrained from publishing; when, however, the remarks come from a responsible official of the S.H.K.A.,* we feel it is time that the matter was ventilated in the *Shetland Times*. . . ."

Despite the many natural, social and economic difficulties Shetlanders have to contend with, they are, on the whole, a hardy thriftful race of people, imbued with common sense and fine humour. They treasure all the more what little can be got from the unkind soil and sea. Nothing is ever wasted, the Shetland fish diets being noted for the great variety obtained from the skilful use of fish-flesh, livers and heads. Fish, milk, meal, butter, mutton,

---

* Shetland Hand Knitters' Association.

eggs and other produce are used by the crofting women in a "frugal" manner. As a queller of hunger and builder-up of stamina nothing can surely beat "liver-heads an' stap," to say nothing of "krappen."

Owing to the lack of industries there is little opportunity for young men. Most have to follow in the footsteps of their fathers and grandfathers, leave home and "hadd fur da suddird!" They become seamen in the merchant ships, sailing the seven seas and visiting many strange lands. "There are reckoned now to be 3000 men (more than half the adult males) in the Mercantile Marine, of whom 2000–3000 are actually away at sea at any given time." (*Historical Geography of the Shetland Islands*, by Andrew C. O'Dell, p. 206, published in 1939.) This again helps to keep things at home from advancing. The women, the elderly and the very young, and sometimes the sick and ailing, are left to look after the crofts and sheep. In the nature of things, they cannot compete with larger holdings whose tillers are able to employ extra labour and get much of the work done by mechanical means.

The fishermen are also kept back owing to irregular steamship services which often deprive them of fresh bait, ice, oil and other requirements. With the erection at Lerwick of an ice-factory, in the winter of 1945, things have eased a lot, the men not now being dependent on ice from Scotland. The fish, iced and packed in boxes for the markets in Britain, is often delayed by bad weather, reaching the markets in poor condition.

The herring industry is on a different footing from the white fishing. The herrings are salted in barrels and shipped in large cargo vessels sailing to the Continent. Changes, however, are coming to the industry. The Herring Board, recognising the high quality of Shetland herrings, have built a dehydrating factory, cold-storage and fish-meal plant, to treat the fish in the modern way. This will compensate for the shrinkage of the salt herring market. The factories began working in May 1946.

To return to crofting. The sheep flocks which each landholder is allowed to keep on the common hill grazings need a lot of looking after, particularly at the lambing and dipping periods.

It is arduous work tending sheep on the Shetland hills. There is little shelter to be found on some hills, and folk sometimes have to be "gja'n aboot da hill" with all sorts of weather. In some cases the flocks have to be kaa'd, or driven, miles over the hills before the krös, or enclosures, are reached.

It is work requiring strength and endurance, work hardly suited to women and elderly people. On every scattald sheep kaains are never complete without the women. Some women can pick out their own sheep at a glance, as they seem to have more "sheep-sense" than men. Sheep-marks are notches, rits, holes and crooks cut in the animal's lugs, every crofter having his own distinctive "mark."

When the young men of the crofts are away sailing, or at other work, "earnin' twa pennies," it will be seen that the fullest advantage of their holdings and sheep flocks cannot be taken by those left at home. Despite all these difficulties, however, a large number of sheep are kept in Shetland, the latest returns showing 2848 owners having dipped 205,278 head of sheep. A big proportion of these sheep consists of blackfaces and other southern breeds. Most of the hill-sheep, however, are of pure Shetland breed, a breed of great hardihood, producing wool of fine, soft, silky like texture.

As has been said, natural and social obstacles hold people back. Land cannot be tilled to the best advantage. Only a limited number of cattle, sheep, poultry can be kept. In some parts a crofter is allowed to keep only four head of sheep, while in others, with more extensive pasturage, as high as fifty head can be kept. Houses and outhouses have to remain without proper repairs, fences and dykes are often lying unrepaired for long enough.

Some toonships are badly served with inadequate roads, children going to school in winter suffering needless hardships through having to struggle over bogs without proper footgear. Outlying crofts only see a van once "in a blue moon," as it were. People taken suddenly ill in outlying places are at a great disadvantage. The nursing and medical services need some improvement, as does the postal service. The physical, moral and spiritual qualities of the people suffer in consequence of the continual grind for a subsistence living taking up all their energies. It follows there cannot be much time or inclination for serious creative intellectual effort. Hence the still discernible subservience shown by some (happily, a dwindling few) towards the landed and merchant class, ministers and officials. From this comes Shetland's dearth of literature, poetry, art, music and plays. Hence, again the fatalistic outlook of "it's laid for us, we cannot make a better of it," which prevents people from combining together to win political and economic advantages from their hard toil in the land of their birth.

The war, however, has had a big share in helping to open people's eyes. Young Shetlanders from the crofts and boats, away on active service, have shared in the cultural and political upheaval caused by the war. They have fought and died so that their country and all its ideals and beliefs may live. At the same time they see their people back home struggling along in the same old way, and they are determined to change things for the better. Something like a minimum of three hundred new crofts will probably be needed to settle men "coming home from the wars." If conditions stand in the way of new holdings being forthcoming in this land they have fought for, trouble is bound to arise. In any bold post-war development programme provision will have to be made to give the land back to the people, with or without compensation to the present holders of big estates. Men who have fought and suffered for homeland and freedom are not likely to remain silent while they see moneyed interests buying up this croft and the next to become sheep farms. On top of this wider outlook of returned Shetlanders, there has been the health-giving commingling of peoples during the war years. Many thousands of strangers have been in Shetland for the first time, they have met and fraternised with the islanders, who, with their usual kindliness, have welcomed the soldiers, sailors and airmen with open arms. A great many homes in "the south" know something of the remote place in which their menfolk had to serve. Many a finely coloured Shetland sheepskin rug forms a souvenir of the war days; many a "Fair Isle" jumper, pair of gloves, beret, or other knitted garment recalls to someone's mind the memory of happy (if at times stormy) days and nights in the "far north" garrison. These "sooth men" brought something of their own ways of life and thought with them. They were often surprised to find such a high level of intelligence among Shetlanders, but what they brought north in the way of culture and ideas was of benefit. Numerous Shetland lasses found husbands from among the men of the services, some Scottish, others English and Welsh, while a good few reforged the ancient ties of kinship by marrying sailors from Norway. While many of the strangers benefited intellectually from their stay in the north, their influence for good was also considerable: the intercourse between "south" and "north" in every way is bound to have a big effect as time goes on.

CHAPTER III

You ask a number of questions about this and that, and it is to be hoped this letter may help to answer some of them satisfactorily.

The Shetland roads are a lot improved nowadays, the Mainland roads especially having been widened and brought up to date during the war. Some of the larger isles, as Unst and Yell, also have serviceable roads.

Almost £250,000 were spent on Mainland roads during the war, the major part of this being spent on new roads and diversion of existing roads, at the two large aerodromes of Sumburgh and Scatsta. A report drawn up by Mr. Dryburgh, County Roads Surveyor, in January 1946, gives some figures of money spent on large engineering works in Shetland. The main items were: Sumburgh airport, construction of runways, £42,005; Scatsta aerodrome, construction of runways, perimeter tracks, dispersal pens, etc., £262,337; diversion of the county road, £3900; defences, £19,000; maintenance of roads and runways, £13,503. The authorisation works cost in all £211,639, which was spent mainly on roads, but which included over £71,000 for war damage reinstatement. Sumburgh was the first big job undertaken by the Roads Department. The work consisted of the construction of an airport from the small grassy landing place existing before the war. The runways, perimeter tracks, dispersal pens, drainage and special lighting were all completed between 1940 and 1942. Excavations included 173,510 cubic yards of sand, 42,000 cubic yards of rock. Bottoming laid amounted to 222,790 square yards; regulating laid, 205,250 square yards; tarmac laid, 224,140 square yards. The number of men working on the site was 225, and plant included 40 trucks.

The Scatsta job was completed in two stages. The first scheme for the construction of a single runway was begun in June 1940 and completed in September the same year. The larger scheme began in July 1941 and included the building of additional runways, perimeter tracks, dispersal pens, etc. The report says: "Scatsta aerodrome formed the largest agency service tackled by the Council, and although smaller in scope than the Sumburgh scheme, the site difficulties were probably the worst in Scotland, owing to the large quantities of peat to be removed, the enormous drainage entailed and the steepness of the ground generally."

The quantities involved were: excavations, 396,000 cubic yards of peat; 66,000 cubic yards of gravel; hardcore laid, 211,000 square yards; regulating laid, 211,000 square yards; tarmac laid, 211,000 square yards; drainage laid, 22,000 yards. The average number of men working was 200, with 9 excavators, 26 dumpers, 38 trucks and much other plant. An average of 120 men were accommodated in a large camp with all essential facilities which had to be constructed. Two quarries were opened at Voxter and Mavisgrind, and a total of 102,000 tons of rock was produced from these sources. For the Army a big programme of defence works was carried out from June 1940, and for three years thereafter. The most notable construction in this service was the building of the "Cork" wall, an anti-tank obstacle around Lerwick, which consisted of 800 yards of stone dyke 5 feet high by 5 feet thick; 300 yards of anti-tank ditch, and two road blocks, all of which were completed in twelve days.

Details of other roads made to camps and air stations are given in the report. One of the most important of these was Skaw road in Unst. This was built up the steep face of a cliff from Norwick to Inner Skaw. The gradients on the original track were from 1 in $2\frac{1}{2}$ to 1 in 7, and after overcoming numerous engineering obstacles, it was possible to give a minimum grade of 1 in 4 on the hill section. Enormous loads were carried by the roads, and damage was frequent, but they stood up well to the test. The traffic intensity in the Scatsta district was 1700 tons daily over the period of the war. War damage reinstatement works, in progress, cover 71 miles of important roads on the Mainland, and up to 150 men were employed bringing them to their 1939 condition before the end of 1946. The surveyor mentioned an incident that occurred at Sumburgh aerodrome. The foreman there, Mr. William Jamieson, and a squad of men were engaged one Sunday in 1942 in pipe laying when the enemy attacked the station. The men had no time to seek shelter, but had to lie on the ground while machine-gun bullets and bombs fell around them, shattering the pipes they were laying, the nearest bomb exploding only 60 yards away. Only a slight casualty was caused, and within one and a half hours the men had the bomb holes filled, and the aerodrome was again free for operation. The Air Ministry and the R.A.F. paid high compliments to the roadmen for their good work.

Yell, Unst and Fetlar, the three North Isles, have quite good roads, motor cars plying for hire between the ports where motor launches and the mail steamer *Earl of Zetland* make regular calls. The most of the Shetland roads are narrow compared with the highways in Britain. They are from ten to fifteen feet in width, but, as has been said, some have been greatly improved during the war. Owing to the broken coastline and the hilly nature of the land, there are few long straight stretches of roads. These generally twist and turn "up hill and down dale" in peculiar fashion, so that really fast motoring is out of the question. Drivers soon get to know the dangerous corners, the narrow brigs over burns, and the places where the road skirts near high cliffs. Accidents are few, although at some bends fatal accidents have occurred. The roadmen, mostly crofters, have the job of keeping the roads in good repair. With heavy snowfalls they have to dig away the wind-driven fanns of snaa to let the traffic get through. At times they also have to help in rescuing snow-buried sheep. In 1912 over 2000 head of sheep were lost to the crofters through being smörd, or choked, in the snow.

D

In the winter of 1944–5 numerous sheep were lost in the drifts.

You mention the "strategic position" of the islands as being in the nature of "stepping-stones" on the route from America to Europe. This is easily understood by looking at the map. Shetland is over one hundred miles west from Norway, and about the same distance south-east of the Faroe Islands, their sister islands.

Two airmen from Detroit, U.S.A., reached Shetland by "hops" from "stepping-stone" to "stepping-stone" in 1931, and in 1933 Colonel Lindbergh called at Lerwick on his great flight from the west. Developments of this kind are sure to make Shetland an important air base in the future.

An interesting article, "Visit of German Fleet in 1904," reprinted from the *Scotsman* in the *Shetland News*, 16th September 1945, touches on the "strategic" aspect of the isles. For diplomatic reasons, the editor's introduction says, the correspondent's reference to the feat of large ships of the German Navy negotiating the narrow north entrance of Lerwick Harbour, was suppressed from publication.

The article, describing the visit of the German Active Fleet, says, the fleet, "numbering thirty-three vessels, under Admiral von Koester, lay in Lerwick harbour for almost four days in the end of July, during which time the harbour, piled out southward almost to the lighthouse with the massive grey turreted walls of the battleships, was an impressive sight. This was at the very height of the fishing season, with all its traffic. Fishing boats sailed, stock and mail boats steamed, trawlers, liners and drifters raced in and out of the harbour; torpedo-boats darted about; the water was alive with the launches and pin- naces of the warships; little sailing or rowing pleasure boats went round the fleet; yet the visit was unmarred by accident. The courtesy and good behaviour of the Germans won the hearts of Shetland. They came ashore in their thousands, shopped, made excursions, took snapshots, and showed generally appreciative interest. The weather was perfect. Flags flew everywhere. Tourists and country folk flocked to the scene. The vessels were thrown open to the public, bands played, and launches were sent ashore for the visitors. In the soft simmer dim of the July midnight the shores and headlands were lined with people watching the memorable spectacle of the battleships aglow with electric lights that trickled in long bright reflections on the water, while over all the rapid signal lights changed and flashed. When on the fourth day, at various hours of day and night, one and another vessel noiselessly weighed anchor and stole away, the harbour looked blank. But they had not left. All night the thunder and blaze of battle surrounded the isles. For almost a week the Germans sounded, reconnoitred, manœuvred, drilled and practised round the Shetland shores. They hovered round and glided here and there. They stole into voes. Startled islanders abroad in the night-time met bands of Germans traversing the country silently and swiftly like companies of the dead."

After asking why Germany should have found it worth while to pay Shetland so much attention, the writer of the article proceeds to compare the lack of interest in Shetland and its many fine harbours on the part of the Admiralty. He says no vessels ever visit the isles, no soundings are ever taken. Then he describes the visit of four ships of the Channel Fleet, under Lord Charles Beresford. He then writes of the sailors' lack of appreciation of the islanders' welcome, and of how, "When Lord Charles Beresford steamed away he left a strong pro-German feeling in Shetland."

Letty Grierson, in an article, "Hard-working Shetland People Love Peace, but they can take War's Vicissitudes in their Stride," in the *New York Herald Tribune* for 17th December 1939, speaks of the strategic position of the islands, and goes on: "In a war in which air raiders have thus far failed to produce the threatened 'Blitzkrieg,' one spot has been consistently bombed. This is the Shetlands, a cluster of treeless rocky islands, lying between the North Sea and the Atlantic. Barren of real industries, populated by fisher-folk and farmers for the most part, the islands may appear queer targets for bombers. In fact, to most Americans Shetland suggests nothing but ponies.

Before the last war, Kaiser Wilhelm II of Germany said jokingly to one of the Shetland landlords that he wished he owned the islands. Their strategic position explains the remark and the present raids. The Shetlands control the 'north-about' passage from the North Sea to the Atlantic. The southerly exit from the North Sea is the English Channel, which is comparatively easy to guard. But in the north there are three possible exits: the Pentland Firth, between Scotland and the Orkney Islands; the Fair Isle Channel, between the Orkneys and the Shetlands; and the wide channel between the Shetlands and Norway."

Three aerial photographs picked up in Germany, after VE-Day, by a Shetland soldier, are of interest as showing the keen attention Shetland and its bases got from the Nazi war chiefs. The photographs, taken in April 1940, show details of the Sullom Voe and Sumburgh aerodromes and landing-grounds. The "anchor-places," for sea-planes, barracks for airmen and troops, "flak" stations, coastlines, distances from Lerwick, roads and other details, are carefully noted in red. At the sides of the maps, scales, distances and the rest are noted in red and black. On the map of Sullom Voe a number of flying-boats can be seen at their moorings.

Some notes, taken at random from time to time, may help to give a picture of things during those early days of the "phoney" war period, when Nazi airmen, in a raid over Lerwick, waved handkerchiefs to the bairns coming from school, and people stood in the streets gaping at the great Heinkels flying past.

A feeling that war was imminent came to Shetland

people in the summer of 1939. Flying-boats paid numerous visits to the islands, surveying voes and anchorages. A large ship, the *Manella*, came to Lerwick with stores for the R.A.F. as early as the month of July. She lay alongside the pier, quite close to some large German trawlers, each flaunting a huge Swastika flag. The Germans were ashore in the town and surrounding neighbourhood, taking everything in with observant eyes. The local Territorials were reorganised in the first of the year. They had route marches and other exercises, and each day that passed saw more young men joining up. Sand-bagging of important (and some not-so-important) buildings began shortly before the war, and the first black-out tests were held on Friday, 1st September 1939.

In the two local papers a week after war was declared, "Interested" wrote letters urging the erection of bomb-proof shelters. The editor of the *Shetland News*, however, thought differently. He added a footnote to the effect that the chances of air raids on Shetland were exceedingly remote.

Less than two months later six Nazi Heinkels raided Lerwick and destroyed a flying-boat in the north harbour.

For about a week or more after the 5th of September gas-masks were distributed to all and sundry at the Central Public School, Lerwick, the bairns having a holiday meanwhile.

Saturday, 2nd September, was a fine bright day. Lorries were running all the time fetching in sand for the bags that were put up around some buildings, remaining there till they burst and began to smell. Sunday, 3rd September 1939, was a warm sunny day, with light southerly wind. The sky was blue, with some billowy clouds, and the sea a sparkling blue. It was fine weather, with the land looking bonny, the late summer greens and yellows beginning to merge into the darker brown colourings of da hairst. It was dull on the horizon, and the hills were a dark blue, da ask* giving a far-off appearance to the

* The haze.

land. Folk waited expectantly for Chamberlain's harsh words that were to bring a cold chill of fear to many. Some people, mostly Shetlanders, had left the cities and came to the isles "for refuge." The black-out was fairly complete that Sabbath night, and people waited for the sound of the bombers. There was little fishing carried on for a week or so, as ice and bait ran short, owing to erratic steamer sailings. An aircraft landed in a field of corn in Bressay and crashed. On Saturday, the 16th September, two large timber-laden steamers came into the harbour. They had come from the Kara Sea, and lay off Bressay for a day or two awaiting instructions. A large Polish steamer lay in the north harbour for two or three weeks. People seemed vague about everything. They did not seem to be able "to make sense of diss waar!" It looked to many as though folk were being "kept in the dark." The almost continuous wireless news bulletins were eagerly listened to. The handful of progressive-minded folk who had been getting the leading newspapers regularly through the newsagents were puzzled to find their supplies cut off. Papers of any sort became very scarce for a time, and once it was about ten days before the steamer arrived with mails, cargo and papers, the news-agents being besieged by news-hungry folk. There was the usual crop of wild rumours almost daily. "Submarines were in the bight of Quarff," "Men were being landed," "Ships had been sunk by the dozen," "Lerwick would soon be wiped out!" and the like, were examples of some of the "news" that went round like wildfire. Saturday, 30th September, was a cold showery day, with fresh north-westerly wind. Three large steamers that had been lying in the harbour for a day or so left the port and headed for the north-east, in line, some distance between each other as they steamed to join one of the first convoys. The hills had begun to take on their drab winter look. Thursday, 5th October, was a stormy day, with strong southerly wind. The lifeboat was called out to look for an R.A.F. launch which went to the assistance of an aircraft forced

down "off Flugga." The boat returned on Friday, the
6th, after being twenty-one hours at sea. The crew were
awarded £2, 16s. 6d. per man. The launch turned
up safely on Sunday. As it came tearing in through
the harbour people thought "it was a submarine!"
The launch had been blown about ninety miles from the
land.

The hairst came on well that first year of the war.
Most crofters had their corn cut, and some had it screwed,
by the 30th. Hirdin took place near Lerwick during the
last week of the month, and lambs were kaa'd from the
hill to graze in parks until they were shipped to the
Aberdeen market. About six hundred lambs were put
into the Twagios parks to await the steamer. The *St.
Clair* arrived on Tuesday, the 10th. On Thursday,
rumours went around about "a fight going on outside."
Aircraft left the station at Sullom Voe, and the *St. Clair*
had to await an escort before proceeding south. It rained
heavily all Thursday night. The Terriers gave a farewell
dance in the Town Hall that night. The mail steamer
and other vessels were painted a dull blue-grey colour like
Navy ships. All that week the wind blew fairly strong, and
there was a fish famine. Two Norwegian steamers lay
anchored off Twagios. People added to the rumours after
dark by saying they had "heard the gunfire!" This
turned out to be true, as people in Unst had heard the
guns of the submarine that sank the Swedish steamer
Vistula on Monday, the 9th. Eleven shells were fired into
her about forty-five miles off Unst. The captain and eight
men were missing. A boat, with nine of the crew, came into
Baltasound on Tuesday, after being twenty hours in the
boat. The war had come home to Shetland in no un-
certain manner, as the story of the submarine attack got
about. The lifeboat went out to look for the missing boat.
The vessel was loaded with pulp for paper. The commander of the U-boat said to the men that there would be
"no paper for Mr. Chamberlain this time!" The men,
after landing in Unst, tramped about three miles from the

shore to a place on a moor where some men were working at the peat-banks. They took the shipwrecked men to their homes, where they were fed and clothed. One man was carrying a tin with a German loaf which the submarine commander had given to them. It was so hard they could not break it, and seemed to have been made from treacle and sawdust. The men were thinking of keeping the loaf as a "souvenir."

On Friday, 13th October, the *St. Clair* left about 5 p.m. She was escorted by an aeroplane and two destroyers. Included among her passengers were about 98 Terriers, 30 R.N.R. men, about 50 men and boys bound for the whaling at South Georgia, about a score of students, and the 9 Swedes. A large crowd of people gathered on the pier to take leave of the first lot of islanders "gjaa'n awa ta da waar." That night the "Merry Dancers" gave one of their "first-class shows." The Northern Lights were brilliant all over the northern sky, right to the zenith and beyond. The newspapers on Sunday, the 15th, and Monday, the 16th, had small news items on the "Black-Out, Knock-Out." *Reynolds' News* headed its par. "Turned Night into Day." It read: "Lerwick, Shetland Islands, witnessed a magnificent aurora borealis which changed night almost into day on Friday. The whole sky was illuminated by great swiftly moving shafts of brilliant yellow, green, mauve, and red lights. A.R.P. wardens threw in the sponge and called it a day."

On Monday, the 16th, the *Royal Oak* disaster at Scapa Flow set folk agog. The *St. Rognvald* had come north in the morning, and some of the passengers reported having spoken with some of the survivors, among whom were two Shetland men. On Tuesday, the 17th, there was an air raid on Scapa Flow, and on Wednesday the air-raid warning was sounded in Kirkwall. Two steamers were reported on the way north, the *St. Clement* bound for Scalloway. Folk in Scalloway that day thought they heard gunfire to the westward. Thursday, the 19th, an aeroplane passed over Lerwick about noon. She came from the south-east and flew towards the north-west. Folk came rushing out on to the streets, where they stood looking upward, some wondering "whether it was da Germans!" Men from the air stations were seen daily in town as they spent a few hours' leave, or hurried about on various duties. People began to get into the way "of the war," ever more men and youths were seen in uniform, the restrictions began to be taken as a matter of course, and the black-out gradually became more complete. Friday, the 20th, saw the steamer *Highlander* arrive, direct from Leith, with cargo. It was frosty in the morning, with south-west wind. An aircraft came from the south about 12.30 p.m. and flew to the west. At half-past six at night the moon was about half-full, shining clearly in the southern sky. The lifeboat left her berth in the small boat harbour at 2.40 p.m. and went out the north entrance. A small crowd of boys and men were on the breakwater seeing her leave. Some men leaned over the rails of the *Highlander* yarning and speculating as to the ill-fated craft the boat had gone to look for. About the same time a crofter from Bressay came into the boat harbour and made fast his small boat at the south steps. The *Highlander*, the *St. Clair* and the *Earl of Zetland* were all lying at the pier. There was something of a stir and bustle about the pier and esplanade as cars and lorries came and went, and folk strolled about with the fine day. A man from the country, with some wool in his bus, was standing near the Market Cross speaking to another man. The country man was saying something about Hitler's *Mein Kampf*. From the Hillhead smoke could be seen spiralling from the croft-rigs at Soond, some three miles to the westward of the town. With the clear air the croftland could be picked out very distinctly. The land seemed sharp and definite, with a dullish "washed" green colour, but refreshing looking as the sun beamed down. Some white fleecy clouds seemed to be motionless up from the western hills. The shadows cast by the sun showed here and there in the hollows under the brows. The road carrying the traffic to the south mainland wound through the Soond lands, very clear and white in the sunshine. The Ness of Soond lay bathed in sunshine, the sea was calm and the Ness was reflected in the still water. Home Service News, at 4 p.m., reported another raid over the Forth. German planes were reported flying to the north and east, chased by British fighters. Droves of lambs were driven out over the road to parks to wait on the steamers. About 5.30 p.m. news came that the steamer *Sea Venture*, laden with coal for Norway, had been sunk off Unst. The lifeboat had gone to the assistance of her crew. At the Picture House that night, Will Hayes was featured in *Old Bones of the River*.

Saturday, the 21st, was dull and rainy-like, with little sunshine. It was reported the lifeboat had been out all night. Another rumour had it that "a submarine had been sunk off Sullom Voe on Friday night." In the forenoon an aircraft was seen flying low over the town. The rain "laid on" passing noon. Passing 5 p.m. the lifeboat returned with the crew of the *Sea Venture*, after being twenty-seven hours at sea. The R.N.L.I. award was £4, 5s. per man. Two Shetlanders were in the *Sea Venture's* crew, numbering twenty-five men. People hurried to the pier to meet the lifeboat. By then it was dry, with clear moonlight. The vessel had been torpedoed off Unst, the men landing there from their own boats. A typical rumour of the time went something like this: A roadman working at Mangaster, in Northmavine, was said to have told some other roadman of how "ida mirknin o' da evenin", he had seen a "well-dressed man" one night at the "Hillswick junction." He had spoken to "da unkan-laek man," but got no response. The man seemed "queer," as if wanting to "hurry away." This stranger was put down as a "Nazi spy!" Another story was that submarines were putting men ashore "disguised as civilians" to "spy out the land!"

It was learned that the *Sea Venture's* gunners had fired on the enemy, and that a flying-boat came and sank the submarine. The boats from the sunken steamer came ashore at Skaw, in North Unst. The plane was said to have sent the wrong bearings, thus delaying the lifeboat.

Three small Norwegian shark-fishers were lying in the harbour on Tuesday, the 24th. Almost every day flying-boats or fighter planes were flying over the town. The folk were beginning to lose their curiosity about "aeroplanes," but gradually came to know the sound of British aircraft. Saturday, the 28th, was dry and cold, with little wind. The moon was nearly full. The *St. Rognvald* "arrived at last," in the early morning. A German aircraft was reported to have been "high over da toon" about breakfast-time. It was said she had been shot at by the gunners at Garth and Graven, in the north mainland. In the voes thereabouts a number of cruisers and destroyers were based. Sunday, the 29th, saw a large flying-boat come down in the harbour, using her searchlight to pick out the mooring-buoys. On Monday, the 30th, it was wet and cold, but there was little wind. About 11.8 a.m. the town crier, or bell-man, in oilskin and beret, with a red flower in his button-hole, rang his bell and shouted: "A drove of lambs and a few good fat yows to be sold at the Market Place at *11 a.m.*!"

November the 1st was a Wednesday. It was fine, cold weather, with hardly any wind. It was reported that a piece of shrapnel from a shell fired at the German aircraft on Saturday came down at the side of Røness Hill, at the Collafirth side. It made a deep hole in the hill, and was a great centre of interest to the folk round about. There was an engagement with a submarine, and fighting reported to have taken place off Sumburgh on Tuesday. Under a new order shops were closing at 6 p.m. People in the streets were beginning to use flash-lamps, and in the pitch blackness collisions took place on the narrow, winding main street. Monday, 6th November, was wet, with fresh southerly wind. The night watchman at the pier, a man over eighty years old, fell over the side of the pier. He got caught in the steamer's hawser just in time, and managed to hang on while men came to his rescue. After this he walked home himself, and returned to work soon after. On Tuesday, about 10.30 in the forenoon, a German plane flew over the town in a north-easterly direction. The plane was fired at from ships in Sullom Voe, the *Coventry* and others. Bits of shrapnel fell at Mangaster where the roadmen were working. They were forced to run for shelter, into quarry holes, peat banks, and anything within reach. One of the workmen, from Eshaness, was agitating for shelters. He was also organising a petition among his mates for higher wages owing to the increase in the cost of living. Shrapnel splinters also came down in the sea. An air-raid warning was sounded. The gunfire was heard by people in North Røe. The folk north about, near the aerodrome, were "in a great wye" over all these happenings. Some women wanted their men to flit somewhere else. A Finnish steamer, the *Eileen*, put into Olnafirth about this time listing badly. It was damp and dull on Wednesday, 8th November. A crowd of R.A.F. men went away on leave with the *St. Clair*. A lot of folk in from country districts were bustling about, "in a shop, an' oot a shop," getting their errands. Near a butcher shop a man was standing speaking to another man and his wife. They were discussing "the war." One said: "They couldn't see nae farther dan da point o' dir nose!" The news came that the big German liner *Bremen* had managed to slip through the Navy's cordon somewhere near Shetland. She reached the port of Murmansk, and afterwards sailed down past the Norwegian coast. The pocket-battleship *Deutschland* was at large about this time. This was a big topic of conversation with folk. Some said "da British" would have a job to catch her owing to the ship's speed, but others thought she'd soon be caught and sunk. The American steamer *City of Flint* had been seized by the Germans some days before. This was another interesting topic of conversation. The "island in the Rhine" that figured in the war news was also discussed. One or two seemed surprised to learn there were "islands" in the

Rhine, seemingly thinking the Rhine was not much bigger than a "bit o' a burn!" The report of the German plane having been over "the Shetlands" on Tuesday, 7th November, was given in the B.B.C. Home Service news bulletin at 9 p.m. The following day it was rumoured that a submarine had been sunk in St. Magnus Bay. This was supposed to have been seen from Papa Stour by three coast-watchers.

Fifty or so airmen went south with the *St. Clair*. Rumour had it that forty or fifty "marines" were going to be stationed on the Fair Isle, at anti-aircraft guns, and that a big aerodrome to hold "twenty aircraft" was going to be made at Graven on the Garth side of Sullom Voe. It was said that some German aircraft had been seen on Tuesday coming in from the west. The local paper reported some bombs having been dropped, but no damage had been done.

It was a westerly breeze and damp on Saturday, the 11th November. The Boys' Brigade organised the selling of poppies. The Finnish steamer *Eileen* was now lying at the coal-hulk in the north harbour. Folk said there was "something of a mystery" about her cargo. *It's in the Air*, featuring George Formby, was the "big picture" at the Picture House. Three *March of Time* pictures also were shown. The first dealt with Mexico. Peasants and workers could be seen being handed books at a library. Some of the books were by Communist and other progressive writers. The conclusion of the film showed the editor of a Tulsa, Oklahoma, newspaper, sitting at his desk dictating an anti-Cardenas article. On Monday, the 13th, "da Germans" were north again! It was a day of heavy rain and low visibility. The "foreign-sounding drone" of a plane was heard about dinner-time. A gale from the south-east came up, with rain. People said they saw "da German" disappearing in the clouds. Official notices dealing with food rationing and licences for shops were being exhibited in the shops.

The National Defence Corps, made up of ex-Service

men, was growing in strength. The men were getting their uniforms and wore glengarry-shaped caps. The planes dropped bombs at Sullom and an unoccupied house was hit. The Home Service news at night spoke of the air raid. It said that some bombs fell in the sea and others made holes six feet deep.

Tuesday's *News Chronicle* had the air raid splashed on its front page under big black headlines:

"4 NAZI BOMBERS TWICE FAIL IN
SHETLAND RAID"

The report went on: "Nazi bombers twice raided the Shetland Islands yesterday, but were driven off by anti-aircraft fire without having caused any serious damage. Four bombers took part in each raid. Some of their bombs fell into the sea, and others dropped on open ground, shattering the windows of crofters' cottages.

"This was only the second time that bombs have been dropped in a raid on Britain during the present war, the first being during the Forth Bridge raid. A German plane flew over the Shetlands last Friday, and a raid was also made last Tuesday. The Shetlands are 600 miles from Germany."

This was the raid that gave rise to the foolish wireless and newspaper talk about "the only casualty being one rabbit!" The inane treatment of this incident caused much resentment in Shetland. Folk saw by this that "the powers that be" did not seem to be taking the war very seriously. The Germans claimed to have destroyed two flying-boats. It was reported by folk living near the base that there were as high as twenty ships in Sullom Voe and other northern voes at any given time. A bomb had dropped on a hill at Brae and made a crater 20 feet wide and 10 feet deep. "The teacher in the Sullom school kept the bairns calm during the air raid by getting them to sing!" This was another "splash" headline by some papers. A piece of stone from the force of the falling shrapnel was thrown through the air to enter the roof of a byre a good distance away where a woman was milking a cow. A shell was said to have come down at Hillswick. A witty hand-made poster was seen in a shop window. It was in ink on a quarto sheet: "Horace the Hamburg Humbug says Lerwick is wiped off the map. Why not come to Scalloway, the New (Ancient) Capital of Shetland, for the dance in Public Hall on Saturday. . . ."

Wednesday, 22nd November, was a memorable day in Lerwick. It was rainy, with a lot of wind on the previous night, and it faired up towards noon. About a little after noon folk heard the drone of aircraft. Five planes were then seen to come in from the north. They flew low over the north harbour and the town. Presently "da Germans" was on every tongue. People saw the crosses—black-and-white—with swastikas on the wings. It was seen the Heinkels were intent on business. They circled the town once or twice, then their machine-guns went into action, and before long a bomb was heard bursting.

A great column of black smoke was seen to rise from a burning flying-boat in Gremista Bight. The four airmen aboard got clear by jumping from their craft. The planes re-formed again, and flew off in a south-easterly direction. A photograph of the planes low over the roofs of the highest buildings appeared in the *Daily Express* the following day.

The vessels at the Fish Quay did not open fire, and the air raid siren sounded only about five minutes after the raiders were heard. The "all clear" went about fifteen minutes later.

Something like eight or ten bombs were dropped, but all fell in the sea. The flying-boat was riddled with bullets and set on fire. The same day news went around that "a German had been brought down at Sullom." Two haddock-boats went off from the docks to the men in the blazing aircraft. The boats made for the wreck while the last of the planes was still over the north harbour.

The fishermen picked up the airmen and landed them at the docks. The town was agog with excitement during the raid, but hardly any panic or "windiness" could be seen. The whole thing had been so unexpected that folk came out and stood about on the streets or lined the dykes near the harbour to "get a better view" of what was going on.

The B.B.C. four o'clock bulletin mentioned the raid over "the Shetlands." They said it had been carried out by "six Nazi raiders," and that the warning had been sounded in "one town!" They said the raiders circled low, dropping bombs, but nothing was said of the destroyed flying-boat.

The seagulls, in great circling clouds, were very excited. They klaagd as they soared and circled, white dots against the great black column of smoke being blown to the eastward over the harbour.

The armed liner *Rawalpindi* was reported sunk off Iceland by the *Deutschland*. The Germans kept up intensive aerial activity over Shetland all that winter, bombing and taking observations. On 27th November Orkney and Shetland were declared as being a "protected area." No person was to be allowed to enter this "zone" without a permit, except members of the Forces, residents and children under sixteen. Residents travelling were to get their National Registration Cards stamped by the local police.

The first soldiers of the garrison arrived in Shetland with the mail steamer, on the 1st of December. Over two hundred soldiers for anti-aircraft and other duties arrived, and were put up in the fisher-girls' huts on stations at the North Ness. The men were of the Argyll and Sutherland Highlanders, H.L.I., and Black Watch. They had six Bren guns, machine-guns and other arms with them.

All over the place coloured posters appeared, telling the people that "Freedom is in Peril, Defend it with all your Might!"

A day or so after they arrived a party of Scottish soldiers marched along the road, singing "There'll always be an *England*!"

MUCKLE FLUGGA LIGHTHOUSE

To face page 64

WEST COAST

Fishermen working the haddock-lines reported a mine as being about "a mile off Sumburgh." Another was said to have been washed ashore at Nesting. Thursday, 14th December 1939, was remarked on for its unusual darkness. It was styled the "darkest day of the year," and it was reported that wells in the south mainland were covered with a dirty film of stuff as if "something had fallen out of the sky" with the rain. On Sundays the soldiers were marched to church, headed by pipes and drums, and watched by crowds of townsfolk. The arrival of escort vessels, submarine chasers, the mail boats, flying-boats, Spitfires and the like were interesting events, and formed topics for conversation, sprinkled with many an alarmist rumour. Uniforms of all descriptions soon came to out-number "civvy suits," and the main streets echoed with numerous dialects. On Wednesday, 20th December, a trawler came in, escorted by a drifter, and made fast at the north end of the mart. She had been badly damaged off Fetlar, where she had been attacked by German bombers. Two men were killed. The wheelhouse of this trawler, the *Star of Scotland*, was blown away, and at six o'clock the B.B.C. reported this attack on unarmed fishing vessels off Shetland. There were no direct hits, but the plane flew low, machine-gunning the crew. The survivors from another vessel were picked up and carried to Norway. The Germans claimed they had encountered, and destroyed, thirty-four small "war vessels." On Monday, the 1st of January 1940, the air-raid siren sounded at 11 a.m. Ten minutes later aircraft flew in a southerly direction. People seemed to know right away that "they" were "nort at Sullom!" The "all clear" sounded about noon. Later in the day folk were speaking of a "German plane" brought down in Yell Sound, and another at "da back a Bressay." The following day the wireless mentioned the raids. Folk said the Germans "nearly got" two ships, the *Coventry* and the *Manella*. The plane brought down in Yell Sound was the result of a direct hit.

E

On Wednesday, 10th January, the lifeboat went out through the north entrance to the assistance of a Greek steamer which went ashore on Unst. Two days later the Greek seamen arrived at Lerwick carrying suit-cases and bundles. Snow fell heavily about this time, with very keen frost. Soldiers joined in the fun of sledging on the braes. In one of the huts occupied by the "Home Defence men" icicles had formed inside the roof, just over one of the beds! Saturday, 20th January, a Norwegian steamer was sunk off Unst. The crew got to Baltasound, and came to Lerwick in the *Earl*. Another ship, believed to be British, was lost at about the same place, "with all hands." There was a lot of aerial activity on Wednesday, the 24th, and bombs were dropped near Girlsta. Two or three planes flew low over Lerwick, apparently reconnoitring. On Monday, the 29th, there was another air raid on Sullom. The anti-aircraft guns were in action, and a shell was said to have landed in a burn at Skea, Northmavine. Another shell was heard whizzing through the air near Voe, in Delting. A crofter, working on the roads, heard the shell, and fell to the ground right away. He said the shell buried itself in the hill somewhere. Two ships were lying in Sullom Voe at the time. Four bombs dropped near them. Folk north about had begun to "get used to it" by this time. An old woman said there "wis a battle ower my hoose, an' I wid a laekit till a won furt ta see hit!" Another old woman remarked very philosophically, "Dey wir come to look at dem again!" About the first of February bodies of German airmen were washed ashore near Mossbank. The *Shetland Times* of 2nd February reported one of the *Athenia's* lifeboats having been washed ashore, and smashed, at the Ness of Sound. The name was on part of one of the boards. A locker fastened to a tilfer (flooring-board) contained biscuits in good condition. On Tuesday, the 30th January, a raft was seen floating in past the Bressay lighthouse. This was one of several that had been washed up or seen floating along the east coast of Shetland. The raft came ashore at the Slates. A Norwegian flag was on it. It was reported that a part of an aeroplane wing had been washed up along the coast. This same week's papers carried the report of the loss, by bombing, of the Leith steamer *Giralda*, with the loss of all her crew of twenty-three, including eight Shetlanders. Her captain was a Lerwick man, John Erasmuson. The boat, with the men, was near the Orkney shore when it capsized. The tragic event was seen by watchers on the shore. The *Shetland Times* of 9th February published its fifth list of names in its "Muster Roll" of Shetlanders serving in the Forces. It contained one hundred and one names, mostly of men in the "Merchant Navy." The second list contained twenty-three names. Among other items from the *Times* was a report of the Town Council meeting, at which five councillors out of twelve attended. The Government had turned down the Council's appeal for a subsidy for coal to Shetland. Milk prices were discussed, and it was stated retailers were selling at fourpence a pint and acting illegally.

The steamer *Highcliffe* went ashore on Forwick Holm, Papa Stour, at 5 a.m. on Tuesday. Her skipper was a Shetlander. Some of the men went ashore on a beach in a small boat. Others were taken off by the Aith lifeboat. The ship was abandoned as a wreck, and the boat was left on the beach. The vessel was a Shields steamer laden with iron ore. For three days they did not know where they were.

Most of the snow had gone except for deep fanns in the hills. Cars were beginning to get through to the town, some after being held up for a month. The following Tuesday a Swedish steamer was torpedoed off Shetland and some of her survivors taken into Sullom Voe. Pieces of bombs and shrapnel were to be seen on show in a shop window. These were picked up after the last "big" raid. The window also had on view the piece of the *Athenia's* name-board.

On Wednesday, the 14th, the air-raid siren was sounded on the ships at Sullom. Destroyers hurried out and went north through Yell Sound. Nine bodies came ashore at Unst and Fetlar. One body was washed ashore at Lunnaness, and was presumed to be that of a Norwegian.

The 15th February issue of the *Shetland News* carried an interesting paragraph about the sentry on duty at the Telephone Exchange challenging someone at the gate. It was a message boy, and he was allowed to "pass friend, all's well!" When he was going out the challenge came again, and the reply was: "You —— fool! It's da sam message boy, wi' an empty basket!"

The "Home Defence Corps" had become the National Defence Corps. Composed mostly of ex-Service men, they were posted for duty to various "strategic spots" throughout the islands. Seeing them march along, it was noticeable that they compared favourably, in height, physique and smartness, with the young soldiers of "this war" who had been sent north from the "mainland of Britain." The N.D.C. men carried their rifles with them when making for home. Some bags of mails were found at Noss. They were from a Danish or Icelandic vessel, and some American mails also drove ashore. Another of the *Athenia's* boats was reported ashore at Faroe. Some of the bodies washed ashore at Fetlar were photographed for identification purposes.

In the papers about this time a report telling of the death of Christopher Tait of East Burrafirth recalled a tragic event. Christopher Tait was ninety-four years of age, and he was the last survivor of the *Diana*, of Hull, the whaler which wintered in the ice and made the "death voyage" to Rønies Voe.

About one hundred soldiers arrived with the mail steamer on Thursday, 7th March. Air-raid shelters were under construction at various parts of the town. Some soldiers, coming from the Naafi canteen, were going along singing "Roll out the Barrel," "We'll Hang Out the Washing on the Siegfried Line," and other topical songs. On Wednesday, 20th March, a Heinkel was seen passing from the east, over the town. The siren sounded, and the "all clear" half an hour later. About five or six fighter planes were cruising around during the raid. It was raining, with a heavy cloudy sky at the time. The next day the alarm went about 2 p.m. On Sunday, 17th March, a Norwegian steamer came into harbour with a great hole in her bow. It was reported she had rammed and sunk another steamer.

On Monday, 25th March, at 10 p.m., the B.B.C. broadcast a feature on "The Shetlands: Life and Work in the Northern Islands." The talk was interspersed with musical items, fiddle playing, the singing of the *Shetland Lullaby* and other songs. Most of the music seemed to be Finnish, probably purposedly stuck into the programme in line with the Government's "pro-Finnish" sentiments. The announcer said the producer had been helped by the "men of Shetland," a remark that caused some comment in Shetland, as apparently very few "men of Shetland" had been consulted.

As a whole, the feature was not badly done, although much of vital importance was omitted. There was the usual "romantic" and "Norn" background stuff. There were such remarks as "The sea!—it is their cradle! . . ." Descriptions of the rocks, sea, crofts, wool, sheep, knitting, men sailing ("Some of the older men have been around the world! They've been at such ports as Shanghai, New York, Yokohama, Cape Town, Rio de Janeiro, etc." "Men are familiar with such-and-such a port").

There was a piece about "the road": the main highway was unlike roads elsewhere. The roads were narrow, winding, near the sea. It told the story of "Atla the Giant." Atla was angry and threw some boulders from some place at Aithsting. They fell into the sea off the west coast. Thus there came about the Ve Skerries. It went on to tell "of anchors found on the Ve Skerries," of bits of wood, etc. The story of the ill-fated trawler *Ben Doran* was told: of how she was wrecked on the cruel Skerries, of her men lashed to the rigging, the lifeboat arriving but powerless to give help. It told of a trawler in Rønies Voe going out to try to rescue the men, but the crew found it impossible to go near the Skerries. Nine trawlers came on the scene, but not one could render any help. Next morning they saw the masts awash and the men washed away.

There was something about a smack whose skipper wanted to be in Scalloway over da helly (week-end). The speaker finished this part of the broadcast by saying, "Not a ship ever got off the Ve Skerries." He mentioned Papa Stour, and about getting a man who knew the Skerries, then went on to speak of "other days—other wrecks." This was the Spanish galleon *El Gran Grifon* on Fair Isle. There followed a bit about the knitting, dyeing of wool, etc. Then a woman's voice telling how to wash Shetland hosiery: "Rinse in soapy hot water, and quickly draw it through the hands, squeezing lightly. If you don't know how to do it, send it to us in Shetland and we'll do it for you."

Previously in the broadcast there had been a woman speaking, again supposed to be a Shetlander. It was noticeable that there was a certain straining after effect, trying "ta spaek Shetlan." This had been about the shawls that could "be pulled through a ring." She said she had some, and that only six or eight women could knit fine fancy-work garments. There was a bit about the greenness of the Shetland grass in April, cutting the peats in May, drying them in June; the "fisherman getting home to take in his crops," and the like. One of the men who had acted in the *Edge of the World* spoke about someone in Foula known as "Jimmy." They looked on him as a "mechanical genius." He had fixed some wires or other for one of their cameras that had "to be in action that very day." They offered him "a contract at Elstree," but "Jimmy wouldn't come!" There were "many like Jimmy in Shetland." The broadcast faded out to a not very convincing rendering of the *Shetland Lullaby*, and the remark about "The sea!—it is their cradle!"

The snow laid on again towards the end of March. On Wednesday, the 27th, it was cold, with easterly wind and showers of wet snow. At times it was "flukkra snaa" and "moories" were frequent. Soldiers marching out the road were covered with snow. It came on a "blinnd moorie" towards night. The next day the familiar "alarm" went at about noon. Two "Germans" were seen, and fighter planes went up. On Sunday, 31st March, the alarm went at about 10 a.m. The B.B.C. said this was the "first Sunday raid" here, but it was the "twenty-first visit from raiders."

In the last week of March about forty trawlers were sheltering in Rønies Voe. There were nine ships in Sullom Voe. On Wednesday, 3rd April, a German plane flew from the south-west in a northerly direction, but the warning did not sound. On Monday, 8th April, at 11.30 a.m., there was an air-raid warning, and about twenty minutes later the "all clear" went. No plane was seen, but five fighters were scouring the sky. A German plane was reported over Rønies Voe. The news came through that mines had been laid in Norwegian territorial waters. Folk spoke of this, and a marked feeling of tension was noticeable. "Something's in the air," and "Wonder what's next?" were remarks heard in conversation. Rumours began flying about. Next day more definite news came through. It told of Germany's invasion of Denmark and Norway. This caused something of a sensation. It was a bright but cold day, with occasional hail showers, but folk were early astir, waiting for "da news." The waterfront, as usual, drew most folk. They wondered what was afoot. Four destroyers of the "F" class came into the harbour in the afternoon, one having a big hole in her stern, "after a collision." They lay anchored off Twagios and the Widows' Homes. Groups of men gathered on the breakwater, pier and esplanade. Men went out along to da Knab, watching the ships. Rumours increased, and people looked grave now they realised the Germans were so near Shetland. The air raids had been taken calmly, but the idea that Norway was actually occupied by German troops seemed to bring the war and fighting to Shetland's brigstanes, as it were.

Stories spread of "a troop-ship off Bressay," a "battle was going on outside," "four or five prisoners from a German plane had been landed." "They'll laekly come an' tak wis next!" and the like remarks could be heard. The prisoners were said to have been landed off the destroyer *Cossack*.

The N.D.C. men were told "to stand by." They had got ammunition, emergency rations, etc. They had to report at Fort Charlotte "when dey heard da bugle!" A group of men stood discussing things as they watched the destroyers. "Weel, it's a' up a gum tree noo, I tink!" said one, gravely. "Nae faer a it," said another, a N.D.C. man, with a rifle slung over his shoulder. He turned to the first man: "Diss country's da strongest o' da lot! Look at da armaments we have!" A young fellow, overhearing the remark, glanced sarcastically at the man's rifle, and said, "Sez you!" A fourth said, to no one in particular, as he agitatedly paced back and fore, "Noo, whaar tink ye wis da Breetish Navy it dey koodna a stoppit dem! Eh?" Another shrugged, struck a light to his pipe, and smiled: "Laekly ida Cattegat, sinkin a' yun ships!" There was a pause, then the fourth man resumed: "I donn know! It looks gey queer ta me. I never thought da Jarmans hed sae monny ships." "It's a bad business, aa da sam," said the N.D.C. man; "only twa hunder miles frae wis noo. Dey kood doe dat in twa days' time wi' dir fast boats. . . . Weel, I'd better hadd nort ower, for da alarm may geng at onny meenit!"

As the day wore on and nothing happened, the groups dispersed, but it was seen by all that "da waar" had taken a new and graver turn.

News came on Thursday, the 11th, that Britain had occupied Faroe, and that Iceland was also to be protected.

More troops, mostly young "militia men," were landed in Shetland during the month of April and first part of May. Guns, lorries and ammunition were brought north. On Sunday, 12th May, three transports were at the Fish Mart quay landing men, cars, guns, stores, etc. There was a continuous running of lorries, cars, guns from the Mart to the huts at the herring stations, where men were billeted, as well as to places in the north mainland. Crowds stood watching the troops and commenting on the exciting events. On this same day the troops were told to "stand by," and ammunition was said to have been issued to them. Destroyers damaged by enemy aircraft during the fighting in Norway came into the harbour for temporary repairs.

On Saturday, 4th May, some Norwegian refugees arrived at Lerwick in the Norwegian steamer *Gudmund*. There were also some Norwegian soldiers on board, and some captured Germans. A Norwegian flying-boat came down in the harbour that same day. Some Norwegians were said to have captured a German plane and flown it across to Sullom Voe. The Norwegian soldiers were enrolled in the local N.D.C. On Friday, 17th May, Norway's National Day, a company of Norwegians, some in N.D.C. uniform, sailors, fishermen, and others, marched from the docks, headed by a piper and two men carrying large Norwegian flags. This was a march to celebrate the "17th May" and all it stood for in courage, independence and the desire for freedom. The Norwegian flag flew from the Town Hall tower.

Barbed wire was put up along the sea front and at all possible landing-places. Anti-tank traps were built on the roads, and the fields and hills covered with wire and all sorts of obstructions. Leaflets were even distributed, giving the "password"—"BLOOD RED"—that was to be used when "da Invasion" started. A curfew was imposed, and folk were fined for being out after 11 p.m. without permission!

CHAPTER IV

FAIR ISLE, mid-way between Orkney and Shetland, stands like a lonely sentinel between the two seas. It used to be said Fair Isle folk could sit at their firesides watching vessels on their voyages between the old world and the new passing the Isle. In the days of the sailing ships men from the Isle made a practice of putting off in their small boats to "speak" the passing ships. In this way they got "news" of the outside world, and often various needed commodities in exchange for fish, mutton and vegetables. A Fair Isle boat is said to have kept up with a sailing vessel as far north and west as Foula before the islesmen took leave of their sailor friends. The first news of such great happenings as Waterloo and the battle of Trafalgar reached Fair Isle from men on board passing ships.

There are numerous references to "the Isle" in historical works, from the *Orkneyinga Saga* and onwards. In an account of Frobisher's voyages there is a reference to the Isle, and in Edmund Vale's *The Way of Ships* there is a drawing of "A fourteenth-century shipwreck of wool-ship on Fair Isle," showing the high "stern-castle" of the period. In the American War of Independence the Isle was well known by Yankee privateers, Paul Jones, the Galloway-born privateer, passing the Isle on his way north "to sack Lerwick."

Many a stirring sight must the people of the Isle have witnessed. Large sailing ships, as the *Pommern* and *Grace Harwar*, yachts, steamers, men-o'-war, have been seen passing the Isle. Trawlers working in huge seas, vessels in distress off the Isle, bearing down helplessly, crashing on the cliffs.

The most famous Fair Isle shipwreck was that of the Spanish Armada galleon *El Gran Grifon*. She crashed in a gio in 1588. The story of how the Spaniards are said to have taught the Fair Isle women the art of knitting coloured designs into their woollen hosiery is already well known. The stories of the "Cross of Castille," "Anchor of Columbus," "Moorish Arrow," "Spanish Mermaid," "Star of Granada," the "Basque Lily," and the rest as being featured in the numerous intricate "Fair Isle patterns" are probably far from genuine; but as folk-traditions with a ring of poetry and romance about them, they are similar to the legends of the "sea-shell," "sea-wave," "fern," "fish-bone," "horse shoe," and other patterns found in the designs of other hand-knitted Shetland woollens, and no great harm is done recalling them here.

The population of "the Isle" is about one hundred, about ninety islanders and six families in the two lighthouses. They have a school, a lighthouse at either end of the Isle, a library, two kirks, and a small mail boat, the *Good Shepherd*, which runs between the Isle and Grutness and Lerwick "in Shetland." They have a distinctive type of open boat in the Isle, called the yawl, long and narrow, like a small Viking longship, fitted with six or eight oars. The men are probably Shetland's best boatmen. The "ward hills" of the Isle were the places on which beacon-fires were kindled to warn the men of Orkney and Shetland of the approach of unfriendly vessels. A JU 88 German aircraft was shot down off the Isle by an anti-aircraft gunner in August 1943. The Germans raided the Isle on many occasions.

Fair Isle is one of the places where you will still hear a fine distinctive speech. Its intonation and idiom is almost purely Norn, or Scandinavian. The isolated position of the island has helped to keep the Norn tongue of the folk very pure. It could be said to be the most "Norn spoken" of the isles, Foula, Papa, the North Isles and Whalsay coming next. In accent and structure the speech is not much different from that of people in parts of Western Norway. They have much the same inflexion, full-throated but not harsh, with the pleasing "sing-song" drawl and melodious raising of the voice towards the end of a sentence as are found among most Norwegians.

A Fair Isle man, in a letter to the writer, in December 1944, writes: " . . . I remember being told that Dr. Jakobsen, when in Shetland, was informed that it was little or no use going to Fair Isle, as, by their contact with the south, Fair Isle people had lost the dialect; and as a result he did not come here. Dr. Jakobsen had an interview with Mr. James Wilson of Kirkwall, who was a native of Fair Isle, but left here when he was young. Dr. Jakobsen got some dialect words from him, but I do not know whether he had any other contacts with F.I. people or not."

This writer sent an interesting list of Fair Isle dialect words, for use in compiling the proposed *Shetland Dialect Wordbook*, in the course of which, commenting on the Fair Isle folk's way of saying "day," he remarks: "In the Fair Isle word for 'day' the vowel sound is different from 'a,' 'ae,' 'aa,' 'aw,' and which I do not know how to write. I have very rarely heard other Shetlanders use this sound. I think it is used in Whalsay. We use it in many other words." On the other hand, he points to certain traits of speech indicating a slurring of the former Norn purity, as, for instance, " . . . I do not remember the 'k' sound used at beginning of words. In regard to 'gj' sound, we do not say 'gjaan,' but 'gaein.' We have the sound, however, in 'gjill' (narrow glen with burn), 'gjimmer' (two-year-old sheep), 'gjo'; and as a common noun, in place-names we almost invariably say 'Gja'."

The list this writer sent gives an interesting guide to the Fair Isle people's pronunciation of vowels, as is seen in the following extract: " . . . pronunciation *aa* as in Haa, baa. *Aald*; *kaald*; *keel* (cabbage); *oag* (to crawl); *oog* (verminous); *mylk* (milk); *been* (bone); *kaa* (drive); *bairn* (child); *tusker* (*tushker* in North Mainland); *tenn* (ten); *baand* (band); *haand* (hand); *heem* (home); *spaed* (spade); *baed* (bed); *dwaam* (sleep); *een* and *wan* (one); *hain* (economise); *blaand*; *shøn* (shoes—*never* 'shunn' or 'sheen'); *ook* (week); *heel* (whole); *aleen* (alone); *yea, yah* and *yiss* (all three used for 'yes'); *stoor* was used until recently for 'big' or 'large'; *muckle* is still common. . . . In Fair Isle the three stars (the 'three stars' in 'Orion's Belt') were called 'Da ladies' ell-waand' . . ." Finally, he makes the interesting statement: "I do not think that there is anything in the story that the Spaniards taught the Fair Islanders the art of knitting designs, etc. The native tradition is that a sailor brought back a shawl with some designs in it, and which the F.I. women tried and succeeded in copying. The designs have, I believe, been developed by one and another from time to time to almost the present day." This list gave a total of 217 dialect words, of which 39 words related to "corn, barn, and mill"; 36 to "boats," etc.; 27 to "birds"; 18 to "fish"; 10 to "utensils"; and 2 to "mammalia." The same writer also compiled a list of 224 Fair Isle place-names. Another Fair Isle man sending a fine list of words, wrote: " . . . There are a lot of place-names here that can't be pronounced properly without the letters ø and *eh*, two letters used in the Danish alphabet. I noticed when travelling in Shetland there are several names in Shetland the same; it needs these two Danish letters in addition to the English alphabet to get the proper old pronunciation which some of the old people used."

The Isle's people are good speakers of English, however, and they are hardy, highly intelligent, shrewd and kindly; characteristics bred into them by the long struggle with the elements. For months on end Fair Isle was often cut off from the rest of Shetland and the world, the first sign of civilisation usually being some ship or other passing the Isle. Well read and up to date with all that's going on in the world, and with keen critical faculties that go to the roots of things, they are very progressive-minded, eager for all the latest in modern "fixings," as wireless and electricity. At the same time they have a sensible thrifty outlook, preserving what's best of the old way of life in their snug little "outpost of the North." Rivlins, or shoes made from untanned cowhide, are not quite obsolete, and oxen-drawn ploughs and carts are still in use.

There is one road, running roughly north and south,

linking up the lighthouses. There are two churches, Wesleyan and Church of Scotland, and as the population is not large enough to make two congregations, it used to be the custom that people able to go to the kirk would go to the Wesleyan Chapel for morning prayer, and to the "big kirk" in the afternoon. Then the following Sunday the order would be reversed; in this way any jealousy was dispelled.

W. Strong Eunson was a notable son of Fair Isle. He was a merchant in Lerwick for some years, and wrote and published his own "paper," called *Sib* (Kinsfolk). He went to Aberdeen to live and turned his able mind to research in connection with the fishing industry. He invented "Scapa Flower," a preparation made from seaweed, which is being used in scientific agriculture. Strong Eunson was one of the first men to place filleted fish on the market, and he discovered and demonstrated the possibilities of block filleting, thus finding a profitable outlet for fish which formerly were cast aside as worthless.

In the middle of June the summer sheep-kaain takes place in Fair Isle. The island kaain is more adventurous than in most places in Shetland, with the exceptions of Foula and Rønies Hill. In Foula they do not "kaa" or "koosh" sheep in the accepted sense for fear of driving the animals over the high cliffs, and at Rønies Hill some sheep have run wild for years, and defy both man and dog. Those in Fair Isle whose sheep are on the green fertile top of the "Sheep Craig" have an arduous time of it ere getting their sheep attended to. They have to go in boats, and then climb the steep cliff sides of the Craig with the help of chains fastened to the rock. The Craig, which is on the east side of the Isle, is like a huge obliquely truncated obelisk. It has ten acres of fine pasturage on its summit. The wind, even the strongest gale, is deflected upwards by the perpendicular cliff sides, this enabling the sheep to graze in safety. When the people need to get sheep down, the animals are lowered to the boat by means of ropes and chains.

It is an interesting point you make about some surnames here being Scottish, and some English and Irish. Yes, that is true enough, and there are even Manx and Welsh names in Shetland, for the islands have always attracted folk from other places, just as many Shetlanders have settled down elsewhere, giving to their new homes a distinct Northern colour in surnames and speech and customs.

However, for all the intermingling of peoples that has taken place, the essentially northern character persists. This is seen in our dialect, place-names, traditions, legends, fiddle-music and, above all, in our surnames. Most of the surnames are of the "son" type, the form in which the Norse patronymics became stereotyped round about the first part of the nineteenth century. Even long after that, traces of the Shetland custom lingered. It was common for folk to refer to persons by their parents' names rather than their Christian names. Magnus Olafsson was Olie's Maansie, Laura Daamarsdaughter would have been Daamar's Lowra, and so on. This Christian name Daamar is the form the old Norse Dagmar (the Day-Dawn) took, and it in turn became Tamar.

As is to be expected, there are numerous modern touches in the naming of bairns here as elsewhere. There are not so many Thorvalds or Olafs nowadays, nor do we find any Gudruns, Sunnivas, or Sigrids. The Oslas, too, are getting rarer. Sigurd, however, still persists in the form Shuard, and Shuardson is a fairly common surname in some mainland districts. Of late Einar, Ivar, Karl, Norman and other northern names have made a welcome reappearance. Magnus, too, is widely used. Even in the matter of surnames changes have taken place, as in the case of the Shetlandic *Johnson*. Far too often this is debased into Johnston, after the Scottish place of that name. Most surnames here are of Norse origin, some being identical with surnames in use in Faroe, Iceland and Norway.

Arcus, for instance, seems peculiarly Shetlandic, as is *Aitken* and *Anderson*. *Bairnson* has the real northern sound about it, while *Bain, Barclay, Bigland, Bolt, Blance* and *Burgess* are often encountered. Burgess is probably from Borgar, a dweller in a "borg." Cluness, or rather Kleniss, is doubtful, and probably Scottish. In some parts of Shetland the name *Coutts* used to be pronounced *Kowtt*, and may have been a Dutch name. *Cogle* is a good Shetland name, and so is *Coupland*. *Cooper* is very widespread in Delting. *Charleson* is not now so common. It is met with in Yell and on the west side. *Cummings* is found in Burra. *Danielson* was generally pronounced Dennilson, and is a North Isles name. *Deyell* seems to be the same as *Dalziel*. *Doull* is another northern name. Davidson is pronounced as *Dauvidson* in the North Isles, and *Daavidson* in the Mainland. It is well known in Sound, Gulberwick and Quarff.

The once fairly widespread Erasmus, or Rasmie, as we know it, gave us the name *Erasmuson*, or Rasmieson as Shetlanders call it. *Erikson, Erlendson, Erlingson* and *Einarson* are not now known; but *Edwardson* is a surname here. *Eunson*, pronounced "Yunnson," is commonly met with, and has been a name in the Fair Isle since the Norse days. This name is probably from the Norse *Uni*, and the old forms *Yaan* and *Yon* are similar. When Jarl Rognvald and the other great Shetland and Orkney chiefs were trading and fighting near the isles, there was a man named Uni in Fair Isle who rendered valuable service to the folk by slokkin the war beacons kindled on the ward heights of the Isle.

Flaus, or *Flaas, Firth, Foubister* and perhaps *Frizell* belong to the islands. *Ganson*, or *Gaanson* (North Isles *Gaunson*), *Garster, Gardner, Gaadie* (or *Goudie*), *Gear, Goodlad* (*Gjullet*), *Grains, Green*, are authentic enough, though Gardner may be from Scotland. *Gear* is akin to *Geir*, still common in Iceland. *Geirhilda* was Raven-Flokki's daughter. She was drowned in the big loch now known as Girlsta, in the year her father Flokki came to Shetland, guided westward by the ravens.

Goodlad is pronounced *Gjullet* in some parts of Shetland. In Lerwick we have a man of that name

CLIFFS, FOULA

J. Peterson

To face page 80

J. Peterson

OFF FOULA

commemorated in Gjullet's Brae. *Halcrow, Harklson* (from *Haakonson*, now known as Herculeson!), *Harrison*, or *Hairison, Henderson, Henry, Hoseason* and *Hughson* are well known here. The name *Hunter* is fairly widespread, especially in Nesting and Weisdale. It was said that there were so many Hunters in Nesting at one time that there wasn't much room left for other folk, so to even things out a bit "da Black sheeld"* took a kishie† full of them and went westward to Weisdale and Whiteness. The bottom of the kishie fell out before he got there, so things remained much as they were. *Haa'* is probably the old Norse name *Hall*, as "Hall of the Side" in Iceland. It seems native to Delting. *Inkster*, thought to be from either "Inge's setr" or Inge's farm, or Inge's daughter, is a Norse name, as is *Isbister*, from the place-name occurring more than once in Shetland. The "daughter" names were common in Shetland up to comparatively recent times, and it is not long since a woman, Naanie Johnster, or Agnes Johnsdaughter, died at the West Side. *Irvine* is a common name here, probably the same surname as the older northern form *Irving*.

Jakobson, or to give the correct form *Yakobson*, is still common in Shetland. The name *Jamieson*, although fairly common in Scotland, is as common in the islands as *Jakobsen* is in Faroe. The name *Jeemson*, to give its local pronunciation, is akin to Jakobson. *Jarmson* is also still with us. It is *Jaurmson* in the North Isles and at the Ness. Another form is *Jeromeson*. *Johnson* is one of our most widespread names, and as stated before, is at times corrupted into "Johnston." The name is from *Yon*, or *Yaan*, and closely akin to Eunson. It is perhaps the case that in almost every parish the name Johnson is met with. It was said of a certain district that almost all the folk were Johnsons, and "tö-names," or nicknames, had to be used to distinguish one family from the other.

Laurenson is another name, the Shetland form "Lowrinson" being from the Norse *Lavransson*. The title of Sigrid Undset's great novel *Kristin Lavransdaughter*, in the Shetland

* The Deil. † Straw basket.

F

dialect would be "Kirstie Lowrinson." *Langskail* is better known in Orkney. *Leask*, or *Leisk* (Shetlandic *Laesk*), is widespread in the islands, although it is not known if any of them managed to get as far as Papa, Foula or the Fair Isle. *Linklater* is another good northern name, common to Shetland and Orkney. *Mail* (pronounced *Mell*), *Mainland*, *Manson* (from *Magnusson*), and *Mann* are well represented here, as is *Malcolmson* (*Maikimson*), the latter seeming to be Scottish. *Morrison* has a northern sound about it, being found in the Western Isles as well as Shetland. *Moar* or *More* is an old northern name. *Mouat* and *Mowat*, usually pronounced *Moad*, is common in Shetland. *Mullay* (older form *Mulla*) is another surname, though not very common.

Nielson (or *Nelson*) and *Nicolson* are well known here, the latter as *Niklasen* or *Niklassen*, being a common Faroe surname. Although *Nisbet* is a good North Isles name, it may be another of the "in-comers."

Odie, *Ollason* (*Olafson*) and *Oman* have a northern ring about them, while a name *Ottison* or *Ottarson* used to be known in the islands. *Peterson*, *Pottinger*, *Pole*, *Poleson* and *Priest* are all Shetland names, the latter common in Unst. *Ratter* is an old Shetland name, as is *Ridland* and *Russland*. *Ringanson* was a surname here at one time. *Robertson* is common enough, and *Russell* is met with. *Rendall* is known here as well as in Orkney, where there is the parish of Rendall. *Sandison*, *Scollay* (older form *Skolla*), *Shewan*, *Shuardson* (from the Norse *Sigurdsson*), *Skae*, *Stove*, *Stickle* (from the German *von Steigle*, or *Fredmann von Steigle*, a sailor who came to Unst and settled there), *Tait* (or *Teit*), *Thomason*, *Twatt* (corrupted into *Watt*), *Walterson*, *White*, *Williamson*, *Winchester*, *Young* and *Youngklaus* are further examples of Shetland surnames.

Yes, it is true that folk find quite a lot of sea-driven wood and other gear on the beaches. With bad weather, and the wind from the south and south-west, a lot of drift-wood is washed ashore, although it is probably the case that wood and "wrack" of various kinds get driven ashore with all the "erts o' wind" that blow, as the islands are in the centre of numerous trade routes.

Some men get a passion for scouring "da banks" and the shore. Even in bad weather with the spindrift dashing over the land some "beachcombers" must go down to the shore to see "what's doing!"

When the gale moderates the beachcombers get busy. All along the shore heaps of seaweed get piled up by the driving sea. These are carried to the crofts to be used as manure. Dead fish are found along the beach; seals, too, at times. The islanders use some of the fish. The seals, if not badly crushed, are skinned and the carcases are thrown away. At one time, though, they were used for getting seal oil. The skins are valuable for slippers, golf bags and other articles. Wreck wood, deck cargo from timber-laden ships, fish boxes, casks, spars, oars, boats and so on, all drive ashore. Of course, most of this is reported to the Receiver of Wrecks, but often wreckage is sold for very little at the spot it comes to land, as it would cost too much to have it transported to sheds in the town. People get firewood from the sea and pieces of wood suitable for roofing, or "stabs," or fencing-posts. A beachcomber on one of the outlying isles almost lost his life trying to retrieve a cask with some paraffin from the rocks offshore. After some strenuous hours he at last got it ashore, only to have it lifted again by a big wave which dashed its staves asunder on the beach.

The wreck of a trawler was confirmed early one morning as a crofter set out to "geng aboot da banks." He found a small inlet jammed with broken fish boxes, some of which were found to bear the name of an overdue vessel. Chests, clothes, ropes, casks, tins, odds and ends of various sorts are flung up on the shore. Some amusement may be caused by the efforts of rival beachcombers. In a certain place one night after the wind subsided two crofters sat up, anxious to be at the shore. Carrying lanterns, they both got to the cliff edge at the same time, and they started quarrelling as to who should go first down the narrow path to the shore, where, far below, they could hear the noise of "wrack wood" among the surge. After some hot words one knocked his rival's lantern from his hand and hurried down, the other scrambled after him; but when they at last reached the shore in the grey dawn the wind veered round and the two were left to watch the spoils being blown out of their reach.

It is quite true what you write about Hermaness. The bird-watcher at this place has (or had up till recent years) one of the loneliest jobs imaginable. Hermaness is a point of land rising to a height of about 600 feet, at the north of Unst, and for about five months of the year he has to stay by himself, looking after the rare bird species on this sanctuary.

Employed by the Royal Society for the Protection of Birds, the bird-watcher has a little hut on the slope of the hill. Coming to Hermaness shortly before the breeding season, he usually stays until the birds are full grown. Reports on his interesting charges are sent to the society from time to time. The first watcher to be sent to Britain's most northerly bird sanctuary was a man named Edwardson. He kept up his lonely vigil, season after season, for about thirty years. The great skua, or "bonxie," made Hermaness its breeding-place, and since the watcher took up his duties this bird has multiplied greatly.

Hundreds of nests are to be found at Hermaness. So well have successive bird-watchers done their job of preserving the loneliness of the place, that sheep-breeders and crofters say that the skua is becoming a menace. It is said the bird attacks lambs. While the birds are tending their eggs it is not safe to go too near their nests. Climbers on the Foula cliffs have been attacked by them, and once a cragsman—scaling the banks for eggs—was almost knocked off the rocks by the fierceness of two big bonxies. He kept them off with stones until help came.

The "Great" and "Arctic" Skuas, and also the

"Richardson's" Skua, are rapacious birds. They live by preying on herring-gulls and other birds. Since "the hermit of Hermaness" began the job of guarding the species, the skua has spread to other places in Shetland, as Noss, Hillswick and Foula. Hermaness is near the rocks at Muckle Flugga, the most northerly points of land in Britain. Here, at Flugga, live other lonely men, the keepers of the "farthest north" lighthouse.

The "bird-land" promontory is named after a legendary Shetland giant, "Herman of the Hills." He was said to have been a "mortal terror," amusing himself by casting large rocks at random. In this way, says the legend, the Fluggas and other isles were scattered higgledy-piggledy. Herman was not the only giant in the land, as not far from his home there lived Saxa, the "sire of Saxavord." Saxavord is a height across the firth from Hermaness. The two giants were always "tullyin," or fighting, life for ordinary folk becoming unbearable, so that some sold up and went north to Faroe to bide. The giants, however, could never abide wet feet, so one day when their quarrelling was more than usually violent, "whole islands" were torn up and thrown through the air. The splashing caused by rocks falling into the sea so wetted the giants that they lost their powers of resistance, speedily being overpowered by bands of men from neighbouring districts. It is said that Herman can be seen to this day sitting, "in an abject mood," at Hermaness; while old Saxa sits unmovable and morose on top of Saxavord hill.

The sanctuary is mostly damp heathery moorland on its low-lying ground. Here the Arctic Skuas nest on the slopes. In a report from Hermaness, the watcher wrote: "I had a surprise visit from my old friend the tame Richardson's Skua with a new partner. The newcomer kept away from the hut at first, and the old one was a bit stand-offish, but is now his usual self. The new one is always coming nearer, and I hope ere the season is over to have her as tame as her predecessor."

From this report it is seen that the bird-watcher, in spite

of his lonely vigil, makes friends with the predatory skuas and other birds. Some of the birds become almost tame, nesting near the hut, bringing out their young right under his nose as he goes in and out of the building. Some of the skuas even come to the threshold, others venture inside. Once the watcher was amused to see an old bird take its new mate a share of some food he had given it.

Of recent years the solan geese, or gannets, and the fulmars have become very common around the Shetland coast, a colony of the latter nesting at the Knab, near Lerwick. During the hairst and winter of 1945 large numbers of gannets frequented the harbour, feeding on the sillicks, or small coal-fish, then in vast shoals around the coast. The "Lerwick gannets," as they became known, grew quite tame. They came into the piers after the sillicks, the piers and esplanade being lined with hundreds of people admiring the graceful diving of the birds. Men with kine-cameras stood on the pier making a pictorial record of the display.

CHAPTER V

YOUR remarks on the film the *Edge of the World* as convey-ing a good impression of island life are to the point.

The film was directed by Michael Powell from his story of the same name. It was inspired by the evacuation of the folk from St. Kilda in 1935. This suggested to Powell the idea of making a film showing the problems of people living on the remoter isles.

On the film's showing at Lerwick in January 1938, great interest was aroused, and people came to the town from all over the islands. Foula folk were debarred from seeing themselves on the screen, as bad weather following on an influenza epidemic prevented the boat from making the crossing.

The picture did not please everybody. Most people, however, were delighted with it. The general impression was that Powell had done a fine bit of work, both in story and film. One man was indignant, and said the film was a "disgrace to Shetland!" Another thought it lacked a really strong "story," while some younger people thought the acting "slow," and the whole thing sort of tame after the usual run of "tough guy" drivel from America. Other young people, though familiar enough with the Shetland scenery and theme of the picture, were very impressed with the cliff and sea scenes, and their comments were favourable.

The film opens with a view of Foula taken from an approaching vessel. It shows the wonderful effect of sun-light on sea and rocks. The opening caption tells of when the Romans sailed north they saw from Orkney an isle like a dim blue haze to the north and called it Ultima Thule. The caption speaks of the "slow shadow of death" falling over the outer Scottish isles, and proceeds to tell that this is the story of *Hirta*, an old Scots name meaning "death."

Then there comes the picture of a sheep and lamb

grazing on a Foula hill. An eagle is seen watching the lamb. The two animals scamper off on sensing their enemy—"Death." But the bird of prey flies after them, and this sequence is a fine bit of photography and "natural acting." The bird is almost over the lamb when the sheep turns to defend her young. The eagle is shot just in time by the yachtsman who has been rowed ashore by two men —one of whom is Andrew Gray, a native of "Hirta" (Foula). Accompanying the yachtsman is a girl, and they wander up over the cliffs, followed at a distance by Andrew (Niall MacGinnis), who had decided to remain ashore when the boat puts off for the yacht lying in Ham Voe.

Presently Andrew comes abreast a cluster of ruined buildings. Here he stops and stands musing sadly on all that's left of "Hirta's" post office, shop and other "biggins" (dwellings), where once strong laughing kinsfolk of his lived. This is an effective scene, and as the young seaman stands watching there is seen a procession of his islesfolk trudging by, carrying bundles of clothes and other belongings as they had done that last sad day when "Hirta" had been left to the birds. Andrew moves along and comes up to a stone on the top of the cliff. This stone has the legend "Peter Manson, gone over," carved on it. This is the spot where Peter had "gone over" for the last time, when—on "da hindmost day"—he had gone to find some eggs for "them fool collectors" and the rope had broken and Peter had plunged to his death. "Bob," the collie dog, had come after him to the cliff, had seen the strands breaking one by one, and tried to warn his friend by frantic barking. Here the film proper begins. The yachtsman and his companion ask Andrew about the stone and what "gone over" means. Andrew turns, and sees on the far horizon "the isles of Scotland" clearly in the bright sun. This he says, the old men said was a bad omen, saying the isles had been seen one time before, as this time, and then there had also been three people together.

The story is then told by Andrew. Of the old life on Hirta, the people, their work and play, problems, trawlers coming near the banks ruining the fishing grounds, the final scenes, evacuation. The "story" revolves round the love of Andrew Gray and Robbie Manson (Eric Berry), a son of Peter Manson's (John Laurie), for the girl Ruth Manson (Belle Chrystal). It is finally decided between the two young men that the question of "evacuation or no evacuation" will be settled by a race "up the cliffs." This "race" scene is thrilling and impressive, but not convincing. Andrew is the winner, his chum Robbie being knocked off the cliff and killed. Peter Manson, a crofter, never forgives Andrew. Andrew cannot bear his animosity, he wants to go away to get a job in a trawler or other vessel. But before the race and Robbie's death there are scenes of the two men arguing the vexed question of evacuation. Andrew says the place has nothing to offer them, Robbie wants the people to remain in their old home. He says Andrew has "gone over to the other side now"; but Andrew says, "It's every man for himself" now, and he for one is leaving. Peter is angry, in the sequence at the pier, where the men are gathered together in the "Parliament," and he says, "Andrew talks of every man for himself now, when formerly he talked of co-operation." Most of the men are in agreement with Peter to stay on in their homes. Andrew says, "Birds were in the isle before men came, and birds would be there when men have gone." Looking to all the drawbacks life on these remote isles entails, perhaps there is truth in this, and birds are the proper "inhabitants" of such rocks. The picture as a whole is fine, succeeding in its object: namely, to show the gradual coming of "death" to isolated places under present social conditions. Perhaps under a sanely organised system such isles would not need to be evacuated unless of course, through time, if young people refused to stay in them.

Belle Chrystal is supposed to be the "unsophisticated" crofting lass Ruth Manson, who is with child to Andrew

Gray. The actress, however, though able enough as an actress, and making the best of a difficult role, does not quite succeed in striking the part of the innocent daughter "gone astray" of a Shetland crofter-fisherman. Even as a film "type" Belle Chrystal's looks were nothing great. Almost any Shetland crofting lass could give some of these film women a run for their money in the matter of good looks. With training some of the girls from the crofts would do just as well, if not better. However, for the film folk, strange to Shetland and Foula, to have done so well after only a short stay in the north, reflected credit on all concerned.

Other principal actors were Finlay Currie, who, as the "Laird's man," elder, and general "important body" of the place, acted really excellently; John Laurie, as the dour "crofter body," also was good; but Grant Sutherland, as a young crofter-fisherman and the island "catechist," was perhaps the star turn of the picture. He acted his part to perfection, and many Shetlanders at first thought Sutherland was a Foula man. Niall MacGinnis, as Andrew Gray, was convincing; and Eric Berry, as Robbie Manson, was good. The actress who impersonated the old "granny" had many islanders guessing when they saw her superb performance on the screen, some thinking she was a native of the isle, so well did she do her parts.

There was some comment that the picture was not entirely satisfactory in certain respects. "All mixed up!" one heard, and astonished laughter rang out in the Lerwick picture house at times, as when some sequences seemed to have got wrongly connected. This was noticed when the catechist and the factor were discussing crop prospects, and one scene depicted the shearing of corn, or bere, followed right away by a peat-cutting scene! Then it seemed to some that the dancing of the Foula Reel to spirited fiddle music came too suddenly after the moving funeral scene. People in the audience were much taken with the funeral scene, this being generally conceded one of the most impressive parts of the film. People were genuinely affected by the "bidding" by "word of mouth" to the funeral, the scene at the kirk, the sad trudge of the men bearing the remains of their dead comrade on oars, and the tramping of feet on the brig over the burn, then the rain falling in the water-lily pools, and Peter and Andrew standing over the grave, lonely and never speaking, rain beating down on them. ... The abrupt jolting of the audience out of a sympathetic mood by the dancing and playing could have been avoided by a short interlude, which could have gradually led up to a more cheerful note. The "bidding by word of mouth" of folk to Robbie Manson's funeral was one of the "high spots" of the *Edge of the World*; the repetition by the catechist and Peter of the invitation: " . . . bidden to attend the funeral of Robbie Manson at twelve noon to-morrow . . ." which then trails off into " . . . twelve noon . . ." " . . . to-morrow . . ." was well done. The tramping over the brig with the coffin on oars was one of the finest "shots" in the picture. It was in keeping with the story, with Shetland tradition, and with the best traditions of the cinema. This sequence was almost like something out of one of the big Soviet films.

One at times had the impression that the best "actors" were the Foula people themselves. They were just themselves, with no "put-on" or other artificialities such as the "leading lady" and others at times adopted. The islanders seemed to be enjoying the whole show immensely. Of course the coming of an entire film outfit and staff of actors and technicians must have come as a bit of "light relief" to the Foula people, helping to dispel monotony, and bringing some welcome enough cash to the isle. The islanders took the film crowd to their bosoms right away, so to speak, and the film folk for their part were delighted with the place, its kindly people and, above all, with the remarkably fine weather experienced during their stay in the north. At times it seemed as if there could be detected in the picture just the faintest glimpses of sarcasm on the faces of some of the islanders, so suddenly brought face to face with powerful cameras and film producers desperately anxious to dramatise them and their ancient home place! When Andrew was leaving the isle to seek his fortune "far away" in the great "metropolis" of Lerwick, and shaking hands with all and sundry, it seemed as if that white-whiskered crofter was shaking Andrew by the hand as if he really meant it.

While on the subject of the impressive funeral sequence, one may say that it might have been more effective and "Shetland-like" if there had been no "keenin'" accompanying it. Just the slow shambling tramp of feet on the brig and over the rough path to the kirkyard, with the rain falling from the haze-hidden Sneug. . . . After all, Shetlanders are apt to take their grief in a much quieter, restrained, philosophical manner than is the case with the more emotional Gaels of the Western Isles and Highlands. The "keenin'" suits the Gaelic or Irish sense of sorrow, but is out of place as "atmosphere" in a northern funeral. However, the film is supposed to be dealing with Scottish isles in general, and "Hirta" or "the last land" in particular. Again, the film might have benefited if the "orchestral" accompaniment had been left out altogether, although the women of the Glasgow Orpheus Choir did their work well.

Andrew's sudden wiping of his face at the grave was impressive. The scenes showing the Foula people at work, such as the rooin, caain', shearing corn, rowing in the boats, cutting peats, cliff climbing, and the pictures of the folk worshipping in the kirk, dancing and the like, were very natural. These parts would have been spoiled by the intrusion of any "acting business." The tolling of the kirk bell added a fine touch. There could, however, have been more "indoor" shots showing something of homely life "by the fireside." There also seemed to be a lack of shots of Foula boats, boats off at sea and men fishing, though there was a shot of one of the "cursed trawlers." There seemed a complete absence of fish in Foula while this film was being made! Not even a "raep o' sookit piltiks" or haddocks was to be seen. Little was heard of the famed "shaalds o' Foula" near the isle where men used to get catches of fine fish.

One saw the trained actress in Belle Chrystal when she went to the burn near the house for a pail of water to "brinnd da coo," and although it was the Sabbath and she was hurrying to "geng ta da kirk," still, she could have taken more time over it. A more realistic scene would have been for the lass to have led the cow to the burn, where the animal would have helped itself. The cliff incidents and John Laurie's climbing—particularly the rescuing of the sheep which had gone over—were excellent, and gave real Foula glimpses. The setting off from the isle, of Ruth with her sick child in a boat was not too convincing. Here there seemed some incongruousness, and what was termed "a' mixed up" in the scenes of wild weather and huge breaking seas running into pictures of small boats being pulled off to the trawler in a calmer-looking sea, then the trawler swept by waves in which few small boats could have lived. Then there was Ruth being tossed about in the heaving cabin clutching the babe—which some little time before could "hardly breathe"—and this was not very well done. Ruth was heard crying on Andrew to come to her, and he was seen to hurry below right away, looking quite clean when, as a fireman at work in the engine-room, he would have been grimy and sweaty, and with the storm that was raging, would hardly have been able to hear the lass's cries.

All this, however, is probably part and parcel of the difficult art of film-making, which, when the main thing is "the story," cannot be expected to conform to accuracy and naturalism in every detail. Artificiality must be allowed in efforts to heighten the effect, to improve upon the seemingly bare and cold world. Andrew Gray in the town looking for a job was hardly satisfying. The glimpses of their own "hame burg" were appreciated by the Lerwick people, some looking for "kent faces," others regretting there wasn't "more of it." The scene where the trawler is shown fishing in rough weather off "Hirta Isle," and Andrew gazing ashore at his old home and wondering what Ruth and the others were doing, was effective. The "doctor" episode was natural enough. The exciting boarding of the trawler, motor-boat shooting past, doctor jumping on deck, and the men, one after the other, holding their breath and telling each other to get "a can of hot water" were good. One of the most natural sequences occurred towards the end when the factor and the catechist go to look for Peter Manson, and there is heard the crying, "Peter!... Peter! Peter Manson..." echoing among the cliffs. This was the real thing. It seemed to sum up the whole idea of death and desolation and heart-breaking loneliness. The cries and plaintive echoes seemed to be the heart-rending cries of people in a place of the dead. The collie dog barking as the strands of Peter's rope break, his trying to edge down the cliff, then returning to bark, was another fine bit of film. The "shot" of Ruth with the Foula women near the cradle on the flower-thick greensward in the dale seemed lacking in something. The island women, healthy and winsome-looking, with their busy fingers plying their knitting wires in a real way, were the actual "goods," as was also the baby sleeping; but again there seemed something unreal in the posing of the actress. The dancing sequence was convincing, the factor adding a fine and authentic touch in the "peerie reel, tight, tight, and peerie wyes wi' da feet!" Peter Manson, standing with the factor looking down at Ruth and the cradle, was good enough, but again there seemed the merest touch of unreality about it. The factor, standing with the laird as they check up on all the goods for export with the mail-boat bound for Walls, and always interjecting remarks on Peter Manson and other islanders, acted the part to the life. The whole sequence was life-like, satisfying, a real touch of "local colour" in every way. The insistence on the "Sabbath," and the factor's "get thee behind me, Satan!" when about to put his pipe in his mouth was perhaps overdone. Foula people, like other isles people, may be religious-minded, pious and well-read in the "Guid Buik," but they are not such strict killjoys as all that. The kirk bell ringing came as a pleasing touch; but the tying-up of the collies outside seemed exaggerated. Nowhere in Shetland do crofters take their dogs to "da kirk" with them. The young preacher—in his blue fisherman's jersey, and without even a hint of a collar and tie—his reading of the "lesson," praying, the singing, and the whole kirk scene—women nodding off to sleep, men yawning (maybe even some popping a pan-drop or "lozenger" into their mouths!)— were to the life. The old "granny" sitting there on the bit chair by herself, outside the kirk, aye straining to hear the sweet singing of the Psalm, the "Twenty-third"—"The Lord's my shepherd, I shall not be in want; in pastures green He will lead me beside the quietly flowing waters"— was remarkably fine. The "parliament" shot down at the pier at Ham Voe, the men arguing and debating over this and that, was not bad, though here again more might have been shown of the cliffs, voe, men in boats, landing and gutting fish, hauling up boats to the noosts, or shelters. About the only sign of fishing activities was the shot at the herring yard at Lerwick. The shots of the wind blowing the burn water back over the cliff, bending the bere on the rigs, rippling over the grassy slopes were fine pieces of photography.

Among the best of the professionals were Grant Sutherland as the catechist, Finlay Currie as factor, and Niall MacGinnis as Andrew Gray. John Laurie as Peter Manson and Belle Chrystal as Ruth Manson acted well. MacGinnis and Laurie, like Chrystal, could not get away from the fact that they were professionals. Some of the "studio-set" stuff hardly fitted into the grandeur of the Foula background. On the whole, the film they made is a splendid portrayal of island life. The artistes, Michael Powell, cameramen and other members of his staff, and the "extras" brought from Lerwick for the dancing, deserve

the congratulations and thanks of Shetlanders. The people
of Foula, too, are to be congratulated on their fine per-
formances in the *Edge of the World*, one of the few worth-
while pictures of recent years.

Another fine film of Shetland life is *The Rugged Island*,
by Jenny Brown, now Mrs. John Gilbertson. It tells a
plain story of Shetland crofters, their life and work, shows
the fine rock and sea scenery, and very creditably gives
authentic "local colour" in the best style of the documen-
taries. A "love story" is the central theme, around which
Miss Brown wove her pictures of island life. The hero of
the story, a Shetlander, John Gilbertson, married the producer some time before the actual shooting of the film.
Mrs. Gilbertson has shot thousands of feet of film in Shetland. In addition to acting in *The Rugged Island*, John
Gilbertson did almost everything, from mending the
camera to repairing an old croft house, used as the sets for
the interior shots. The unit consisted of ten people, the
derelict croft being used to represent three houses. This
Gilbertson did by making three different types of fireplace,
changing white-washed walls to wallpaper, varying
pictures, furniture, clocks, dishes, and the like. The themes
of depopulation and emigration, occurring in Powell's
film, also occur in Miss Brown's picture.

The Gilbertsons' home at Hillswick has a fine atmosphere, having been furnished in a modern manner without
destroying the old-time appeal of the croft. Mrs. Gilbertson has recently made several short pictures from all her
material. The *Harvest of the North*, and *The Crofter*, two of
her latest, have been showing in cinemas throughout the
country. Mrs. Gilbertson says the most exacting part of
her job is to cut her own film. She says one cannot forget
all that has gone into the making of each shot. During
a lecture-tour in Canada Mrs. Gilbertson showed her
Scottish films to child audiences numbering from 50 to
1250, their ages ranging from seven to eighteen. In
Saskatchewan she met Miss Evelyn Spice, the two

having numerous adventures on the great prairies making a two-reeler, *Prairie Winter*. The temperature was twenty degrees below zero, and the unit wore every article of clothing they could find while riding around the country in an open sleigh taking shots.

CHAPTER VI

THE antiquities of Shetland, about which you ask, are many and varied. The most important are the stone brochs, or "Picts' Castles," as they are called here. The brochs date from the pre-Norse period, and are found all over Scotland. *Ancient Emigrants*, by Professor A. W. Brøgger, has much of interest to say about the stone "castles," and it may as well suit your purpose to give some quotations from this authoritative work.

"The number and variety of monuments from the pre-Norse period scattered over all the islands north and west of Scotland, and on the Scottish mainland itself, are so great that this alone bears witness to a considerable population in ancient times.

"There are cairns, most probably dating from very early times, widely differing in form and dimensions, with and without chambers, which presumably belong to the Stone Age and which, to some extent, correspond to the Bronze Age of more southerly countries. In many places they are supplemented by earth mounds which were thrown up at the same period. They are apparently characterised in all parts of the country by the same high situation, look-out stations, and mounds.

"Of their connexion with the people who raised the great standing stones, stone circles, etc., cromlechs and so on we know very little. In the Shetlands they are comparatively rare, but the Orkneys possess some of the most imposing examples to be found anywhere, such as the stone circle at Stennes with the beautiful centre table, and some distance away that enormous circle known as Brodgarringen, which was originally composed of thirty-four standing stones of great height." (*Ancient Emigrants*, p. 42.)

"The Scotch name of broch, which is now customarily applied to the old stone, towers is a corrupt form of the old Norse word for them of *borg*. It is interesting and valuable evidence of the fact that among the things which created the greatest impression upon the minds of the Norse emigrants were those towers of stone. To the historian and archaeologist of to-day they are also one of the main links with olden times in these regions.

"Of the hundreds which at one time existed, not many now remain which are not in ruins. Unique, therefore, is such a well-preserved and obviously complete tower as the Mousa Broch in the Shetlands. No one who has once seen this tower and entered its dark interior can forget the impression created by this mighty pile. It is not by any means. the largest of the towers, but it is instructive because of its perfect preservation. Its grey mass of stonework rises up from the shore of the little island of Mousa on the eastern side of the Shetlands. It is 15 metres in height, circular in ground plan, and built of flat, slaty grey stones, without mortar. The mere fact that this tower remains unimpaired after hundreds and hundreds of years, proves that it is the product of real technical skill in building, the more so since within its round, smooth walls there are a variety of arched rooms, stairways and ledges. I willingly confess that it was with a feeling of apprehension that I entered these rooms and mounted the stairways, dank, dark, and cold as they were. Even the open room imparted an unpleasant and melancholy impression in spite of the light from above. The magnificent view from the wall over the whole of Mainland down to Sumburgh Head was worth all the feeling of discomfort I endured. . . .

"Altogether, these brochs are relics of a remarkable civilization. They are the expression of a high standard of technique with primitive means, in a military epoch which knew no other long-range weapons than the bow and arrow, stone missiles, and the like. They are solid, well-balanced architectural works, equipped to withstand even the most powerful blows of the stone missiles of olden times. Finally, it must be emphasized that they imply the use of considerable manpower, great numbers of slaves who dragged the stones to the spot, shaped them and, under a technical director, carried out the building operations" (*Ancient Emigrants*, pp. 43–45).

Brøgger gives the number of brochs in Shetland as seventy-five. Discussing the old place-names Brøgger writes: " . . . the total number of Norse place-names in the Shetlands probably amounts to about 50,000, or perhaps even twice that number" (*Ancient Emigrants*, p. 60).

On page 72 of the same book he has a very interesting passage on the old names. "The elements most frequent in the names of the old farms in the Shetlands are very re-stricted in number, and occur in those names which have -*ster*, or simply *setr*, as their second syllable, and also in names in combination with -*bister*, -*sta*, -*gaard* and -*land*. A large number of others, such as *vik*, *voe*, *ness*, *hamar*, *by*, *lee*, etc., are of so general a character that they do not repay an investigation which has for its object the discovery of sources of origin." He then gives a footnote here. "In 1860 Arthur Laurenson (in *Annaler for nordisk oldkyndighed*) published a survey of the distribution of a total of 854 names which he had studied in the Shetlands. The figures are to some extent representative and are therefore repro-duced here. *Setr* (including *bister*), 176; *gaard*, 115; *hus*, 60; *ness*, 59; *land*, 55; *vik*, 44; *fjeld*, 42; *dale*, 32; *sta*, 29; *burgh*, 24; *firth*, 23; *brake*, 21; *voe*, 19; *toft*, 16; *lee*, 16; *ting*, 15; *wall*, 11; *gardie*, 11; *gord*, 11; *quoy*, 10; *hamar*, 9."

The excavations at Jarlshof, at Sumburgh, however, are the most important relics of antiquity in the north. A lecture given by Mr. James Richardson, H.M. Inspector of Ancient Monuments for Scotland, at Glasgow, in August 1943, is interesting in this respect. At Jarlshof, Mr. Richardson said, there existed perhaps "the most fascinat-ing archaeological site in Britain, for there to-day lay ex-posed to view buildings dating from the early Bronze Age, through the Iron Age, Broch Period, Viking times, and minor constructions of mediaeval date, the whole arrange-ment being capped by the ruin of a building of the late sixteenth century. In a late Bronze Age dwelling was found a metal-castor's shop, from which were recovered the clay moulds for socketed axes, swords, and other implements. The Viking sites in Orkney and Shetland were visited by Norse and Danish archaeologists, and had it not been for the war the Danish Government would have sent an expert to assist in the elucidation of the buildings of these settlements."*

Jarlshof is the scene of some of the actions in Sir Walter Scott's romance *The Pirate*. Scott visited Shetland in 1814, and spent some time gathering material for the novel, which appeared some years later. Near Sumburgh Head and to the westward rises the gaunt Fitful Head, another place figuring in Scott's novel. Here lived "Norna, the Rime-Kenner of Fitful," a wise woman who was thought to have the power of bringing on storms. *The Pirate* is perhaps the earliest known "Shetland novel," and in spite of some inaccuracies as regards places and ways of life and work of the people, it gives not a bad impression of the southern "side" of Shetland during the period. Fitful Head was also the place where "Black Erik, the man with the Iron staff," had his hiding-place. He was an outlaw, stealing folk's sheep and scaring everybody for miles around. George Stewart, a Dunrossness man, used the folk-tale of Erik the outlaw as material for one of his "Tales" in the popular Shetland book, *Shetland Fireside Tales*.

Traditions survive in the "south country" of invasions of the Lewis men from the Hebrides. Those invasions are said to date from a feud between the Shetland men and the Western Isles men during the ninth century. In one of the Sumburgh battles, when sixty persons were slain, Olaf Sinclair, a laird of the estate of Brew, escaped from death by leaping over Sumburgh Head on to a patch of grass in a cleft in the rock. About one hundred and seventy years ago the wind and sea exposed a heap of human bones on Sumburgh Links, said to have been the vestiges of a traditionary "final war" with the Islesmen, in which they were wiped out by "the Ness men" under one of the Sinclairs of Brew.

* *Shetland News*, 2nd September 1943.

Foula, as you probably know, is the "bird isle," and also the "Ultima Thule" of the Romans. The film people's title of "Edge of the World" is perhaps the most apt of the lot. It is a lonely, isolated place, with a population of barely one hundred. A small motor-boat runs between the isle and Walls on the west mainland, with mails, passengers (quite often there are passengers), goods and stock. With stormy weather, however, the isle is often cut off from the other isles for weeks on end. In the winter of 1937–38, for instance, Foula was isolated for more than a month. Some provisions and oil were running low, while an epidemic of influenza made for an urgent need of medicines, the nurse's supply having run short. Attempts were made to get across to the isle, without success. Things were getting a bit desperate when the Highland Airways mail-plane flew over the isle, dropping some goods, mails and medicine by means of small parachutes made of flour bags. A day later the Fishery Board drifter made the crossing from Scalloway with goods and paraffin.

The houses are on the east side of the isle. The west side rises almost sheer from the sea, the highest point, the Sneug, being over 1300 feet. Numerous birds frequent the cliffs, fowling at one time being greatly carried on. The Foula cows and sheep are among the best of the Shetland breed, the Foula women, mostly all expert spinners and knitters, making good use of the wool roo'd from off the sheep. Fine fishing-grounds known as the Shaalds o' Foula lie to the east of the isle. Foula men, like the Fair Isle, Papa Stour and Skerries men, are skilled boatmen, and knowing everything of tide and wind, they get many good catches from the Shaalds.

Sudden gusts of wind of great force often sweep the isle; but the houses are built of stone, with thick walls and low roofs, and are thus secured against the wind. The boats lie snugged in sheltered noosts, well up from the tide-line, when not moored in the shelter of the little breakwater in Ham Voe.

The Shaalds o' Foula are fishing grounds to the east of

the isle. A song named *Shaalds o' Foula* is sung to the tune of *The Foula Reel*, a fine island dance.

The song is as follows:

> Here we're met ta wylkim in Yule,
>> Up wi' a light fit an link it awa, boys;
> Send for a fiddler an play up da Foola reel,
>> We'll skip it as light is a maa, boys.

> *Chorus.*
>> Da Shaalds a Foola 'll pay for aa,
>>> Up wi' a light fit an link it awa, boys;
>> Da Shaalds a Foola 'll pay for aa,
>>> Da Shaalds 'll pay for aa, boys.

> Da hens 're amung da kye i' da byre,
>> Up wi' a light fit an link it awa, boys;
> Link up da pot an pit on a guid fire,
>> We'll sit till da cocks doe kraa, boys.

> Noo for a pipe an a pot a guid beer,
>> Up wi' a light fit an link it awa, boys;
> We'll drink a guid fishin again' da neist 'ear,
>> An da Shaalds saal pay for aa, boys.

Foula was one of the last places in the north where the people spoke the old Norn. In the seventies of the eighteenth century a ballad was recited in Norn by William Henry of Guttorm, and taken down in writing by the Rev. George Low, then touring the islands. It was found to be a version of *Hildina*, an old Norse court visick, or poem.

Einar Seim, a Norwegian, visited Foula in 1935. He is one of the compilers of the dictionary of the Nynorsk language, which, based on the old dialects, is competing with Dano-Norwegian as the national language of Norway. Seim came to Foula for the purpose of studying the remains of the old northern language there. An interesting article by Seim, "Ultima Thule," was contributed to the 1935 number of the Norwegian Christmas annual *Jol i Sunnfjord*, and was reprinted in the *Shetland News*, February, 1936, under the title "A Norwegian in Foula."

Seim found much in Foula that was of value for his work.

He writes: "The Norse lived longer in Foula than any-where else in the west. . . ." It was still possible to find Norse words and more Norse traditions in Foula than in any others of the isles. "In spring and summer Foula is peaceful. A hallowed place for man, bird and beast, in the bosom of the sea, and in the blue infinity. Day and night merge into one. In holy midnight hour voices of birds and beasts are silent. In the early dawn the sun rises over the low Mainland hills, to the east. At late evening it drops into the ocean out in the north-west. Those seasons of the year all are busy—people and birds. I saw men working in the rigs at eleven and eleven-thirty at night. Very early in mornings the 'bonxie,' or 'big skua,' had been to the loch under Hamnafield for a morning bath. I counted as many as 100 bonxies on the tiny loch. Kittiwakes, lesser skuas (Richardson's Skua) wash in lochs near Stromness. The fulmar petrel ('maallie') and other species contented themselves with bathing in the sea below the rocks where they build and live."

He says rabbits were everywhere. "The Foula folk were sick of this pest. They eat up grass from sheep and cattle, come into kailyards, destroy growing crops, even gnawed their way into corn stacks in the hairst and winter nights. One day when I had been at '*Stjol in Heimtun*' talking to old people there, I sat down to rest by the stream when I went away, and I counted the rabbits feeding on the *cultivated* field near the house. On tiny slope counted 25." He found few trees or flowers in Foula now. Tradition says there was a wood in *Efra Fendal* in olden days, but that the Lewis men burned it down on one of their raids on Foula. There were many species of beautiful flowers, also good grass. Seim got one kind of food in Foula that he had never tasted, but a food that was well known in the west of Norway a couple of generations ago. One evening as he sat in the "but-end" a woman asked him if he would taste a genuine Foula dish "for foklaskap" ("for fun"). He got a bowl of milk and a wooden plate with "burstin" (dried beremeal). He had then to mix the meal in the milk according to taste, and eat. They often used such food in Foula. It was the same kind of food which they called "drøsta" in Nordhordland. Seim came in mind of a local verse: a pedlar man came in to a woman in her house and wanted to buy some food. The woman set down drøsta—dried oatmeal mixed up in milk or water. As the pedlar sat looking at the dish the woman burst out: "What's wrong? Is the man daft? He doesn't want to eat drøsta!" This became a byword, and only in that way had he any acquaintance with this kind of food before coming to Foula. "*If the meal is dry and good one need not turn up one's nose at this dish nor look at it like the pedlar. I finished what I got.*" He goes on to write of the foods they ate in early days—dried fish and butter, dried flesh and drøsta, such food is what they termed "raakost" (ready food), and, "when, in addition, they drank whey, ale, and cod-liver oil, the Vikings might well indeed have been strong-stomached, whole-toothed and hardy." He says it was forty years since Dr. Jakobsen was in Foula, and "yet there is still a mass of Norn words used in every-day speech of the people." Seim managed to hear many Norn words Jakobsen had not noticed. "I knew previously that the Norn speech had survived long in Foula, but I had no idea that a mass of Norn words would still be in use. Dr. Jakobsen believed that the use of English in school would soon cause the remnants of Norn speech to disappear. And now it was forty years since Dr. Jakobsen was in Foula. Strangely enough, however, I managed to hear many Norn words which Jakobsen had not picked up.

"It sounds odd, but there are words and phrases used here in Sunnfjord which I did not fully understand till I went to Shetland. For example, in Dalsfjord they speak of having something 'i vonavare.' They say of a lad, 'he has a girl ashore' ('uine i fjera,' lit. in on the beach), 'i vonavare.' What was meant by that I never rightly knew. But in Shetland they use exactly the same phrase—'to ha'e avonavara,' have in reserve. Also, 'to ha'e avonavara'—to go on chance: O.N. 'a von ok vara.'

"I had a kind of hope that I might find some of the old sea-terms still in use in Fula. That too was the case—people remembered them all right, laughed a bit at some of them, but paid good heed to them nevertheless. At sea they call the minister 'upstander,' the church 'baenihus' (prayer-house), a woman 'hustikk' (house-bitch), the horse 'gjonger' (gang-er), the dog 'beinibiter' (bone biter), the cat 'firføtter' (four-footer), a cow 'drynja,' pig 'bursi' or 'sungi,' land 'da klumper,' boat 'far,' sun 'glida' or 'gløda,' moon 'glonter,' halibut 'gleida' (squinter), conger-eel 'sliki,' etc., etc. It may be seen that these are old Norn 'kennings,' or periphrases, all through. Some Gaelic, Scotch and Dutch-German words also have been used as sea-words (tabu terms)—*e.g.* 'skjaan' for tully or knife, 'frau' for a woman (instead of 'hustikk,' 'moia' and other Norn pet names for a woman)."

Papa Stour, about which you ask, is a small, not very high isle, of great fertility, lying about three miles to the west of Sandness at the west mainland. Papa Sound is the stretch of water separating it from Sandness. Like Yell Sound it is agitated by rapid tides, so that only local boatmen can navigate the channel in safety. There are about one hundred people in Papa. The name is said to mean the "large priest isle," as it was thought to have been one of the refuges of priests from St. Columba's mission in the north before the time of the Norsemen. A sword dance, with seven dancers, made up as the "Seven Champions of Christendom" is peculiar to Papa Stour. Its intricate movements, to old Shetland tunes, are very striking, as the dancers carry imitation swords, which towards the climax of the dance are formed into a star-shaped "shield." This is dashed to the ground at a command from "St. George of England" and the dancers bow while "St. George" recites the final verse of a whole "book of verses" he has to memorise and recite. It is really a masque, or drama, probably dating from before the Reformation.

To the north-west of Papa lie the Ve Skerries, bare jagged reefs where numerous ships have perished. A whistling buoy was recently put up on one of the skerries as a guide to ships. Papa Stour, like Foula and Skerries, now has a wireless-telephony installation, a much-needed benefit to the people of these exposed isles.

The second largest Shetland isle is the north isle of Yell. It is roughly twenty miles in length and about four or five in breadth. It is covered by deep deposits of peat moor, the heather and grass of the hills sustaining large flocks of sheep. The soil is not so fertile as in its more northerly neighbour, Unst, or in its other neighbour, Fetlar (the "garden of Shetland"); but there are numerous crofts in the isle, some worked by elderly people and women. Most of the Yell men are seamen. They are usually away from home for long periods. It has perhaps more master mariners to its credit than any other part of Shetland.

The steamer *Earl of Zetland* makes regular calls at the main Yell ports of Burravoe in the south, Mid Yell, and Cullivoe in the north.

Mid Yell is the most important district. It is a well-populated neighbourhood, with shops, a church, school and public hall.

Gardie is the name of a croft which used to be the home of the noted Shetlander, the northern scholar, the late Laurence Williamson. He was one of Dr. Jakobsen's greatest helpers in 1893–96, at the time the distinguished Faroese philologist was engaged in rescuing what remained of the Norn speech that had at one time been the only speech of the Shetland islanders. Laurence Williamson was a man of great learning, with a remarkable memory, who all his life had interested himself in the study of the place-names, speech, history, genealogy and culture of Shetland. With other scholarly-minded men, as John Charleson, Robert Jamieson, Robert Cogle and others, Laurence Williamson was able to provide

Jakobsen with a mass of valuable material. Most of this was published, the folk-speech material in a large dictionary and the place-names in smaller works. English translations were brought out some years after Jakobsen's death in 1918. Professor Gudbrandr Vigfússon, the Icelandic scholar, also visited the Gardie scholar, being in Shetland in 1886 on philological and historical research. Laurence Williamson had a great knowledge of almost all the families of the North Isles. Himself of Fetlar parents he had made a special study of this easterly Shetland isle, its history, legends, place-names, speech and folk-genealogies. He could trace the kin of many of the Fetlar families for generations back. His own family's genealogy was worked out from the time of Olaf Nicolson, who was udaller of the lands at North Dale, Fetlar, in 1540. According to the tradition Fetlar was one of the first places in the north to be colonised from Norway, and among those first settlers of the seventh century "who came to Finni" and then "peopled Strand and Grøtin" were the ancestors of Olaf Nicolson. Laurence Williamson died in April, 1936, at the age of eighty-one, and was buried in the kirkyard of Fetlar. His people had been forced to leave Fetlar through the evictions from the crofts. The landlords were needing the crofts to make large enclosed farms for sheep grazing, so the people had to make a shift elsewhere. A big part of Fetlar was "laid down" to sheep farms and the grass grew over the ruined walls of the houses.

CHAPTER VII

THIS letter will strive to give a fuller account of some of those intellectual giants, men known as crofter-scholars, and more particularly of Laurence Williamson of Gardie, perhaps the most remarkable of them all. It is no wonder you are keenly interested to know more of Williamson, as it is widely held he was one of Shetland's most outstanding intellects. These biographical details and extracts from some of his manuscripts may help to give a glimpse of the man who held "da toon a Gairdie" in Yell, and whose friends included such famous scholars as Gudbrandr Vigfússon and Jakob Jakobsen.

It is not often that the death of a crofter arouses any comment, and outside the immediate family circle the "man that's awa" is soon forgotten. Go anywhere in Shetland, however, especially in the north isles—Yell, Unst, Fetlar—and you will yet hear folk speak with reverence and admiration of the tall, grey-blue eyed, rosy-cheeked man who tilled the rigs of the "toon a Gairdie." This croft was about thirteen acres in extent, half of it outrun land.

Outside of Shetland, too, particularly in scholarly circles, people remember Laurence Williamson, not perhaps from his having been a crofter, but from the fact that with his passing a chapter of northern history may be said to have closed. Laurence was perhaps the last of that fine company of men who were known as "crofter-scholars," men to whom the book and pen were as familiar as the spade and tushkar, how and sickle.

At Nissetter in Northmavine parish, over sixty years ago, there lived a crofter, Robertson by name. His library of scientific and philosophical books was unequalled in the north. A free-thinker, this crofter was a close student of Herbert Spencer, and keen-minded youths from all over the north mainland visited his croft as in old Athens young students gathered around Socrates. After the day's work ida rig or hill, the little croft biggin became a veritable "university" as the crofter expounded the famous "First Principles" to the keen youngsters.

Another crofter of a contemplative turn of mind would get annoyed with his wife at times, as she had a habit of using his "big buik," a copy of Kant's *Critique of Pure Reason*, for "shoardin up" her broken-legged spinny-wheel; and in one herring-boat at least, two fishermen used to pore over a well-thumbed paper-covered copy of Edward Aveling's *The Student's Marx*.

Here and there in Shetland it is still possible to meet crofter-fishermen with rare intellectual gifts. There was an old haaf fisherman living in Northmavine not long ago whose mental powers in arithmetic were amazing. He was able to give ready and correct answers to complicated "sums" that had floored even "da minister" with the magic letters "M.A." ahint his name! In Burravoe again, John Robertson, a seaman, has studied astronomy all his life. John can tell you the names of any of "da staurns," and their position at any time of the year. His lectures on the subject are concise and accurate. One of John's neighbours, John R. Rendall, of Ulsta, is another man of remarkable intellectual gifts. A rationalist, Rendall was for long a seaman in Australasian waters, and while there met many of the brilliant minds of the famous Industrial Workers of the World.

Another brilliant man, largely self-taught, was William Johnson, mentioned earlier in this book. He was a stone-mason to trade, but could turn his hand to almost any task. Of a scientific cast of mind, Johnson wrote a book giving the result of years of his study of physics, with some of his poems appended. Like many geniuses William Johnson was often misunderstood by people not given to "thinking things out for themselves."

George Stewart was largely self-taught, and after a time as a teacher at Levenwick, he left Shetland for Edinburgh, where in 1877 he published the *Shetland Fire-*

side Tales, one of the first books to be written largely in Shetlandic.

Many of these men gathered knowledge by themselves, as did Robert Cogle of Cunningsburgh, who taught himself Icelandic after the day's work about the croft had been completed. He was one of Dr. Jakobsen's helpers when the latter was in Shetland on research work into the Shetland Norn tongue.

There was also Robert Jamieson, of Sneusquoy, Sandness, who learned his Latin "ida voar rig," as, with others, he bent to the spade. Eventually he became master of Sandness school, many master mariners receiving their first "laer" under "aald Jeemson." He was another of Jakobsen's assistants.

Two other self-taught men of laer belonged to da Herra, Yell. They lived at Stivlar, Mid Yell, in the eighties and nineties of last century. They were John and David Charleson. John Charleson, though blind, had acquired a great store of philological and historical knowledge, a store that was of great value to Laurence Williamson and Dr. Jakobsen when they travelled through Yell and Fetlar on their important researches.

David Charleson was born blind, but John was not. Blindness came on him as a young man. He was very strong as a youth, and often carried great "back-burdens" for long distances. David Charleson seemed to sense his surroundings. He even knew the meads (landmarks) at sea. He would go off in the boat with other young men, and after a time would ask them where they were. He would then tell them the correct position and how to set their course. Olla Charleson was their father. He was a good fiddler, but his son John was "timmer," and unmusical. John had a great memory. He could tell a story "oot o' his head," after having had it read or related to him. He could do this for hours. John was wont "ta geng him luif-aleen," and folk would hear him speaking. When he came to some empty barn or house he would go inside and "praech a sermon" to himself. In a manuscript headed

"The Herra, Yell," Laurence Williamson has a remarkable testimonial to his friend: " . . . During the year there have been 3 deaths. The first was John Charleson, the blind man. 'He was the very embodiment of the spirit of the north,' said Dr. Jacobsen. He had dwelt from youth in the next district. Common sense, kindly, genial, his store of Northern things was boundless. Mr. Burgess or any writer on old Shetland life would have been well advised to have thrown all their other Shetland gatherings aside in exchange for his. He died after 6 weeks' illness, aged 80. . . ."

Laurence Williamson, as a man of thirty-eight years of age, took Jakobsen to Stivlar to interview John Charleson, then seventy-two years old. Jakobsen made frequent visits regarding old words of which John had an extensive knowledge. He had the makings of a scholar, and was not inclined to a seafaring life; but he was a storehouse of traditions. David, on the other hand, could walk anywhere by himself so long as he had a stick to feel his way. John was intensely fond of children and stayed at houses where there were young bairns, minding them while the parents were away. Dr. Jakobsen was a very pleasant man, and would romp with the bairns of the house, so it would have made a homely scene with Jakobsen, the two blind men and Laurence discussing the old days, traditions, speech, place-names, while they "held da bairns oot a languor oot an in atween." Olla Charleson's father was Charles Laurenson, as the old patronymic system was still in use. John Charleson's maternal grandmother was Catherine Gargees, her father being Gaan Frederick Gargees. He came ashore in Unst, with other shipwrecked men, as the Stickles and Priests, supposed to have been Germans. John is said to have turned up the part of the Bible from the place the minister had taken his text, and knew to "a laef" any particular portion of the Scriptures.

Unlike the Charlesons, Laurence Williamson had the benefit of a teacher from the age of seven to seventeen.

JARLSHOF

To face page 112

C. J. Williamson

PICTISH BROCH, CHICKIMIN

This was Andrew D. Mathewson, or "Auld Mathewson," of East Yell. "Auld Mathewson" was one of the most outstanding intellects Shetland has produced. Partly self-taught, Mathewson had read the New Testament right through when only six years old. He learned Latin while harrowing in "da seed coarn ida voar rigs" of the toon of Houll, Nort-a-Voe, Yell. When he was eight he was teaching older bairns than himself, the bigger boys having agreed to keep order in the class. Mathewson taught in Fetlar, and then at East Yell, where his schooling lasted sixty years. A talented draughtsman and surveyor, he was employed in surveys all over the islands, being called in by the landmasters to make records of their estates, chiefly about the time when "da laund was plannked," as the reorganisation into separate crofts after the end of the semi-communal runrig system was termed. His land-maps, some of which still exist, are admirable examples of their kind. A lay preacher in the Established kirk, Mathewson is said to have had stones set up at various spots, the better to guide him during fog and snow on his tramps through the hills to the kirk at South Yell. It is said that he could name all "da staurns ida lift," and that one summer he started to count the bones in a herring. His wife was not of the same intellectual turn of mind. She wrought about the croft, knitted, and did all the ordinary "skutterin wark." Once in the twilight when she was haepin tauties she saw her husband approaching. Before he came into the rig he stood looking at da staurns, as was his wont. Folk near by heard her say: "See ye him staundin gaunin ida Heevens!" Mathewson was a fine handwriter, and is said to have written the Lord's Prayer on a piece of paper the size of a sixpence.

Laurence Williamson was born on Sunday, the 11th of March 1855, in the "Auld Haa" house at Linkshouse, Mid Yell. His father was James Williamson, merchant, Linkshouse, son of Laurence Williamson, udaller of Ruster, Fetlar, a fertile isle, and the most easterly of the

H

Shetland group. Mary, or Mally, Gardner was Laurence's mother. Her folk also were udallers from Fetlar. Both the Williamsons and Gardners suffered from the policy of croft-clearance that emptied half the crofts in the north isles of people in order to make room for black-face sheep.

The Williamsons were of Norse stock, their forbears said to have come to Funyi in Fetlar in the seventh century in one of the first "Danish ships that came." While still a youth Laurence got from kinsfolk in Fetlar a store of genealogical lore enabling him to construct a fairly complete record of his father's folk from 1540 when Olaf Nicolson was udaller of the lands of North Dale, Fetlar. Synnovo Williamsdaughter was Olaf's wife. She died in 1615. Their sons were William Olafsson and Erasmus Olafsson, William succeeding to the North Dale lands.

The Gardners were a Scottish family. They were thought to have come to Orkney and Shetland as fugitives from the terror that followed in the wake of the Covenant.

Laurence's sister, May Barbara, was born at Linkshouse in 1857. She was, like her brother, remarkably handsome, with strong will power and "a way of her own," but not so drawn to things of the intellect, although sharing his love of everything Shetlandic, as the following extract from one of his letters to her shows:

Sat., 18 Dec., 1897

I am sending you the *Shetland Times*, with the Bordeaux wreck, also L. J. Nicolson's latest poem. . . . I also enclose John Charlesson's photo [taken] by J. M. Goudie at my suggestion, lest Jakobsen . . . use it for his book; its very like him also. I send also Dr. Jakobsen's carte sent by him to me. Its exactly him, and a pure typical Norseman. But his hair having a tinge of red it looks dark in the photo, whereas its very light & yellow. Dr. Jakobsen published a book on Shetland language in Danish 192 pages, when he was made Dr of languages (philology) on 27 April 1897, and sent me a copy. His 2 lectures on same subject delivered in Shetland, were published by Mansons' Lerwick in Oct. His big Dictionary on Shetland tongue is not yet published. Theres a Shetland story out *Prisoners of Conscience*, by Amelia A. Barr, gifted American authoress. They are attacking it for incorrectness in *Times & News*. Also J. J. H. Burgess is about publishing *Tang*, a new Shetland story; and theres a translation by Miss Irvine from German of *Helga*, a Shetland story in verse. Thats all the Shetland things this year. I mention it as it used to be interesting. . . .

His sister worked mostly about the house and outside on the croft. For a time she was in Edinburgh and London, at service, but their mother's failing strength compelled her to renounce this congenial work and return home. All three were devoted to each other, and when, in 1906, their mother died at Gardie, May kept house for her brother, doing much crofting work while he engaged in his studies and writing. She died in 1934, and, like Laurence, was buried in Fetlar's kirkyard.

Being a "Sunday's bairn" Laurence was favoured as a boy. His parents adored their son, and early showing signs of more than average intelligence he was sent, at seven, to "Mathewson's" at East Yell, at that time the foremost seat of learning in Shetland. He had, however, learned to read at home, and beside his parents' folk in Fetlar, and at Gossabrough, East Yell. The old home-place was loved with an intensity of feeling, and Mally Williamson visited it almost every year. On these journeys the boy of Gardie heard lore and legends of the old days, and listened intently to everything. Since his early years he noted place-names in Fetlar, gradually amassing a list of about two thousand names, most of which are to be found in Jakobsen's *The Place-Names of Shetland*.

Laurence took to "laer" easily and was downcast when circumstances hindered him from going to school. Mathewson, seeing his aptitude for learning, gave him every help. Later on he referred to Laurence as one of his two best pupils. The other was John Spence, who became 'a teacher in Nesting, and wrote *Shetland Folk-lore*, thought to be one of the best works on the subject. Laurence had to travel six miles to reach the school, the road leading over bare hills and spanning burns, which in winter ran in torrents. On rough days Mathewson would send one of his daughters to carry the boy on her back over the snowy wastes.

Mathewson himself was acquainted with northern languages, and had much knowledge of Shetlandic speech, lore, legends, place-names and genealogy. Seeing his pupil's interest in these subjects, he encouraged him to concentrate on the study of the Shetland Norn language, as it was spoken in the North Isles of Shetland. Early acquaintance with the gifted Charleson men of da Herra led his mind in the same direction. His mother, too, had a remarkable memory, and a love for "da auld wyes," so it was not surprising that Laurence had written down many of "the rare beautiful words" from the lips of people visiting his father's shop before he was fourteen years old.

James Williamson was inclined to be more reserved than his wife. She was some eighteen years his junior. He was, according to Laurence, "the Norseman, conducting his affairs with even regularity; my sister was like him . . . ," but his mother, on the other hand, "had a greater versatility of mind." He observed that he could generally "see a connection between what my sister said and what had been discussed before. In the case of my mother I as a rule could not. . . ." And yet it was from his mother that he got many of the Norn words and phrases, that later on he gave to Jakobsen, and which go to form an important part of the Faroe scholar's *Dictionary of the Norn Language in Shetland.*

With his precise scientific ways Laurence began recording the folk-speech heard daily at Gardie and elsewhere in Yell and Fetlar. During his stay at Hillswick, Northmavine, in 1888, while instructing the staff of John Anderson & Co.'s shop how to operate the telegraph just newly installed, he did the same, under the heading "Northmavine Gatherings." In this way some of his manuscripts are almost a daily record of the life and work of the people, as he gives his informant's initials, the place, time, activities, and often the weather conditions. The result forms an interesting and valuable piece of Shetland literature as absorbing as any novel.

Omitting some phonetic marks, the following are transcriptions of a few entries:

"... 77. Da wis gin ben in gin ta bed, in da lasses in da beirns wis laid dem dun. Andw. wis gyin i da barn in Mam wis sitin at da fire makin af' ir sock. I fan heavy in laid me owir i da restin sair [sair; *shair*, or chair, P.J.] in I drew owir me een in I tawt. ...

"78. The wind is rising down yonder by the marshes and speaks soft & dull tonight as if its voice was thick with tears.

"79. Stitched, yes stiched wi silk linin i da inside, lek a man's coat. J.G. 11 Mr 85.

"Bind da kay [kye, P.J.] wair [*whair*: where, P.J.] du sees ony meat. 'bind dim i da damp *l*oags.' M.G. 26 Ju. 91.

"No break, no change, no alteration more din de wir it he commenced. His kovin da voe (upstairs, W & by N gale). M.G., 10.2 a m, 8 Fb., 94.

"Hitl be ower hard for de *tanyiks* (Dog & bone, at tea). M.G., 22 Jr 94.

"If is a muir-kovi, we miyt skri by wi whats in bit dats no a. ... Da bodim is ut o dis kezis: da bodim wis ut o dis in. I wis gain til a rivd im bit. ... M.G., 11.58 a m, 25 Jr 94.

"Der *bladed* da sem is if did bin sheep-etn (Kil). M.G., 2.41 p m, 25 Fb. 94.

"Hits da ald gantry [pronounced jantry, P.J.] its at da fire: der plenty o dim if de kud be gotn ta da hus ir gotn ta. ... 'Da job is getin dim ta da hus. Del *low* is lang is da *taw* i dem lasts, til de burn ut. Bit dir ne duration in dim.' (Kirning, but, fire bright.) M.G., 10.35 p m, 17 Jl 94.

"Hits a *Karlsom* job (Layin up on unkin mare), M.G., o—p m, 25 Jl 94 (1 st run).

"I tuk a bit o bred, it wes wan [*whan*: when, P.J.] I wis him (Güd miyt it du de). LW. & MG., 3.0 p m. 28 Jl. 94.

"Il *Koml* dis boil for da Katl lik it in destroy it. L.W., 9.32 p m. 28 Jl 94.

"Wat [*what*] aels de Mŭlda? [Pony] Der laid ower heavy upo de last time. Du'l no *Kommis* o dat puir object. M.G., 11.25 a m., 30 Jl. 94.

"Wan [*whan*: when] i *dimmers* dun, dul no see im—da rül (At tea). M.G., 9.15 p m, 31 Jl. (94).

"If it bies mony niyts o da kind it is bin for a wile [*while*] hitl sün kut-up da utliers. M.G., 9.45 p m, 30 D 94.

"25. (Boats) An upo Moninday he wiz blain fre da nort a day, an at night, dun after sinset he fell plat calm in we gud ta 'Glup, in whan we wir drain up wir lines, me uncle kem ashore wi da boats.

". . . fa buird side . . . ta mak im up i da sud wast, jüst is mukl wind is *su* [*shu*: she] kud keep da sea gain fram a da time . . . as mukl is keep 'ir at da keib, in da ling comin up at da forehead. . . . Da sun wiz just gettin ut o da water when we lifted . . . only on da edge o a time cud we get a glimpse o dem.—layin ta da norder.

"(Da sea wiz gain muntins high.) Da gale aye seem'd ta harn, an ne tryin ta andu, just gain lek a *k*ap i da water. I canna see da pobies bit de might be fog on dem. (J.G.

"Der hadin a *malutska* for da gantri [jantry: gentry, P.J.]. MG. c, 0.45 p m., Th., 17 D. 96 (geese—In byre)."

The merchant and his capable wife did all they could to encourage their son in his studies, for they too were of more than average intelligence, James's library containing a number of valuable books. He was a highly respected man in Yell society; Lady Franklin, at the time of her visit to Shetland during the search for Sir John Franklin's ships, is said to have met the Williamsons at Linkshouse.

They loved the boy "Low," as his mother called him, his early years being happy ones as his natural bent for

studying got full rein. Although never lazy or "awkward"
he did not occupy himself much in early life with croft or
shop duties. His mother was a very "managing body"
and saw to it that the croft and animals were always
well kept.

At Mathewson's school the candle had been lit, the
restless light of the intellect fanned, that set his feet on the
straight and narrow road of knowledge he was to follow
till the end of his life.

Even in 1872, the year of his father's death, when he
records the sad event in his last school exercise book, and
he left Mathewson's, his own inclinations were never
hindered. His mother and sister did a lot of the "skutterin
wark" about the croft. Thus Laurence was more or less
free to develop his talents, and started to lay the ground-
work of his methodical system of folk-speech and place-
name recording that has saved for posterity a large
amount of Shetlandic lore and tradition—a heritage of
riches only now beginning to be appreciated at its true
value by Shetlanders.

His guiding principle was a saying of his teacher's:
"To understand a thing you must understand its history
and every word has its history if we but knew it." To him
every face and type of face had its history. He considered
his own mind to be some combination of Celtic and Norse,
by Celtic meaning the Gaelic, supposed to have been a
fair people from Ireland which came across and ruled the
Pictish people. He recited poetry to show the difference
between the Norse and the Celtic mind. How each
handled the same theme, yet the greater touch of charm
and imagery seemed to be with the Celtic song. To a
friend in conversation Laurence said: "My mind tends to
the philosophical and ideal; the Norse to the practical."
On being asked what he meant by the philosophical, he
replied: "The philosophical seeks to trace things from the
cause to the effect." Discussing genealogy he made the
interesting comment: "The Norman French are not now
numerous in Shetland, but at one time they multiplied

enormously, becoming numerous as well as prominent, every village toonship having its Ha'; but there is a fair amount of their blood among the people. . . ."

Discussing the oppressions of the Scots in Shetland, he once recited a ditty, running something like this:

> "Their coming to Shetland was naked and bare,
> Their stay in the land brought trouble and care;
> Where have they gone and how do they fare?
> They did well here, they'll do well there."

The "things of the world," as money, possessions and the like, had little appeal to Laurence Williamson. At times it seemed as if his mind dwelt on the pinnacles, far removed from the bustle and sweat of the day. It is said he was offered "£10 a week" to do some clerical, or surveying, work in connection with the Crofters' Commission in 1889, but could not bring himself to accept the offer of "a' dat money." Where other men were "tearin' at," getting the muck spread on their voar rigs, Laurence's mind would turn to mathematics, and like Mathewson and the herring bones, he tried to find the exact number of heaps of muck required to cover a rig of such-and-such proportions. Similarly, in hairst, the corn of Gardie often stood late, unshorn, on the rigs, while the crofter was engaged on some intricate mathematical problem; or, suddenly minding of something in connection with his philological or genealogical studies, he would lay down the sickle and travel, perhaps miles, on his quest. No one need have remonstrated with him then. "Yea, I maun geeng!" was all the reply forthcoming. Again, when "leadin" home the peats, in "meshies" on pony-back, he might take a notion of calculating the number of "meshies" transported on each "run," and the total number brought home from the hill, and is said once to have calculated the number of peats in all. Some seasons they had boys to help them with the peat-work, the boys generally dining with the family at the same table when they did not take their meals at the peat-bank in the hill. To Laurence this was "lightsome" work, for he met folk at the various banks, hearing many expressive words and phrases. He "wanted to understand" rather than "do" things; although he was capable of sustained work both manual and intellectual.

When a youth, with men coming into his father's shop, he heard "many discussions, narration of events, grievances: saying what they thought wrong or right, what should or should not be done, among them many Norsemen. I didn't hear any of them say they wanted to understand. . . ." He spoke as if there was a vastness, mysteriousness, glory and interest in the universe and in things around him. "When young," he told a friend, "I think I was dazzled by the glory of the picture." When talking on any subject he tended to emphasise the extent and difficulty of the matter. He pondered long on a question, or idea, spending weeks, even months, hunting out older folk, getting them to pronounce a word, phrase or name, over and over again; or tracking down some detail of genealogy, or other thing most folk thought "of little worth." As a woman from the mainland of Shetland who settled in Yell said: "Loard bliss me, I tout da man wheer! He met me an started ta wheestin me da wye we pirnooncd da nems o' lochs an hills athin wir place, in he'd aye say: 'Say dat ageeng, sae's I gjit da vowels. . . .'" He knew an old woman in North Yell who could sing the ballad, with the refrain ". . . *Skowan orla grun* . . ." thought by scholars to have been an old Norse song; and he was always going to bring someone to her with a knowledge of music to have it written down. It took fifteen years, however, before a suitable person was found, and by then the woman was past singing.

In a letter to a friend, dated "Monday, 25 July 1892," he writes: " . . . But I was little interested in it [genealogy] till say 1870 onwards, when we [A. D. Mathewson and L. W.] talked much on it—what he [A. D. M.] could then mind. After his death I spent several days sorting up his papers, but never got through them. There were among them several genealogical matters. I have also acquired much genealogical information in my time from old folk, now mostly gone. However, my interest in it as many have supposed was not a dry-as-dust antiquarian one, but for its human interest—for its connection with people whom we loved or knew interesting things of: & the light thrown on the past of our people & island home. But like all other riches, intellectual wealth takes to itself wings & flies away; & the cares, perplexities & distractions of life have gone with much of mine . . . ," and further, " . . . about 1813 for several years the brothers Grimm collected in Germany their wonderful folk-tales which my friend Dr. Gudbrand Vigfusson (who was here in 1888) says in his introduction to the Edda, 'will go down to be the pleasure of the young & the wise for all time' along with their prose version of the Eddic songs 'told in the inimitable style. . . .' Mr Asbjornsen did a like great work for Norway. Who will do it for Shetland? It is now or never. . . ."

As a boy and youth Laurence was intensely interested in poetry. On one of his papers are a number of poems, the first dated 1868, beginning:

> "Hoo sweet it is on a May morn
>   Whan da sun's shinin fair,
> An smilin on da brierin corn
>   Doon troo da mornin air;
> Whan Zephyrs light early breezes
>   Come slowly glidin bye,
> Drivin da snaw white-tapped cloods
>   Across da bright blue sky."

A poem "To B——" is dated 1874:

> "My first and only love and choice
>   My heart alas hath found it,
> Thy dark eyes steadfast gaze on me
>   To thee hath won and bound it.
> Restless pours the sea dividing
>   Thee and Fetlar all from me,
> Here thou neer mayst meet me more,
>   Stranger I may seem to thee."

The poem "On da Vord eld," begins:

> "O every window o my soul
>   Did drink da beauty in,
> O da days sae lang gin,
>   Whisperin thus its lüe ta me;
> O da four in twenty fairies dancin
>   In a circle roond da player,
> Hoo itil grey steens de turned,
>   Whan da daylight lit the air. . . ."

and

> " (thinking) of the ancient saga tellers,
>   And their thrilling legend lore;
> Of our brother Iceland dwellers
>   In their land of ice and fire;
> Of a Lapland afternoon. . . ."

He did not concentrate on poetry, however, though remaining interested in the subject all his life. Instead, he turned to ethnology, folk-lore, philology and genealogy. In these subjects he held a leading place in Shetland's cultural life. Men like L. J. Nicolson, the poet; Haldane Burgess, author and scholar; James Inkster, author and scholar; Peter Greig, Shetland's ablest journalist; Magnus L. Manson, law clerk, the brains of the Shetland Socialist movement in its formative years; James Irvine, Mossbank, scholar and genealogist, and others acknowledged his lead, and more than one sought the advice of the "crofter at Gardie." The toon became a mecca for all those interested in the north and its people.

He had the post office at Gardie for some years, but eventually gave it up, thereafter finding more time for crofting, and what was more important to him, his studies and writing.

A philosopher, thinker, and at times a dreamer, more than a man of action, and without a trace of vanity, Laurence Williamson did not seem to be ambitious in the matter of publishing the result of his researches. He was immensely happy when the Faroese scholar, Jakob Jakobsen, came to Shetland in 1893 and outlined to him his plans for a dictionary and a book of place-names. Without any idea of reward, other than the soul-satisfying thought that at long last his material was to be used by such a gifted student, Laurence gave Jakobsen most of his manuscripts, and in conversation what "was athin his skullt," as Haldane Burgess once smilingly remarked. The scholar acknowledges L. Williamson's help, also that of the crofter's mother, with deep gratitude in the Foreword to his important book, as well as acknowledging John Charleson's help in the huge task.

Jakobsen* was twenty-nine when he first came to Shetland. He was born at Tórshavn, in the street Gongin, near Eystara Vag, close by the sea. He was the son of Hans N. Jacobsen, bookbinder and bookseller, and Johanna Maria Hansdotter from Sandur. Jakobsen left Faroe for Copenhagen as a young student. He had a brilliant university career, his doctor's thesis being his first book on the Shetland dialect and place-names. He was in Shetland again in 1894, 1895, and finally in 1906. Completing his great Dictionary, it was published in Denmark in 1908–21, an English translation appearing in 1928.

A letter, dated "Lerwick, 17th May 1895," is interesting as showing the warm friendship between the two scholars. It reads:

My dear Friend,

Excuse me that I have not written you yet, although it is a good while now since I came back to Lerwick. But I have always had you in my mind. It is with rather strange feelings that I write this letter because I have to leave Shetland now in a few days; it is quite certain that I shall long [to be] back; there are so many remembrances. I shall never forget you and your mother and your kindness. Yesterday James Goudie and I were a trip to Tingwall especially to see the tingholm in the loch. Although it was very blowy I enjoyed the trip.

To-day I go to Scalloway to see a few people there.

I cannot write just now, cannot get the words out I am wanting to say: sometimes when you have very much to say you can get nothing said.

* Dr. Jakobsen spelled his name JAKOBSEN, his father JACOBSEN.

You have probably seen the reports in the papers about my last lectures. I mentioned your list of Fetlar names (1500) and thought there would be about 2000 on the whole in Fetlar. Do you think that exaggerated? I always thought there would be more than 1500.

It will probably be sometime next week that I leave for Leith. The three past years of travelling are already like a dream to me.

If you have anything to write me or ask me about, a letter from the Yell north can reach me still, before I leave (c/o James Goudie or John Irvine).

My Copenhagen address is: Mr. J. Jakobsen, c/o Widow Anna Horsbøl, Grundtvigsveg 5, 3rd floor, Copenhagen, V, Denmark.

I shall send you a paper in a few days, containing some information about the Doulls.

Kindly remember the "Finnigord dyke," I mentioned it shortly in connection with your name in the lecture. Have you written your sister in Granton? My kindest regards to you and your mother and also to W. Brown,

Yours sincerely,

J. JAKOBSEN.

Two of the proudest and happiest events in Laurence Williamson's life occurred in 1886 and 1888. In 1886 he was honoured by a visit from Dr. Gudbrandr Vigfússon, the Icelandic scholar. He visited Gardie on purpose to meet the crofter-scholar. Two years later Laurence was in Lerwick, and was again honoured by the author of numerous works on Icelandic and Norse subjects, the two meeting at the house of Leog, the residence of Arthur Laurenson, another famous Norse scholar. Vigfússon was Laurenson's guest at Leog, where in the rigs near the house the folk grazed a cow or two. Miss Kate Tulloch, Laurenson's niece, in a letter to the writer, tells of how, as a girl, she saw the Icelander one day laughing heartily at one of the kye, in a frisky mood, tearing around the fields.

Another proud day in Laurence's life came when Jakobsen stepped off the *Earl of Zetland* on a summer day in 1893, and the two shook hands and sauntered "up da toons" to Gardie in animated conversation. Almost fifty years ago he spent some months in Scotland, the libraries and bookshops of Edinburgh and Glasgow being visited by him many times.

Though scholarly studies, crofting work, and his ever willing help to crofters needing their land surveyed, or other clerical assistance, besides other writing work, took up much of his time, Laurence always tried to spare some time for social activities. He had a pleasant, genial way, could laugh and joke with the rest, despite a seeming brusqueness of manner. There was hardly a house in Fetlar and Yell that did not delight in welcoming him, for the folk were then sure of some highly interesting discussions and debates, notably when some of the older folk would "traep wi' een anidder" over details of genealogy. It is said he knew the genealogies of every family in the three north isles, besides that of many in the east isles —Whalsay and the Skerries—and in the north mainland. Among his correspondents were Karl Blind, Dr. Joseph Anderson, Dr. Jakobsen, L. J. Nicolson, the poet, Rev. Thomas Mathewson, and other men of learning. In a letter to the writer, W. Fordyce Clark, the Shetland author, writes: " . . . I never had the pleasure of meeting Mr. Williamson, nor did I ever have any correspondence with him. I did, however, once see a letter he had addressed to the late Mr. L. J. Nicolson (the Bard of Thule) and was so struck with the contents of same that I made a few extracts. Here they are, and they are sufficient to show that the writer was possessed of a fine sentiment, and that he had the power of expressing it in felicitous language: 'Isles locked in everlasting dream'; 'Northern skies like a rested fire'; 'Valleys aburst with life'; 'The complaining cry of the lapwing'; and 'the dissonant scream of the gull'; 'Fetlar men speaking as if in a gale of wind'; 'Childhood and its sorrowful thereafter'; 'Dim, far-off delectable mountains which we can get glimpses of but never delineate'; 'My heart within me was a wilderness in which no flower could grow, tho' I knew the rain would awaken the roots. . . .'"

Some young people, of course, hardly understood why Laurence spoke so much of the olden days and the sturdy Northern race; but though his talk may have tended to bore some youngsters they all instinctively respected "the man frae Gairdie." Older people respected him, some even revering him, not a few "tinkin lang whan he bedd awa'." His friends at Errisdaal, South Yell, always looked forward to his visits, Jarm Henderson, the crofter there, being a man after Laurence's own mind, full of lore of the old days. Laurence took Jakobsen to Jarm's, the three having interesting discussions, and once Jakobsen sang a Norn song in Jarm's ben room. It was at Errisdaal that Laurence boarded during the ten months in 1919 he taught at Ulsta school. Here one morning he found some books that interested him, and forgetful of his class of pupils he sat down to read, the books in a circle around him on the floor. He hastened out to work only when the good-wife of the house came in from milking the kye to tell him "da time a day he wis!" Before this, in 1915, he taught at da Herra school. It was from Errisdaal that he once carried a bag of seed corn all the way to Gardie, over twelve miles distant.

Teaching high-spirited bairns their "Ah-bay-say," however, did not appeal a great deal to him. He was, in the eyes of some of the pupils, "too auld-fashioned," but to others he seemed an ideal teacher and first set their thoughts to an appreciation of Scandinavian history and literature. One of his Ulsta pupils, now a seaman, tells of their singing lessons, when Laurence loved to get them to sing old folk-songs, including many of Burns's, whose works he treasured. He often told them of Shetland's history and lore, of the old kitchen-midden folk, the broch-dwellers, the udallers of Fetlar, the cruelty of the sheep-clearances, the depredations of the naval press-gangs and other vivid episodes from northern history.

The Mid Yell Debating Society was formed in 1908, and Laurence regularly attended its meetings, taking part in the debates and discussions with an arresting vitality that held his listeners spellbound. His memory was phenomenal, and he had knowledge of a great many subjects. He gave three lectures to the Society, one entitled *Shetland Folk-lore*. He wrote, as "A True Shetland Man," a graphic account of local reactions to the Parliamentary Election in 1902, when the three candidates were Cathcart Wason, MacKinnon Wood and Mr. Angier. He liked to go to dances and other social functions, and to regattas and cattle-shows. The Fetlar cattle-show hardly seemed complete without a visit from the Gardie crofter, his striking personality often dominating the scene. At these gatherings he met and studied people—their faces, heads, speech, build and gestures. Once to a friend he described minutely the peculiar ways two girls had of opening a "grinnd," or gate, each having distinctive mannerisms.

He seemed to know which part of Shetland anyone hailed from and whether their parents had been Shetlanders or "incomers." Once he surprised a young girl teacher at one of her first social appearances by correctly telling her name and the birthplace of her parents. Laurence, although a lover of solitude and peace in which to concentrate on his studies, was not a misanthrope. He took part in every phase of social and religious life, and loved to hear the fiddlers playing at the "rants" and "foys." These were held during the winter months when most of the young men would be home from sailing, and it was the period of weddings and gatherings of various kinds. He was one of the original committee that raised funds for the building of the Mid Yell Public Hall. He compiled lists of fiddle "springs," and noted down old songs, one of the lists being headed "Da Picts' Tunes." Another manuscript is headed "Old Verses from Yell & Fetlar, Shetland," some of the material in it appearing in Jakobsen's "Fragments of Norn," in his *Dictionary of the Norn Language in Shetland*.

SHETLAND SUNSET

C. J. Williamson

To face page 128

WINTER SUNSET

J. Peterson

To face page 129

"... Many persons, it is said, while they lay on a knoll, or went by a hillside, have heard the fairies playing and dancing within, and often learnt their tunes.

"*Fair an lucky*. Two fiddlers played at a Delting wedding for a silver fiddlestick, and could play all the same tunes till the Delting man played 'Fair an lucky,' which he had heard as he rested on a knoll coming through. So he won the bow. My informant sang the air and words."

Here Williamson gives some incomplete verses of the song which had a Norn refrain something like " Skowin örla gründ, where yortin han grenorla," or "Wher giorten han grun oerlac." The MS. version is rather difficult to reproduce on account of the number of phonetic symbols used. A book, *Rambles in the Far North*, by R. Menzies Fergusson, published in 1884, gives another incomplete version of the song:

> "Der lived a king inta da aste,
>   Scowan urla grun;
> Der lived a lady in da wast,
>   Whar giorten han grun oarlac.
>
> "Dan he took out his pipes ta play,
>   Scowan urla grun;
> Bit sair his hert we dol an' wae,
>   Whar giorten han grun oarlac.
>
> "At first he played da notes o' noy,
>   Scowan urla grun;
> An dan he played da notes o' joy,
>   Whar giorten han grun oarlac."

"Fiddle springs. Shetlanders are much addicted to fiddling. Formerly there were large numbers of Fiddlers in each parish. Weddings were usually in winter and lasted three days, and frequently there were several fiddlers to play. The chief amusement was music and dancing & fiddlers followed them to church striking up tunes as they went along. Rants were balls open to every comer. They were held in winter and very frequent, and on almost every one of the 24 (?) Holy nights of Yule, and old and

I

young wended to the spot for miles and miles around. A whole family would even shut up the house & go miles away where their relations stayed. And in the long winter evenings the fiddler would play to the children around the fire. Some Shetlanders who were in the navy were fiddlers to the seamen. And each Greenland ship used to carry a fiddler, sometimes a Southern, sometimes a Shetlander, to play to the men while at work to enliven them. And sometimes the fiddlers from several ships would meet & try their skill. And I think I have heard of a Shetland fiddler competing with the Dutch from a buss or ship. No wonder that tunes are so abundant, several of them are fairy tunes and likely very old; many are of Norse or native origin & many Scotch.

"And many of them must have been learned from the sources indicated above. There is even a *Yaki** tune. The tunes had usually two turns, some had more. Some had different names in different parishes. I add an imperfect list of tunes and some have verses attached. . . ."

And on another MS. he writes: ". . . Most springs have 2 turns; many have 3 & 4 and tunes 'Da ald reel' and 'Est nyuk o Fife' are said to have once had 24 each, but only 5 or 6 are extant.

"Dey wir a lok o Fidlers playing afore da wheen; an among da rest wiz a ald Shetland Fidler. An every in o dem hed dir turn at da fiddle an nin o dem cud rus her til da A.S.F., played 'da ald way,' etc., an dat roosed her. . . ."

Laurence's rough notes are, of course, mainly in pencil and hard to make out, jotted down hurriedly as they were, and on any bit of paper handy. Some of his manuscripts, however, are carefully written in ink in neat, minute hand-writing. This neat writing enabled him to get about four thousand words on both sides of a small quarto sheet, almost a small book in itself. In his genealogical manuscripts again, a great amount of material is given in a limited space; on four sheets, for instance, over three

* Eskimo.

thousand names are written. His library contained over one hundred books, as well as many magazines, pamphlets and newspapers. Some of the books were important and valuable ones to him; as, for instance, Sweet's *Primer of Phonetics*; *History of Church and State in Norway*; *Comparative Grammar of the Languages of Further India*; Schlegel's *Philosophy of History*; Chaucer's *Poems*; *The Ancient British Church*; *Elements of Gaelic Grammar*; *Sturlunga Saga*, edited by Vigfússon; *Corpus Poeticum Boreale*, Vigfússon and York Powell.

His great friend, Thomas Mathewson, afterwards Scottish Episcopal minister of Rhynie, Aberdeenshire, had a book-selling and publishing business in Lerwick in the nineties. He was a student of northern literature, and is said to have wanted Laurence to "publish a book," or even a series of books. He published works by Haldane Burgess and other Shetland writers, and being a very business-like man soon had the various editions sold out. He did get something out of his friend the crofter at last. It was an extract from a letter written 10th June 1902, revealing again the poet that might have been, had not the fine mind turned instead to more logical and scientific pursuits.

"I remember your reminiscence of your early visit there, and the pleasant memory of it—the boats, the men, the lodges, the summer days, the summer dim, the clang of the seafowl, the lady-hen singing, the banks, the beach, the sea, the ceaseless comings and goings, the homely sober-kindliness of the men, their friendly nearness. . . . I can see it all."

The bookseller had this printed in red alongside a photograph of the fishing station of Fedaland, at the extreme north point of the Shetland mainland, and published it as a postcard.

The poet's hand is again seen in the following extract from one of his early manuscripts: "6. 'Bern whair bides du?' 'At Kubal.' 'What's dee nim in wha as dee?' ' — — is my nim, in my fedir is — —, in my midir is — —.' The stranger clasped her around the neck. He kissed her.

The tears ran down his sunburnt face, and he said, 'My child, my darling child.' At length the stranger turned to his son & said, 'Kiss her too, she is near, very near indeed to thee!' The lad complied. The girl had submitted without a word, and her face had a softened & puzzled aspect, and she said in a very friendly tone, 'Uncan man whair com ye fre? Ir ye come fre far?' 'Yea, very far, come thou with me.' He took 'ir by the hand & his son went by their side and (leading her) without speaking a word they went eastwards, the old man taking the paths as if they had long been familiar to him. When they neared the house of Kubal the stranger stopped, and pointing to his son, he said, '—— that is Ura lingi, and that is Hammerafield, and there is Kolbastaft & here is Stembirshul. . . .

"'I pleaded wi da Lord for a sight o dee eens mair, an ta lay my bones i da eart in I hupid for mony a year, an at last I lippened ne langer.' Then after a pause, he added, 'Bit He has heard my cry, tanks be to his name—Let me kiss dee, ins meir.' (L. W.)."

And in part of a letter his command of language and fine sense of imagery are revealed.

GARDIE, MID YELL,
Tuesday, 11th March, 1884.

DEAR . . .

I got your letter, on Christmas een, and it made me sad, and yet happy all next day. It was the happiest day I have had for long. I was thinking long—thinking long for —— ——beholding yet again that beauty which adorns her—a beauty that can only be perceived or imagined when the heart is pure and humble. It is a joy that the mind when it is proud cannot picture forth even as possible—tho' it can remember having had it, and believe in the bliss of it. Thinking long—what a strange thing it is, a pain—a pleasure, both combined. You remember what like Christmas morning was. A dark and gloomy sky, and how the day broke with a strange, weird fiery redness all along the east. I wondered if you would play the ba' at the Links o Tresta according to the time-honoured custom of our people. It became a very "distressful" day. Some of the little boys were at the ba, but it was too bad a day to join them. The S—— lasses were to come over to spend the evening, but they did not come, for the weather. We had made a good deal of preparation, but it was in vain, and we were disappointed. I was hardly ever out all day. Yet I felt that strange calming longing. It was better than almost any company. It seemed as if —— and the thousands of little beauties that cling around Fetlar, when the eyes are open, could never be compared with Yell. Even the "lasses" admirable voices seemed as nothing, and all their freeness in comparison. What a number of poetic "delightfulnesses" cling to our own old Fetlar. It is like the beauty of the great outspread ocean—the old sea as the Norway men call it—when you look at it from Strands hill on a glorious July evening, when the sun has just sunk behind the crimson clouds beyond the north end of Unst. It is like the starry sky on a frosty evening this time of year. The firmament is a transparent indigo. The stars twinkle, twinkle, twinkle with a living peace—they move not, no they stir not, yet they are intensely alive, each one as it twinkles is so magnified, so bursting with life. They dwell serenely in the peace of heaven. The geometrician of earth finds few circles or squares or ovals among them. Yet to the open eye, a divine order reigns there. No picture on earth can outvie their majestic simplicity. Joyful are they, and their joy passes into the sympathising beholder.

> " While the stars that oversprinkle
> All the heavens seem to twinkle
> With a crystalline delight."

There is a unity among them—like an assembly of friends— like a company of the blessed. There is an infinity about every one—some wonderful connection with every other one of them, with the boundless ever farther stretching space. Is it not this that helps to give them their wondrous unity & life? Again it is like the inside of the house when every one has gone to bed on a calm winter night. The fire is rested. The things about the house are all at peace. Their day's work is done. The chairs with the out-carved backs, the tongs that set up the fire, the pot that boiled the bere-meal gruel for supper, the brand iron that fired the bread, are all at peace & all alive, and in silent conversation with the old Dutch chest, and the sailor lad's chest & the lasses chests, and the old long press. And look at that spit of haddocks. What a quaint strange story they are telling of their life in the ocean. You cannot but believe that they are still alive— yea almost at home in the sea still. It is like the little springs that gush—ever old yet always young—living and life-giving, among the stones at Mongersdal. . . .

And in a letter written in March, 1915, inquiring about the Stewarts, he lists fifteen questions, and goes on: "Would you just take a pencil & paper, or if it wearies you, get one of the boys to do it—ask your aunt about the Stewarts, & scrawl down the answer any way, never mind the spelling. Put down the very words of the answer, just as they say it—I always find that best.

"You know there is no money in these things, but one longs to know about one's own people, and people that one comes in contact with in one's youth. And often while the old people are alive we can learn it from them, and also preserve it for others who will want to know in future, and not have our chances. It may take a little trouble, but when the old people are away it can't be got any more."

In 1893 Laurence Williamson prepared a "Shetland Calendar," giving a list of the "Merkis Days or Retts o' da Year" still observed in Shetland. This was published in the *Shetland Almanac*. It lists the old style "Saint" and other important days at one time widely recognised in the north.

About this same time Laurence represented the Udal League, afterwards Udal Rights Association, as "Ward Secretary" in Yell. This was founded by Alfred W. Johnston and others, having for its object fairer treatment for landholders. Some of its members even wanted to see "udal rights" restored as a protection against the "feudal-minded land-masters." They organised a petition in 1889 against payment of double land tax, in the form of Skatt and Scottish land tax, and got 1025 signatures in Orkney and Shetland. The petition was sent to the Secretary of

State for Scotland. Minor readjustments were made, and after a few years the Association became moribund. Johnston then founded the Viking Club, soon after renaming it the Viking Society for Northern Research. Williamson became a member of the Viking Society in 1907.

Laurence Williamson led what might be termed a strictly puritan, almost Spartan life. His needs were few. He abhorred anything unclean, and was a teetotaller and non-smoker. He was of good physique and healthy. The many heavy burdens of various crops, stock, provisions, water and the like most crofters have to carry (sometimes for long distances) he shouldered ungrudgingly. His pockets always contained a pencil or two, note-books or other writing material.

As a young man Laurence fell in love with a young Fetlar lass, but although respecting him as a friend the girl did not return his love. As he wrote earlier, of a Northmavine lass of striking beauty: " . . . She is the most attractive girl I have seen here, not that all the attractions of the world cd. depend to attract my heart, but I like to see anything beautiful, simple & pure, in the human face divine:

> My love was a cold chilling star,
>   And life is a long lonely night,
> Serenely she smiled from afar
>   With an alien heart numbing light."

So it was with the bonny Fetlar lass. Their acquaintance was a happy one, like cousins, but she could not bring herself to love the austere, at times brusque scholar, whose gentle vision-filled eyes burned with love of her. After a time she met a lad of her own age, and they both found happiness as man and wife. Recognising this, Laurence resigned himself to his austere, often lonely, life, the quest for truth in the intellectual sphere blunting his sense of loss. He never lacked friends, and after his sister's death he was kindly attended to by a neighbouring family, in whose house he died.

Another letter reveals L. Williamson's fine sense of imagery:

GARDIE, MID YELL,
12th March, 1881.

DEAR——

It is a fortnight tonight since you & I went across Fetlar together neither of us will be likely to forget that Friday & that Saturday especially in the light of after events. Tonight I have been almost across Yell. The homeward journey has refreshed my spirit, like a drink from some crystal "Kelda." And while the musical cadence still warbles across the harp-strings of the heart, I will try to convey some idea of this night in the black hills of Yell. The way lay eastwards over the long "Kaims" and hills & valleys that run in Yell from north to south. I came down a long hillside & then over a valley where 2 burns ran. After ascending a bit on the other side I stood still to listen & look, and the heart was opened to the underlying beauty. It was just as if you were standing below Haggart & looking eastward. But all was reversed, north was south & east was west. The hill in front, the hill on which you stand & the wide valley between run to the right hand & to the left till you see them no more. Away where the "Ruster Know" should be but farther away yet just in the same way you see the overtopping section of the wild sea banks. Still farther to the right is a giant knoll like Stahaberg, on the hither side of it is a dim green patch. This is the hill town of Bouster. Miles & miles up the valley leftwards a dim gray hill locks up the valley like a sea-worn boulder in a great grind, and oh how lonely. Years may elapse between the times that a human foot crosses that widespread wilds to the left once that the day is down in darkness or in moonshine. To-night the sky above the . . . hill is of a hazy blue in which Sirius twinkles clear & aloft.

CHAPTER VIII

The fine effects in the northern sky are perhaps among those things of an almost "spiritual" quality, visitors to the islands are most intrigued with. There is something of a witching charm about summer sunsets and sunrises, "hairst blinks," and winter "Merry Dancers," together with fine cloud displays, caused by the pure air, that holds both visitor and native enthralled.

During summer there is hardly any darkness. The Simmer dim, the afterglow from the setting sun, comes to banish night from the land. The 14th day of April is known as Simmermal Day, or Summer Day. This is the day that is said to foretell the weather all summer. The day ceases setting at Simmermal until Laurencemas in August. This is the period of the Dim. It is seen to advantage on clear nights. When the sky is inclined to be "grumbly," or full of clouds, the dim cannot be seen so well, but some of the best effects of the dim are seen on these cloudy nights with the sun gilding everything in many-hued beauty. Long before the official start of British Summer Time a natural saving of daylight is experienced by Shetlanders. Even as the sun sinks, his golden-red radiance lingers on in great shafts until midnight and after. All kinds of outdoor sports are possible during the summer evenings, midnight parties being organised for rambles over the hills, sailing on the firths, tennis, golf, swimming. Photography is even possible at midnight during June, the shops selling postcards of the Town Hall with the clock at midnight, and showing the shadows thrown by the lingering sunlight.

The Midnight Sun may not be seen in the isles, but the Simmer Dim runs it a close rival. This period of continuous daylight known as "da Dim" transforms the cold northland isles into places of magnetic attraction for visitors, as the phenomenon is probably unknown in any other part of the country. At first it takes a while to get used to going to bed in "the heart of daylight" and hearing seagulls calling long after midnight. In the isles of nightless summer, as Shetland has been aptly named, it is rare to see house-windows with their blinds drawn on summer nights. Folk would think anyone lighting a lamp and pulling down the blind during summer as daft! In the country districts where the crofting people live, so well known are the different families to each other that doors are hardly ever locked or barred. It has long been a tradition in the north that it is unlucky to bar or bolt the doors at night, especially during summer.

It was held that the summer nights were the nights when the "trows" or fairy folk of the hills and caves came out from their fastnesses in the knolls and dells to pay visits to the houses of ordinary mortals, the "cow-keeping people." Therefore the folk kept their doors ajar, or unlocked, and the windows unblinded and open, as it was thought to bring good fortune on any house visited by the trows, possessed as they were of powers for good and evil.

Pails of fresh water were carried from the wells before the household retired to rest, fresh blaand, or sour milk, had to stand in the churns, the peat fires were "rested" with fresh fuel and ashes, the house was "reddid up," dishes washed and everything placed in order so that if "da peerie hill-folk" by chance came in while folk slept and found everything to their liking they would depart in peace and leave a blessing on the house.

If, however, the trows found a house "in an uproar" of untidiness, pails empty of water, or containing dirty water, and the fire black out, then they said, "Ill-health on this house!" or "Graceless beings bide here!" Those were their curses as they fled from the "graceless folk's hoose." So the untidy, unprepared house, its croftlands, cattle, and everything were witched for a year and a day.

The summer dim, dancing over the hills and firths was thought by the older people to be the trows coming to make their rounds of the houses. The tinkling of the sluggish "simmer burn" was the trowy music, the heat "mirl" over the fields, the trows dancing. Many legends sprang up around the eerie beauty of the summer evening, for in Shetland there is darkness, cold, and gloom during the long winter. Many crofts "never get the sun" from November to March owing to the lie of the land "under the hills." It was little wonder then that after the pall of darkness lying heavy on everything during the winter months, the coming of the summer, with its birds, flowers, light, gaiety, should have been regarded as a gift from another world. Accordingly, the "other-worldly folk," the trows, had to be appeased, and even honoured. Midsummer is also the time of the blossoms. The Johnsmas Flowers grow on field and hill, and the lasses used to arise with the "break of the Dim" to pluck and lay up the flowers which brought good fortune in courtship.

The effect of the simmer dim on the hills, in the valleys, and on the hill-locked voes and firths is one of sheer breath-taking loveliness.

There is the stillness of the evening, the golden-violet-reddish colour spreading over the western and northern sky to reflect on the still sea and the sleeping land. It spreads out in a dancing movement like a magic veil being thrown from the heavens. The cliffs are transformed, appearing blue-brown, or golden, in colour, the seaweed fringing the land looking like burnished gold. The waters of firth and loch sparkle and reflect the many hues, the fields of corn, rye and bere are rainbow-tinted, the summer breeze ripples over the rye in velvety folds. The white-washed croft houses, with spiralling peat-reek rising from the lums, look like elfin-houses. Over everything broods the summer quiet. Birds may be heard softly calling as they flit among the cliffs or scamper in the solitude of the thick kowes of purple heather. Subdued sounds may be heard as if loath to break the harmony of the dim-haunted world. Soft lowing of cattle, the timorous yaarmin' of sheep, the creaking of oars as some boat comes in from the sea, the quiet murmuring of fishermen hauling nets ashore, the lapping of the waves against the boats swinging with the tide. The tide sends up a thin white ring round the skerries, plashes sleepily on the ayres and cliffs, the wash of the sea setting up the only sad-seeming undertone. A night which is but the continuing day merges in an hour or so with the new day, heralded by the gulls, their crying the first sign to people that the "dim has riven" and the sun is up.

"Hairst blinks" are small flashes, like lightning, usually seen on hairst, or autumn, evenings. The folk called the blinks the trowie flaachts, likening them to the trows "kindling their lanterns" ere setting forth on their wanderings from house to house. In the twilight, or hümen, these blinks give a vivid flash, suddenly lighting up the countryside, so that at lonely places folk tramping along often got a bit scared and thought they were "seeing things!"

On autumn nights the sea also gives off a light all its own. This is called marild, or sea-fire. It is caused by phosphorus, and can be vividly seen as the oars cut the water, and on the fish in the holds. Hairst blinks, fire-flaachts and marild have inspired some old folk-tales and poetry.

The Aurora, or Northern Lights, are seen very often in Shetland during the autumn and winter. The folk call them the "Merry Dancers," or "pretty dancers," saying their weird movements are like the trailing of dancers' gowns.

Some people say they have heard the Aurora. Scientific inquiry in Canada has revealed much data, all from different sources, testifying to the persons concerned having distinctly heard the movements of the heavenly lights. Much interest is taken in Shetland in these investigations, as the islands seem to be favourably placed for bright displays.

Especially with frost do the lights shine clearest, and then, with big displays, it is said there can be heard a sort of "swishing" sound like the rustling of muslin. In the winter of 1926 there was a magnetic storm in Shetland, and during the disturbance a very bright display lit up the northern sky from horizon to beyond the zenith. The nights of the storm were otherwise still, great crowds of people remaining out-of-doors to watch the fine spectacle as streamers shot up, and broad ever-changing curtains swept the sky from east to west, receding towards the horizon then as swiftly shooting up again, filling the night with varicoloured light. Some assert that the sounds do not synchronise with the movements of the lights, as the phenomenon known as the Aurora takes place at a height of sixty-two miles above the surface of the earth, where the air is so rare that it would be impossible for sounds to be generated which could be heard on the earth. The Dominion Astrophysical Observatory, Victoria, B.C., has collected many letters which go to confirm the appearance of very low, and audible, auroras. In his *Low Auroras*, Dr. G. C. Simpson, F.R.S., writes: "A certain number of trustworthy and intelligent people, some of them with a sound scientific training, are sure that they have heard sounds accompanying displays of aurora extending down to the ground. On the other hand there are people, of whom I am one, who do not accept these conclusions, but deny that the aurora ever penetrates into the lower atmosphere and doubt any connection between the sounds heard and the aurora."

In January 1938 there was a vivid display of the lights that helped to banish darkness for an hour or so. That night it was very cold, with frost.

There are numerous books setting out to give glimpses of the Shetland Islands and the life of their people. Some are very good, as, for instance, Tudor's *Orkneys and Shetland*, now out of print, Joan Grigsby's *An Island Rooin*, and one of the best of the lot, Andrew O'Dell's *Historical Geography of the Shetland Islands*. One or two books have been written by yachtsmen and others who paid fleeting visits to the islands, the picture they give being incomplete, to say the least. Joan Grigsby is a keen yachtswoman, but came here by the usual route, on board one of the mail steamers. She camped out on a small island, Stenness, off the coast of Northmavine in the north mainland. Her companion on the isle, where they hoisted "the Jolly Roger," was Jenny Brown, then just starting her work as an amateur film-maker. Both women went to Stenness on work and pleasure combined, Jenny Brown to film the birds and their nests, and Joan Grigsby to gather "local colour" for her book. Jenny Brown has made some score or so of pictures in Shetland, some of which she has shown on lecture tours in Britain and America. Joan Grigsby's book was published in 1933 and met with success right away, as by her daily contact with the life, work and thought of the islanders she had been able to understand both place and people, writing of them with the sincerity and beauty of one who had come to love the north.

A book published in 1937, called *Dirk III: Jottings from the Log and Camera of a Cruising Yachtsman* ("made and printed in Germany"), gives a good account of some thrilling yachting voyages in northern waters, and some descriptions of places visited. Its author is Hans Domizlaff. There are five pictures of Shetland interest: "Trawlers in Lerwick"; "Cave dwellings at Jarlshof, in the background Sumburgh Head, the southern point of the Shetland Islands"; "A prehistoric tower, known as a broch, on the island of Mousa"; "Typical cloudscape in Blue Mull Sound"; and the "Northernmost part of the Shetland Islands on the edge of the Gulf Stream." A chart shows the course of the cruise of the yacht, whose owners were members of the Imperial Yacht Club. They started from Kiel, sailed up the east coast of Denmark, thence to Sumburgh Head, and Lerwick. From Lerwick they went along the east Shetland coast, through Blue Mull Sound to the south of Sudero, and Trangisvaag in Faroe.

Some quotations from the book make interesting reading. " . . . Brilliant sunshine promised a good voyage. . . . The sea was calm. Fishing lines were out on both sides, with small success. Little by little, minds stirred to activity by shore life settled down again. . . . At short intervals we encountered two big four-masted sailing vessels flying the Finnish flag. Both had originally been German ships. . . . The time is coming when yachts will be the only survivals of the romance of sail, and of man's dependence on the elements. At midnight, Skagen lighthouse was still visible after more than twelve hours at sea. . . . Not until fifteen hours later, in the latitude of Songvaar, did a fresh breeze get up and blow steadily from ENE. By the following midnight we had reached Listerland, and I then came out with my plan to visit the Shetland Islands. . . . As the sun passed the local meridian, it was kind enough momentarily to show a sharp lower rim to enable us to take a reliable observation. It proved possible to take an observation in the afternoon as well, which was particularly important since I expected to see Sumburgh Head Lighthouse on the horizon at nightfall. . . . At last the wind moderated but the sea remained angry, and there was no sign of Sumburgh Head light. . . . I had just listened to the time signal at one o'clock and entered the chronometer reading when suddenly I heard the long expected hail—'Light ahead one point to port.' We bore away at once, making for the entrance to Lerwick Harbour, and then found the distance by taking two bearings. . . . The seas were now exactly abeam, and it became uncomfortable on deck. Although we were travelling slowly, and the sea offered little resistance now that the wind had fallen, the lee side was very wet on this course. It seemed as though the waves, repulsed by the near but invisible coast, fought with the new sea, and our ship was exposed to an oceanic cross-fire. The boom kept snapping relentlessly at the main sheet, and the prospect of encountering land before we had gone ahead far enough was so unattractive that we put out a little more to sea. . . . At about three o'clock the outline of the Isle of Mousa emerged through the darkness. The other lighthouses shown on the chart were invisible, and the Bressay

fog horn was silent. Unfortunately, we had been unable
to obtain a harbour chart of Lerwick, and when at last the
entrance light, now extinguished and recognisable only by
its tower, lay abeam in the cold morning mist, we took in
the mainsail, started the motor, and moved slowly into
the great bay which frames the capital of the Shetland
Islands. The surrounding scenery struck us as dismal and
depressing. Hundreds of grimy little trawlers lay along the
quay, backed by a grey wilderness of stone. The marking
of the channel was so indistinct as to be impossible for the
uninitiated to make out. Since the long rows of trawlers,
piled up five or six deep, left not an inch of mooring space
for weary mariners, we preferred to stay out in the bay
until dawn came to dispel the fog. At a safe distance from
the numerous coal barges and the tangle of mercantile
shipping, we let go the anchor with a feeling whose only
expression found vent in the bitter query: 'Why were we
such fools as ever to sail into these godforsaken parts?' . . .
The trip from Skagen to Lerwick had taken something
over four days, which for a yacht is pretty smart work. . . .
All round us the eye could see nothing but steamers, and
yet more steamers. Over them hung a pall of smoke, and
over that again reigned the fog. A motor-boat that had
run into the harbour with us had pitched on a bad place
to anchor, and was forced to make a second attempt. . . .
We were at first so overcome by the monotony of the Island
that we strove to find its unattractiveness attractive so as to
carry away with us some lasting memory as an achievement of our trip. . . . The German consul enlightened us
concerning the sights and customs of the place. He was
very proud of his non-English descent and described the
Shetland Islands as a part of Scandinavia. It is significant
of the natives' feeling of independence that no crowned
head has ever visited the islands; neither an English nor
a Scottish King has set foot there. . . . This feeling of
independence pursued us throughout our stay as characteristic of all the inhabitants. They all protested at being
regarded as English or Scottish, or even as British subjects.

Even their War memorial was confined to a list of the
fallen and bore only the fact of their death, with no word
of sacrifice or heroism, of duty to King or country. Ex-
service men would begin their narratives with the words:
'We were made to go. . . .' At the present time, Gaelic is
spoken and assiduously cultivated in the Shetlands. . . .
We listened with polite indifference to many emphatic
declarations of independence while we drove around the
island in a couple of cars. The one thing which really
interested us, the famous ponies, apparently no longer
enlivened the monotonous landscape. When the word
Shetland is mentioned in Germany, it always calls to mind
those hardy animals, but our driver had a good deal of
trouble in producing a couple of specimens. . . . One of
our two drivers seemed to have studied local history
rather more carefully than had his colleague. He advised
us to visit the southern part of the main island, and see the
excavations of the Jarlshof on Sumburgh Head. He even
gave us an introduction to the archaeologist in charge of
the excavations, and as a farewell gift, presented me with a
prehistoric axe head. . . . But first we wanted to see something of the northern Shetlands, and take some photographs of the east coast, described by Baedeker as very
picturesque. . . . We anchored for the night in Mid Yell
Voe. . . . A fishing boat came alongside and offered us a
large quantity of fish for a shilling. The fishermen's faces
were set in expressions of anxiety and distrust, as though
they wondered whether a stranger could possibly be in-
duced to part with such a sum. I gave them two shillings,
less than the fish was worth, and that cheered them up and
made them more friendly. The population of the Shetlands
is very poverty-stricken. . . . The Shetland Islands are a
sunny paradise compared with the Faroes. . . . While we
lay there, it rained; then the sun would come out for five
minutes, or suddenly, for a change, dense mist would
blot out the rest of the world; but the chief feature was the
rain. The German yacht *Sleipnir* had been in Trangisvaag
two years before."

K

As will be seen, these German yachtsmen were very observant, although a bit inaccurate when they say Gaelic is spoken in Shetland. Their views on our "poverty," too, are wide of the mark, although Shetland, in 1939, had an unenviable high percentage of workers unemployed. The observations on the "independence movement" in Shetland are amusing and rather inaccurate. Nazi propaganda, however, early in the war, did try to make something of this non-existent "independent Shetland" movement. In 1904 the German High Seas Fleet visited Lerwick. While ashore the Germans were seen taking a great interest in everything, taking photographs, soundings and all the rest. The German freshing steamers shortly before the war, as well as numerous herring trawlers, had not a few keenly observant men among their crews.

CHAPTER IX

As you know, the majority of young Shetland men have to go away "south" to sail in ships of the Merchant Navy in order to make a living, so uninviting has their homeland become after decades of landlordism. There is little chance of earning a decent living in Shetland, where everything is hampered by landlordism and big mercantile interests. Of some score of members of the County Council, something like sixteen are either merchants or landlord-merchants, or their stooges. As can be seen, those interests will do little to better conditions for the mass of the people; being well-off themselves they naturally tend to take things easy, unless it is a question of wages, when they get all hot and bothered about "the high wages being paid."

Crofting and fishing, it is true, employ large numbers of islanders, but at best crofting is a subsistence only, a traditionary way of life; and unless modern methods are introduced, and housing conditions greatly improved, it cannot appeal to young people. Of recent years the fishing has gone from one depression to another, so that under existing conditions it holds out little hope for ambitious young people. The knitting industry, too, had slumped to rock-bottom prior to the war, but with the war things have improved a good deal. New markets have opened up, and with the organisation of the Shetland Hand Knitters' Association, knitters are at last getting something like a square deal. How the Association will be able to face up to the inevitable after-war slump remains to be seen, but it is already assured of markets, and with the willing co-operation of all knitters and every person of progressive outlook there seems reason to believe it will weather the storm.

A similar organisation, aimed at developing handloom weaving, has recently been formed and has attracted many members, although new looms are as yet slow in appearing.

Another co-operative organisation, the Shetland Fisheries Co-operative Society, was set up in the summer of 1946 to develop all aspects of the industry, after a well-attended public meeting had turned down the idea of starting a joint stock company on the usual capitalist lines.

Other progressive plans are under consideration, but are hampered by the apparent neglect of the Government.

Unless new vision and enterprise are imbued into public bodies, new programmes adopted and vigorously pushed, to bring industry and life back to the islands, they will soon become depopulated unless for the sheep and wild birds. Fortunately Shetland people are beginning to realise this, and a number of proposals have been outlined, such as the Shetland Labour Party's programmes for crofting and fishing, the S.H.K.A. programme and others. These, however, will stand or fall to the extent that Shetlanders organise and press for their implementation. This, again, will call for a measure of national legislation, and the putting of this into effect depends on a substantial Labour and progressive vote at elections, with a real desire on the part of the Government to get something done.

For generations the "sea" has drawn young Shetlanders, not from any mystic charm or romance that may enshroud ships and the sea, but from the all-impelling economic reason to make a living. Shetland men were "pressed" into the ships of Nelson's navy, over one hundred Fetlar men alone serving in the French wars. They sailed in the whaling ships to the "West Ice," and Greenland. The "timber ships" of the Western Ocean were manned by Shetland crews, large sailing ships on the "West Coast" of South America trade had Shetland men in their crews. The Australasian trade attracted Shetland seamen, the Iceland and Faroe cod fishing was largely a Shetland concern, the "tramps" trading here, there and everywhere had Shetland men and boys in their grimy, bug-ridden fo'castles. To every quarter of the globe, to hundreds of ports have Shetland men sailed, so that in almost every island household the names of strange lands and cities visited by some son or brother are as familiar as the name of "da next toon."

While ships continue to "plough da ocean" there seems reason to believe Shetland men will still be sought after by masters, although recent changes as regards pre-sea training may have a restrictive effect on the indiscriminate "signing-on" of hands formerly in vogue. At present it is reckoned that something like three thousand Shetland seamen are away sailing at any given time. Shetlanders have a fine sea-going tradition, and it is likely this will always remain. Shetland women know of this tradition only too painfully, as frequently there comes news of some loved one lost at sea. During the 1914–18 war scores of seamen were lost, and during the first half of the second great war Shetland seamen suffered heavily.

To most Shetland mothers there comes the sad day when they hear the half-eager, half-wistful, "Mammy, I'm goin' awa' ta sail. . . ." Knowing there is nothing much at home for the boys to do, the women have no proper answer to give, but after trying to get them "ta bide hame a start yet," they see it is useless saying more.

They get clothes and other gear ready with as cheerful a mien as possible. Then the day of departure soon comes, and the mail-boat steams from Lerwick harbour. . . .

Two friends have given their impressions of their first "sea-days" and subsequent adventures, and as both are writers themselves, the rest of this letter is made up of their own interesting narratives.

The first writes: ". . . I went to sea, of course, for the old economic reason, to make a living. I left Lerwick sometime in the first of February 1930, immediately prior to the depression. My feelings as the old *Sunniva* nosed around the Bressay light were mixed, a bated expectancy tempered by a sadness at leaving home.

"The run south was very fine. Soon I found myself in a Leith boarding-house, with a house full of Shetlanders,

many of whom were tipsy from a too liberal supply of
strong drink. To a question that night, 'What I thought
of things?' I answered, that 'I was just feeling my way yet.'
Next morning I discovered what like a cobbled dock was,
and some of the 'ropes' in approaching mates for a job.
After about a week I got fixed up in the *Coronda*, supply
ship for the South Georgia whaling station.

"The Master, mate, and 2nd mate were all Shetlanders.
Previously, I had worked on a croft in Ulsta, Yell, and at
Gunnista, Bressay, with a fairly adequate knowledge of
small boat work. My father had been a seaman—herring
and small boat fisherman. My grandfather, whom I was
brought up with, was an old Greenland whale-fisher and
Haaf fisherman. My grandfather's father had been an old
sail seaman; he had been in the first of the Australian gold
diggings, and I heard tales both lurid and animating of
his experiences in my boyhood.

"The fo'castle in the *Coronda*—she still sails despite
enemy bombing, I am told—was somewhat cosy but not
flashy. The crew was composed of a number of Shetland
and Leith seamen. The work was not inspiring. Outward
bound the weather was good. We bunkered in the Tyne,
where they 'tium' the coal as Shetlanders tium water.
Then we set out for South Georgia. I was reading Plato's
Republic on my first voyage. I had picked it up in a second-
hand book shop in Leith Street, where I had also bought a
Norse-English dictionary, or rather a dictionary showing
the influence of Norse on the English language. This book
I gave to a young Norwegian, Sigurd to name, who was
also one of the *Coronda's* crew. He was learning English and
made rapid progress. My duties on the *Coronda*, as O.S.,
was generally standing by to answer whistles—that is not
the general O.S. duties in most ships. I first had a trick
at the wheel after we had cleared Ushant going down the
Bay of Biscay. I could steer from my first attempt. I
believe ——, Whiteness, 2nd mate (he is Master now, I
think) was in charge of the bridge. Our watches then were
4 hours on, 4 off, with a change over from 4 to 8 p.m.,

when the watch was split up into two 'dog watches.' That gave you different watches every day.

"We carried coal and stores out, and guano and whale oil home. We discharged in Harborg just on the outskirts of Hamburg. The *Coronda* is a ship of some 12,000 gross tons, a big ship as cargo ships go. Leith Harbour, South Georgia, is a very interesting place, with Coronda peak towering above you, and a glacier within a quarter of an hour's climb. The smell of blubber is just a trifle offensive. Our wages then were £4, 10s. per month.

"I had a scare, though, shortly after leaving South Georgia. We ran into heavy weather, and one dark wild night, with a heavy sea running, the 3rd mate and I were sent from the bridge to examine the steering gear aft. As we left the bridge ladder a really heavy sea broke aboard. The 3rd mate leapt back up the ladder. I seized a ventilator in my arms like a drunk man hugging a lamp-post —the water swept right up to my chest and had me gasping, but I held on, and when the ship righted herself it was found that a good lot of damage had been done. The food was not of a high class quality, and the men growled and groused about that. In that ship there was no real agitation—not like some others I have served on—about anything. The firemen were a hard case lot, and drank copiously in Harborg, finally leaving well in debt to the café proprietors. I liked Hamburg very much. A very clean city, the people ever so homely and helpful. I remember one night on returning to the ship I lost my way, and on asking a passer-by the direction to the docks, he immediately came with me to a café where he said some of our crew were bound to be found, although it was ever so far out of his way. He could speak English and referred to the insanity of the last war. The then Seamen's Union there, as it is everywhere, among seamen was universally condemned. The Union has completely lost the voluntary spontaneous support of its members. The policy of collaboration has earned it the disgust of its members and the plaudits of the shipowners.

"I have spent a lot of breath and ink fighting against the bureaucracy of the N.U.S., without avail. . . . My first voyage lasted about 4 months, and I was again in Leith, out of work. I have sailed in something like 12 ships altogether, for varying periods of from a week to 2 years. I was on a ship that traded to Norway, Denmark and Sweden for two years, so I know Norway especially well. I have been in all the principal British seaports, and like and know London best of them all. There was a vastness and commingling of life in London that was really awe-inspiring. I delighted in the panorama of ships and commerce, and the shrill Cockney blasphemies as they loaded, discharged and went their ways.

"Of the Dominions my favourite is New Zealand, which I claim to know something of. . . . I have seen a fair enough slice of the world's chief seaports. The American continent I know pretty well; also Europe and Africa. Russia, India and the Far East I do not know so well, although I have visited ports in all of them. I have, I am pleased to say, never been ship-wrecked, nor have I ever had the experience of taking part in a rescue at sea. Shetlanders get the *Times* at sea, but not regularly—older men of a thoughtful disposition usually do, younger men rarely. A big number of young Shetlanders during their first years at sea fancy themselves as potential officers, and a fair proportion of them make good that ambition, and from my experience of Merchant Service officers, only a small percentage of Shetland officers are cantankerous, difficult men to serve under. Almost all of them desire to man their ships with Shetland seamen.

"There are plenty of smells in ships. People with acute olfactory organs should steer clear of fo'castles, especially of cargo vessels and oil tankers. Seamen very quickly get conditioned to smells, the pleasant and evil ones alike. I really cannot describe many pleasant ones at sea; they are all, almost without exception, fumes from closely packed cargo, consequently foetid and disagreeable. The worst smell of all is that of a fo'castle infested with bugs. They are the limit in vermin, and I have been in few ships without them; as shipmates they are execrable, in warm weather attacking at night, leaving the skin all hugged up in blotchy spots. Another insect very common is the cockroach, which makes galleys and store rooms its chief haunts. Rats are plentiful, especially in grain ships; seamen readily attack and kill them, but are still superstitious about them leaving a ship. On fruit ships small snakes have often been found among the cargo. To give the names of the red light districts in the various ports is beyond me. I have a very poor memory for people's, and place, names; although Skipper Street in Antwerp, St. Pauli in Hamburg, Skiedamskedyke in Rotterdam, Bute Road in Cardiff, and East India Dock Road in London are so commonly known among seafarers as to be indelibly stamped on the memory from the yarns of old salts.

"I think my longest voyage was from Immingham to Auckland in the *Port Dennison* around the Cape down 'Roaring Forties' to New Zealand. I forget the actual time, but it was over 40 days. The 'Roaring Forties' are very strong westerly trade winds that you can follow almost right around that latitude belt. The weather is cold, snowy showers, hanging threatening sky, strong wind, heavy sea but very helpful east bound. Solitary albatross hover ever above and around the ship; after you clear the Cape pigeons, a species of speckled gull, Mother Carey's chickens, follow the ship in flocks to pick up the souls of deceased seamen before the bodies pass into Davy Jones's locker—so sailors say.

"The Doldrums in comparison are very depressing—no wind, no lift in the sea, bright sun, though sometimes overcast.

"I have passed and stopped at Pitcairn about a mile off. Natives come off in boats and (load?) up provisions. They are actually a very indolent class of people; even the bananas and fruit just grow wild, consequently stunted; they can't be at the bother to cultivate. They do carve

some rare things from wood, make nice walking-sticks and
straw bags. Their skin is dark, the women are fat, they
speak a gibberish of their own, also an indifferent English.
They handle their boats with skill, often in heavy weather.
They always sing the hymn 'God be with you . . .' when
the boat leaves for the shore. Tristan da Cunha I have
not had the pleasure of seeing. I have been with some very
able men at sea, voracious readers of good books, and some
thinkers. Most young Shetlanders of any ability, and some
of only moderate ability, go in for navigation, and consequently do not have too much time for anything else.
One Shetland chap of quite exceptional ability I was shipmates with for a 9-months' voyage. He is —— of ——,
West Yell, now resident in ——. I have just recently heard
that he has been in 5 ships sunk by enemy action since the
war began. . . . But good-natured and a very good shipmate; somewhat impracticable in matters that require use
of the hands, brilliant in matters of the brain. —— had read
extensively in philosophy, psychology and some theology.
He had been brought up in Yell after the last war when a
breath of mental curiosity and free-thinking science had
been sent around by the example of J. R. and others.
Since then many hard technical works have been mastered
by ——, and woe betide the man who tackles him on his
pet subjects. He and I used to argue about Plato, Lucre-
tius, Kant and Marx, Darwin and Jeans, Freud, Joad and
Watson, while painting the ship's side on a stage. To
show you the power of his memory I will cite an
instance.

"... did not bother to keep a note of his overtime, so at
the end of the 9 months he sat deep in thought one night
calculating it up. When he came to sign it, though, he
discovered that the mate was 6 hours out; so—immediately started from memory to recount every hour and
half-hour that he had worked overtime during the voyage;
the mate made a note of each, consulted the ship's log
and found —— to be correct. I considered it a remarkable
feat of memory. When I sometimes relieved him at the

wheel he would set me a problem: 'Calculate mentally the number of seconds in this voyage so far. . . .' I never could do it.

"... I recall a shark hunt in the Caribbean Sea on the deck of a broken-down merchant ship, with a squint-eyed Welsh cook the chief star in the drama. On this occasion we had fixed a hook on the end of the patent deep sea lead wire, and with the ship crawling along at 3 knots a shark took the bait at daybreak and every one was roused by the clamour. This cook, an inveterate prater of trifles, was of a high-strung excitable temperament, and this hot sultry morning he appeared on the well deck brandishing a meat chopper. From the vantage point of a guy I witnessed the scene. Most of the men's faces were transfigured with expectant emotion, the cook was completely carried away. As the shark was slowly but surely pulled closer to the ship, he started to chop the bulwarks; this went on, only increasing in intensity and speed until the shark was made fast alongside and hoisted aboard. Someone then shouted, 'Come on, Cook, cut off his tail!' But poor Cookie was in a state of complete exhaustion, his chopper shapped in the face beyond grinding. The shark lashed and writhed its body until the Bosun, a Swede, delivered the fell stroke with a sharp knife. I have often pondered over that episode since—the old man dancing about full of restrained energy, the mate, engineers, firemen, sailors, stewards and the cook, everyone moved beyond normal excitement by the spectacle of a trapped shark. Others, as well as the cook, showed a keen desire to do bodily harm and draw blood. Rather strange to what depths of animal emotion people can (go?), especially in a ship where they have been cooped up for a period, and beginning to get raw. I was the only Shetlander there, and that night on the look-out I mused on the old 'whale hunts' and wondered what motive, as in this instance only to blow off steam, or that of stern necessity for food, impelled our forefathers in their task.

"... *The Shetlander* may have been known in South Yell

by—and others, but it was never known among the young population. I much regret that now. The —— I told you about is still at sea and has lost five ships in the course of this war. He once told me a remarkable story of a South Shields funeral.

"He had been on a ship, the *Liberton,* or a name like that, with a hard case Geordie bosun. When they paid off, the bosun informed them that his wife was very ill, but that did not prevent him from getting drunk along with the rest. A few days later the bosun made a round of the pubs to invite the boys to his wife's funeral—she had passed away in the time that the bosun had been drinking. So a few of them promised to attend, and the bosun promised them plenty to drink and maybe a party after. At 3 o'clock on the day appointed they set off (along the) 'Neptune,' 'Norfolk Suffolk,' and some other places on their way there, and were consequently late. When they did arrive they found the bosun well sprung, directing operations in the window—the door had been found too small for the coffin. After his few days' burst up his memory had lapsed, and when he saw most of his old crew around him he thought they were putting out the gangway on the ship. —— said that even the clergyman smiled. 'Steady now! Hold on there! For'ard a little with your end, launch! Damn you, why don't you do as I tell you, you blasted fools!' When the job was over they all repaired back home with him and found an abundance of whisky and half a dozen questionable females that he had booked at the same time as he asked the mourners. ——, an agnostic, said it was the most irreverent scene he ever witnessed."

The second seaman, a year or so younger than the other, writes: "A 'green' Shetland boy, newly away from home, finds the great world rather a novel place and picks up impressions which stay with him all the rest of his life. I shall never forget a certain windy night in South Shields, when a hard-bitten old Danish bos'un picked me out of a crowd of youngsters as green as myself and offered me my first job. She was only a collier, but I strutted into my lodgings that night as though someone had presented me with an extra-master's ticket. Those were great days. —— of Mid Yell and I were together in her for nearly a year, during which time I learned some seamanship and quite a lot about almost every port of any size between the Elbe and Brest.

"... With regard to the story about the 'Shetland men only' notice in the Liverpool shipping-office, it might easily have been true. Some skippers do prefer Shetlandmen and will ship nothing else if these are available. On the other hand, you do occasionally meet a captain who has a prejudice against Shelties and will not have them at any price. As a rule, the reason is not far to seek, and the latter skipper is a good man to avoid. The average Shetland seaman will not stand to be either brow-beaten, or imposed upon, and you will usually find that the man who has an antipathy to Shetlanders is inclined to be something of a bully. I knew of one instance during the terrible depression round about 1931, the roadway outside the shipping-office at North Shields was crowded with seamen of all kinds, when the shipping clerk sung out for 'six A.B.'s for a tanker, *Shetland men only.*' He nearly caused a riot, but he got his crowd.

"Some ship-owners (*i.e.* the Ben Line, and, to a slightly lesser extent, the Blue Funnel) want our lads in their ships, and many of the bos'uns in both companies are Shetlandmen. I made a voyage in a 'Ben boat' where the lingo spoken in the foc'sle was pure Shetlandic, and the only two Southrons 'before the mast' were themselves speaking a very good imitation of the dialect before the eleven months' trip was over. We derived much amusement from teaching one of them a dialect poem (culled originally from the *Shetland Times*) entitled 'Mansie's Crö.' His pronunciation of some of the old words was awfully funny.

"(Impressions of my first days.) There would, firstly, be the parting from friends and relatives at home—rather a painful episode, this, since it is your first leave-taking, but tempered by the anticipation of all the wonders which lie ahead.

"Then comes the steamer's sailing from Victoria Pier, the crowd on the pier-head, etc., and later on, old Sumburgh dipping below the horizon—your last glimpse of the Old Rock for many a day.

"Your shipmates in the steerage would mostly be sailormen and the talk 'salty' in the extreme. Perhaps one would be going to join a whaling ship for the South Shetlands; another, a Ben boat bound for the Far East. Still another would be a Port Line man, who would talk largely of 'Down Under' and the New Zealand coast. You listen to their talk with something akin to awe, and wonder where your ship will be going to. In due course you arrive at Aberdeen (incidentally your first glimpse of 'big town'), but since there is, of course, no shipping there worth speaking about, you will follow the steamer to Leith. Arrived there, you would put up at the excellent Sailors' Home, or perhaps seek lodgings with one or other of the numerous Shetland families settled there. Next morning you would sally forth to seek your ship.

"By this time some old hand had put you wise to some of the tricks of the game: to keep your hands out of your pockets, to address a mate as 'sir,' and, in particular, not to smoke in the dock area (this last is a heinous crime in Leith). Your first impression is one of rather confused wonder at the bustle and traffic of dockland, and the number of the ships. Being green, you do not discriminate, but board every ship you come to. In response to your shy inquiry, 'Do you need any ordinary seamen, sir?' some mates will give you a curt negative; others will tell you that they are sorry; while others will try to be facetious, and tell you that what they require are extraordinary seamen. But the answer is always more or less the same, and by the time you have been right round the docks you are tired, more than a bit homesick, and distinctly fed up; also, you wonder if there is any outstanding physical defect about you of which you have not previously been aware.

"About two or three days of this sort of thing, you come to the conclusion that neither Curry nor Gibson requires your services and decide to try your luck at the Tyne. The train journey is, of course, quite an event. South Shields is busier than Leith and ten times dirtier; your first impression is not a very cheerful one. You wonder if this can be the port of which you have heard so much. However, if there is more dirt, there are also more ships, and you realise that you are in Sailor-town at last.

"There were lots of boarding-houses here a few years ago, some of them kept by Shetland folks. The old dialect makes you feel more at home. Things are livelier here, and by and by there comes the day when at last you get a ship, perhaps something after the fashion which I described. Supposing that she is a collier, you join her at Howden Dock (North Shields), or Harton (S. Shields). Wherever you join her, she will probably be under the loading shoot, with a steady stream of coal pouring into her and everything inches deep in coal-dust. There is no gangway and you black your hands climbing on board, not having learned that the proper way to climb the steep ladder is to walk up without using your hands at all. An officer interrogates you (the second mate, perhaps): 'Who are you?' 'New ordinary seaman, sir.' 'All right. Foc'sle's on the port side,' he says tersely. 'Get them glad rags off and turn-to as quick as you can.' The foc'sle is small, but considering the mess on deck, quite surprisingly clean. You dig a suit of dungarees out of your bag, pitch the said bag into the only empty bunk you see, and are soon out on deck, doing your best but feelin' kinda 'unkin'!

"You probably sail at some ungodly hour in the morning bound for Rouen or Rotterdam, London or Hamburg. Reeling up a kinking wire on the foc'sle-head, in the dark, you begin to wonder if this sailing is all it's cracked up to be. But then you think of the strange places ahead of you and are thrilled again. Your first impression of your shipmates is not a very favourable one. There is a fusilade of oaths and obscenity in the foc'sle which disgusts a lad brought up in a decent home. A man tells of a girl he has met, and describes his adventures in amorous detail. The others tease him about his lack of success. You sit shyly in a corner, not yet having discovered that underneath their rough exteriors your new comrades carry kind hearts.

"In the morning you start to wash down. This is not the haphazard swill which some sea writers would have you to believe is the normal clean up on board a coal boat. You wash and scrub and polish until she shines like a new dollar, and it dawns on you that you have joined a ship and not a coal barge. Then comes your first trick at the wheel—something of an ordeal the first time, a pleasant task for the next few watches, and a source of infinite boredom for ever afterwards. One by one you pass the milestones, Whitby and Scarboro'; steep Flamborough Head, and all the string of lightships—the East Dudgeon and Haisbro', the Cross Sand and Kentish Knock—until, by daybreak another morning, you are coming through the Downs with Deal and Ramsgate on your starboard hand and the piers of Dover ahead. You pass the white South Foreland and round Dungeness, and, since you are bound for Rouen, take your departure from there for Cap d'Antifer on the French side. You sight the powerful light on the cape long before daylight, and in the dawning are rounding Cap L'Havre with the French coast lying green for miles, and busy Havre Roads opening in front of you. A fleet of little French fishing-boats come darting past you, and you are thrilled when you remember that this is your first glimpse of a foreign land. In the estuary of the Seine the Rouen pilot comes on board, and soon you are threading the multitudinous windings of that beautiful river. On your starboard hand are rolling meadows, with cattle and horses grazing; to port are high chalky banks; with here and there a small village—a cluster of red roofs and narrow streets and the steeple of a little church.

"The orders have come on board: 'The New Quay,' says someone. 'We'll be away to-night.' You are disappointed; you wanted to see the town. At last you sight the town, its roofs shadowed with a haze of smoke and the spire of the cathedral towering. The ship is moored. Instantly the discharging starts (you have been stripping hatches and making ready all the way up the river), and it seems to you that the ship will be empty in a couple of hours. But there is a shortage of railway trucks; you are not to sail until noon to-morrow; there is a wild scramble to get shore togs on. Everybody seems to know Rouen; they discuss the various places of call—the Café Copenhagen, Syd's Bar, the South Wales Bar, the White Star (a wild joint, this last one)—and offer to show you round. But though you are green, you have a certain amount of common sense; you decline to be taken round the dives, and say that you will probably walk up later on to post a letter.

"Your first impression of a French town is rather a mixed one. There is much to admire and much to disgust you. The streets are dirty, down in dockland, and the gutters are foul. There is a fine bridge across the river, but the loafers on the bridge are a revelation of how humanity can fall. The cathedral is magnificent—and the 'red light district' lies right alongside it. Of course, you make a few purchases, a bottle of perfume, a couple of ornate silk handkerchiefs, for somebody at home. On your way down to the ship, an old woman cries to you from a doorway: 'You come to my house, John. Plenty pretty girl here, dearrie.'

"Coming down the river in the afternoon of the following day you confess to yourself that Rouen is a bit of a washout. However, your shipmates, most of whom straggled on board after midnight in a somewhat elevated condition, seemed quite satisfied. You are, perhaps, going back to Hartlepool in ballast to load for Hamburg.

"Such is the way of the greenhorn. . . . It is so long since I was in those Continental ports that I am beginning to forget about them.

". . . We loaded general cargo in London in the late August and early September of 1940, and experienced the

L

first night of the big London 'blitz.' One night of it was enough, and we sailed next morning, exceedingly thankful to get away with whole skins. Various convoys took us up the coast and round the north of Scotland, and we were not attacked, though we watched Yarmouth getting a beautiful pasting as we passed. Incidentally, our ship was a ten-thousand ton tramp, and we were bound to the east coast of Africa. We picked up the 'ocean convoy' off the Skerryvore Light—the Halifax convoy—and followed them until we were well out of soundings when we went on our own down the North Atlantic. In spite of several S.O.S. signals, including one from the *City of Benares* (the 'sea-vac' ship), nothing bothered us, and we had a more or less uneventful trip to Freetown and Cape Town. From the latter port we went to Beira, in Portuguese East, thence to Dar-es-Salaam and Zanzibar, and so right up the coast, discharging and picking up small parcels of cargo in each little port. Our last place of discharge was Port Sudan, where we got rid of our outward cargo and loaded cotton for home.

"The Italians were still in Eritrea and Somaliland then, and air-raids were so common in Sudan that we scarcely bothered to wake up in the night when the siren went. We went from there to Beira again, took the cotton out of her, and loaded a few thousand tons of copper underneath for stiffening, then put the cotton back. By this time we had been six months out, and were badly in need of an overhaul, so were ordered along to Durban. After a very pleasant month, we left there, ostensibly for home; but we had a breakdown off the Cape and were two months in Cape Town repairing. Two weeks out of Table Bay and just north of the Line we 'got it,' and left the poor old lady for good and all.

"A Dutchman picked us up that same night and landed us at Freetown next day. . . . The actual torpedoing was not too pleasant, since we lost four men, had seven others wounded (one of whom subsequently died), and had both our lifeboats smashed. I was at the wheel, at four bells in the forenoon watch, when it happened, and have a some-what hazy recollection of a terrific shock (you don't notice the actual sound so much) and the ship listing till I thought she would turn turtle; and the stink of burning oil, and a pall of smoke which hid everything. However, we got clear of her all right on rafts and in the small boats, and, as I have said, were lucky enough to be picked up the same night. It was five weeks before we eventually got to Britain, five weeks of danger, boredom, and prolonged unpleasantness; and Shetland, on the still summer night when we eventually arrived home, seemed like a glimpse of Heaven. . . . I try to forget about it as far as possible and look forward. . . . Convoys are a sore point with the 'powers that be,' and a friend of mine got into trouble, quite innocently, not so long ago. There should be some interesting seafaring stories told after the war is over, and some books well worth reading. A young cousin of mine was in a ship which was sunk in a running fight with a raider in the Tasman Sea. Thirty-eight, of the ship's company were killed, including a young shipmate of mine belonging to this district, and my cousin has been three years in the Marlag and Milag prison camp in North Germany.

"Two hundred of us, all torpedoed men, came home from West Africa together, and in the course of the long passage I heard some wonderful stories of hardship and adventure.

"During my last long deep-water voyage, I had kept a comprehensive log of the whole trip with the secret am-bition of possibly being able to publish it after the war as *A War-time Voyage*. We were in many queer and interesting places—Zanzibar, Dar-es-Salaam, Beira, Mombasa, Aden, Port Sudan, etc.—and experienced quite a few of the vicissitudes of seafaring in war-time, and all the time I had kept my log religiously up to date. For three days after we crossed the Line and entered the danger zone off the West African coast I had carried the books in the breast of my shirt. But on the morning we got bumped it had been raining, and, while changing before going to the wheel, I laid them on my bunk and forgot them. Twenty minutes later we 'got it,' and my books went with the ship. I could have forgiven that submarine skipper for the loss of my gear and various silks and curios, but I did curse him for the loss of that log. It is, unfortunately, quite impossible to replace it from memory. . . ."

CHAPTER X

Life in Shetland, as you will have gathered from these letters, is not quite like city life. There are no huddled houses, noisy streets and din of smoking factories and workshops. There are open spaces and fresh air, light, sunshine. Even in the town there is comparatively little reek, except when a large fleet of steam drifters is lying in the harbour. There is no great noise, either, but for the sound of cars and lorries. Out in the country the loudest noises in some places are the din of the swarming birds on the cliffs, or the lowing of kye and bleating of sheep. At times the kye and birds are silent, the sheep quiet on the hills, and but for the echoing cries of some crofter sending his dog after some stray sheep a kirkyard quiet seems to brood over the place.

This may give you the idea that things are a bit "primitive," and some folk still wearing skins. This is not the case, as with the passing of the haaf fishing days the last of the sheepskin clothes worn by some fishermen passed with them. Stone hammers and querns were in use until comparatively recently, but now they are museum pieces. There used to be broch-dwellers here, if not cave-dwellers, but they too have vanished. And yet, in a way, housing conditions are bordering on the primitive. You would see slum houses in some of the old, narrow, stinking "klosses" in the town, while many of the croft houses are one hundred years behind the times. A County Council sanitary inspection carried out shortly before the war revealed the following unsavoury picture:

Total number of houses examined	.	.	4,038
Unfit for human habitation	.	.	1,136
(28·13 per cent.)			
Without water or sink	.	.	3,794
(93·9 per cent.)			
Without water or earth closet	.	.	1,742
(43 per cent.)			

In August 1946 the Shetland Labour Party called the attention of Mr. George Buchanan, M.P., Under-Secretary of State for Scotland, to the desperate state of rural housing in Shetland. They urgently requested him to pay a personal visit to the islands to see things for himself, so that something could be done to speed up the housing programme. The letter reads: "We feel that the desperate state of rural housing, and in particular crofters' housing, is not understood by the Government, and we would urge you most strongly to visit the islands and see the position for yourself.

"Scarcely any of the crofters' houses in Shetland can conform to modern standards—dry-stone walls without a damp course, absence of water supply and drainage, inadequate window space and ventilation, over-low rooms and conditions of over-crowding are commonplace—and at present there is in existence no scheme which holds out any prospect of an early improvement in the situation. The terms of the Housing (Financial Provision, Scotland) Bill with regard to agricultural workers' housing, while admirable in farming districts, are of no help to us in Shetland. The Shetland crofter, often with no more than 3 or 4 acres of arable ground, has never received any assistance in improving his house, other than what was available to a landlord to improve the tied cottage on his estate. In what other community would members of the working class be expected to provide their own houses with a grant of only £200 from the Government?

"With regard to water supply and drainage, the scheme submitted by the Zetland County Council, based on the Post-War Survey of the Department of Health for Scotland, has an estimated cost of over £1,000,000, and in view of the rateable value of the County is utterly impracticable without a 100 per cent. grant. Even if this is made available, some years must elapse before it is put into operation. In the meantime, the relevant sections of the Rural Water Supplies and Sewerage Act, 1944, virtually prevent any house-building in most rural districts in Shetland.

"Rural housing among the non-crofting community is, generally speaking, in a rather better state, and legislation is available whereby, once the water supply and drainage problem has been solved, the local Authorities can provide the houses required; but even here the position can only be described as desperate. A survey of these houses carried out by the Sanitary Inspector and submitted to the Zetland County Council on the 18th June 1946, reveals that out of 1,249 houses, 333 are regarded as unfit, and that, of the fit houses, 166 are overcrowded, making a total of 499 houses, or 40 per cent. of the houses, other than crofters' houses, in Shetland, which are unfit for one reason or another.

"While we realise your manifold commitments and the many demands on your time, we are confident that even the few facts set out in this letter will convince you that you must inspect local conditions for yourself. For our part, we are convinced that only through your personal intervention can we hope for the necessary action, legislative and administrative, to solve the housing problem in Shetland."

Shetland has another bad record, in that it has one of the highest tuberculosis rates in Scotland. Before the autumn of 1939, the islands had a high percentage of unemployment, some months previous the figures touching the 1,300 mark.

Although things are far from satisfactory, you will find modern innovations here, but, of course, trains, trams, theatres, concert halls, modern libraries and the like are not to be found. Recently, however, a large hall, used as the Garrison Theatre during the war, has been taken over by the Education Committee for use as a concert hall and cinema, while another fine building has been turned into a community centre. There is electric lighting in the town, a picture house, modern schools and hotels, fine shops and stores and other signs of progress. The large Town Hall, at the North Hillhead, overlooking the old town and harbour, is one of the sights of the north. Apart from a few small plantations, there are no trees in Shetland. Since 1921, when the citizens voted the town "dry," public-houses and licensed grocers have become things of the past, although a considerable reaction in favour of reverting "wet" again seems to have set in, and a " Local Option " poll may take place soon.*

There is only one town in the northern islands. This is Lerwick, with a population of about 5,000, roughly a fourth of the islands' population.

The Dutch fishers and merchantmen of the sixteenth and seventeenth centuries found Bressay Sound to their liking as a fine natural sheltering place for their great fleets of herring craft; a fine meeting-place for the luggers and other vessels whose crews ran up the red-white-and-blue flags and pennons preparatory to holding their feast of Johnsmas, in mid-June, after which event fishing activities could start in earnest, and the thousands of miles of nets be "shot" over the side in the waters at "the back of Bressay."

Each summer saw the Netherlanders' fleet fishing in the seas around Shetland. The earliest maps and charts of the islands and the adjacent seas were the work of Dutch navigators and cartographers.

The fishers made Bressay Sound their headquarters for the season. They put up rough-and-ready booths on the western shore of the Sound, on land then forming part of the "East Ness of Soond," the common grazings and peat moors of the crofting settlement at Soond.

This collection of a dozen or a score of rough booths known as "Leirvik," from the muddy nature of the "vik" or bay, did not flourish very well at first; or, rather, it flourished in a wrong sense.

This was in the latter years of the sixteenth or first years of the seventeenth century. It was probably in those first few years in the nature of a summer "fair ground" overlooking the broad sheltered harbour, with conveniently placed landing "bergs," or piers, at numerous out-jutting rocks along the foreshore.

The "fair" attracted people with croft produce and

* At the poll in December, 1946, the "wets" won by a large majority.

live stock. They exchanged their goods and animals for various articles brought ashore from the Netherlanders' ships which could not be got in the islands. In addition, the Hollanders were glad to get ashore, to stroll around and stretch their limbs, or lie in the hills, after long weeks in the luggers and yaggers. They found some relaxation and amusement ashore on the heights of the "East Ness." People brought ponies there, and the Hollanders had pony rides down the slopes at the Mound, Twagios, the Hillhead, Knab and elsewhere. Smuggling of brandy, gin and tobacco, with other goods, went on.

During the summer months with thousands of fishermen swarming all over the place, the settlement by the seashore became a very noisy place.

The fishermen's loud cries were heard from one end of the Sound to the other. Indeed Brand, who wrote of the islands in 1701, said the Hollanders were anchored so thick in the Sound that it was possible to step dryshod from Lerwick to Bressay, from one ship to the other.

The singing and shouting and on-carry of the men and their companions scared both sheep and decent crofting bodies from the Hillhead and near the Mound, with its ruined fort, which was to arise, later on, duly restored, dominating all the harbour.

Smuggled goods were hidden in passages and caves, or in "hoidy holls" under the flooring of lonely crofting houses far from the harbour. The revenue officers, it is said, often went in fear of their lives, for brawls were frequent, and knives would flash, fists shoot out, clogged feet lift to kick.

All in all, it was getting to be a scandal. It was in the nature of a "sink of iniquity," and an eyesore to most of the godly crofting folk of the neighbouring toonships of Soond, Freefield, Holmsgarth and Gremista, while the udallers of Bollasetter, where the Sooth Kirk Kloss and parts south by, now stand, must have been "fair scunnered." Complaints were made, and an ordinance was passed by the Court at "Skallowaybankis," the then

capital of the islands where, but a few short years before
the booths of Lerwick arose, Earl Patrick Stewart had
lorded it as ruler of the Isles from his fine baronial castle
near the pleasant waters of Scalloway Voe.

This ordinance was to the effect that Lerwick, "quilk is
a desert place," was to be utterly razed to the ground
"and destroyed."

The decree, issued from Scalloway in the year 1625,
crippled the "fair ground," and Lerwick dwindled away
to nothing.

Then for some years the "West shore" of the Sound was
almost bare of houses. The Hollanders and Bremeners lay
in the Sound as usual, and the men came ashore to buy
and sell, smuggle, amuse themselves, and look about for
ponies and women. The crowded heights and foreshore,
with the Sound black with shipping, proved too much
for the crofting people. They could not let slip this
opportunity to make something out of "da Dutchies."

Phoenix-like, Lerwick arose from the ashes of its burned-
out booths and sheds. Soon the shore witnessed new
booths, houses and shops, and lodberries* were built. Piers
were made, trade grew apace. A merchant class developed,
doing great commerce with the Netherlanders. Lerwick
took shape, at the South End, where more and more of the
old crofting land of Bollasetter became covered with houses,
near the Cockstool-rock, at "da foot o' da Burn" (near
the site of the present Market Cross), at the North End,
and North Ness. The town grew and forged ahead, Acts
of the Scalloway Court notwithstanding.

In a few years narrow closes were branching off from
"da Shore" or "Street." The "klosses" followed old, well-
trodden "gaets" or folk-ways up over the steep slope of
the high ground to the south and west of the foreshore.
The closes climb up to the top of the height, or Hillhead,
which overlooks the harbour to the east and the crofts of
the ancient settlement of Soond, and the Staney Hill to
the south-west.

* Rough piers with enclosed yards near them.

During the first years of the Protectorate, Cromwell ordered the building of the Fort. The townsmen were very pleased over this. It meant a sense of protection; the garrison of soldiers increased their trading turn-over. Above all, it put their rivals in the decaying "toun of Skalloway" in the shade. The roof of Scalloway Castle was falling in, the roofs on the buildings in "da Gerrison" were only going up. Before long, they said, Lerwick would be the Capital toon, Scallowaybanks nowhere.

The population increased, and a kirk was built. This soon proved inadequate, and a "meeting-place" was built for the soldiers of the garrison at the south end of the town.

This "meeting-place" gave good service for some years, then a new kirk was put up. By this time the town was growing, the fishing was bringing ever more and more ships to the port, shops and trading enterprises of various kinds increased. In 1716, the town had about two hundred families, all mostly engaged in trading with the Netherlanders and other seamen and fishers, as well as buying produce and animals from the crofters.

Throughout the eighteenth century Lerwick grew until it was able to boast a "Street," several "Closes" and lanes, a Tolbooth, several lodberries, the Fort, Kirk, manse, Market Cross, and numerous shops. Some of the shops had secret passages underneath the street for storing kegs and demijohns of Holland's gin and brandy, landed at dead of night from the vessels riding in the Sound.

The "Street" began, as did the "klosses," in a haphazard manner. They all followed the already well-worn gaets (paths) to the Cockstool-rock, "Craigie's-stane," and other landing-places and lodberries at the shore, the centre of life and commerce then as now.

No plan was followed when the early townsmen resolved to have a "Street." Indeed, "the Street" just "happened" to be there. The folk just used the run of the twisting and skirting, climbing and dodging footpath following the line of the old foreshore, so much so at places that they were half in the sea and half on land. At the low-lying place near the present Market Cross there was a beach, and north by this a "brig" had to be placed over the burn flowing down the slope of the hill. As the sea came almost to the brig, with flood water, a big part of the "Main street" was awash. The "Street" was known as "da Shore a Lerrook" up to quite recent times. Boats were said to have been moored by shop fronts, and Dutch vessels beached for repairs had their bowsprits almost on the shop-shelves. At the Sooth End, the oldest part of the town, people opened their kitchen windows to catch fish, only a half-hour or so standing between them and a tasty dinner. The Dutchmen had big iron mooring rings fixed in rocks and in the walls of houses by the sea. At a place known as da Cockstool, at the south part of the present Esplanade, a big rock was one of the principal landing-places of the port. The "sooth steps" inside the break-water, where the Bressay folk land from their boats, is no great distance from the old Cockstool-rock, where generations of Bressay folk used to make fast their boats when they had occasion to visit the "East Ness."

The Tolbooth, or "town-house," was almost awash with high seas, the spray dashing in through the iron-barred windows behind which prisoners gazed wistfully seaward. Vessels and houses, shops and sheds seemed intermingled in confusion. Over all hung the smells of herring and cod, ships and tar and nets; so that, with Amsterdam, Lerwick can rightly say it is "built on herring bones."

Towering above the huddled houses and the jostling Holland ships rose Fort Charlotte on its Mound at the high rocky northern part of the town. It was begun about 1665, and by 1685, in Lerwick, there was already a kirk, preacher and session, with numerous houses and trading enterprises. The townsmen came to regard the Fort with affection. They looked up to the grim walls and the shining cannons, well pleased with themselves. The Garrison, with its smart red-coats, would teach a lesson to any stray privateer or other adventurer seeking to steal into da Soond and work havoc with the shipping. They were proud of their Fort, the "Street," Kirk, Tolbooth, lodberries and shops. The place was thriving. New houses were being built yearly, more and more shops were opening, new workshops opened, cod-fish were exported in increasing quantities.

Then the wars with France came. Lerwick was hard hit, for a French force set fire to the Dutch fleet off the coast. The Fort was of small avail against the big men-o'-war, who kept well out of range. Trade stagnated for a time and the population fell. Things took a turn for the better fairly soon, trade expanded again and the town grew. Houses were creeping ever farther to the north and west.

In 1778 Paul Jones, the American privateer, was in northern waters and heading for the port. On the same day as his ship approached Bressay, some women from Soond wearing red petticoats were on the heights tending their kye and sheep. Seeing what looked like red-coated soldiers lining the cliffs, and not too sure of himself in face of this "garrison," Jones decided to turn about. He did not tackle the shipping in the harbour, nor the Dutch vessels off-shore, but headed south, leaving the islands in peace.

Lerwick's fine natural harbour, and the shipping it gave anchorage to, brought plenty of trade and industry to the town, so that by the year 1814, when Sir Walter Scott visited the north, it had become quite a fair-sized place. The leading merchants and citizens gave the great writer a warm welcome. He saw the big Greenland ships in the harbour paying off the Shetland men forming the bulk of their crews. He wrote of the noisy, riotous scenes in the town as the men came ashore, got drunk and started quarrelling. Scott tells of how he rode on pony-back down a hill near the town. He met two women named Campbell, one of whom taught music lessons to the daughters of well-to-do citizens. On his return south Scott bought a piano and sent this north by packet-boat to the music-teacher. Eventually this piano landed up in Yell, and it was said a small pig was once seen tethered to one of its legs. It afterwards became the property of "Auld Mathewson," the celebrated teacher.

Scott's forthcoming book *The Pirate* was to show something of Shetland life in the southern half of the main island. At the same time it gave rise to the legend about the "wild hill ponies," whose hunting and taming were said to afford thrilling sport to adventurous men.

Four years after Scott's visit the town was erected into a Burgh of Barony. The first Town Council election took place in the late 1880's.

That the legend about the "wild ponies" has still a good grip was illustrated a few years ago, when some American tourists visited the port on a conducted tour. Coming ashore, they were keen to be off on a "pony-hunt" in the "wild hills" of the "interior"!

Somewhat disappointed when told the real state of affairs—that Shetland ponies were remarkably tame and intelligent, and, forbye, belonged to private owners—the Americans shrugged their boredom, and went and did the next best thing—hired "push-bikes"! For a few hectic hours that fine summer day the streets of the town—not very wide or straight at the best—were lively with young Americans tearing through the place at break-neck speed. Staid townsfolk coming up from the Fish Mart, or on their way to the shops, were a bit astonished. They took it all in good part, smiling upon the Yanks, whose purchases of knitted woollen goods had helped to clean out not a few shops.

Since being made a Burgh of Barony, with a coat-of-arms of its own, and all, the town has never looked back. Its Main Street retains its old-world appearance. At parts it is barely ten feet wide, and twists and turns and then suddenly opens up to reveal picturesque glimpses. It has been said that two or three crofting women with kishies on their backs, and milk-pails and parcels in their hands, can hold up the traffic while they yarn together about this and that. When motors crawl along the street, at the narrowest parts folk just have to squeeze into the nearest shop-door to let the traffic pass. Both sides of the street are lined with shops, offices and warehouses, while at parts steps lead down to the Esplanade. Sheep and kye and ponies awaiting shipment at the main pier sometimes break loose and stampede over the Esplanade and street. The din and confusion of the subsequent "round-up" make for a somewhat exciting half-hour or so—a real touch of "aald Lerrook" life. The kye are generally hoisted aboard the steamer in slings.

Although the street is much the same old-world folkway it was, unless for minor improvements here and there, the rest of the town has changed a good deal. Neither Brand, nor Low, nor Scott would know the "pleasant little town, with its Town-house and Spire . . ." if any of them were to come back to life and pay another visit to the north. It has spread out: to the south, north and west. Commodious and well-planned Council houses stretch right to the edge of the Staney Hill and the march-dykes of the croftlands of Soond, the toonship of which it was said:

> "Soond was Soond when Lerrook was nane,
> Soond'll be Soond when Lerrook is geen."

Although the town has grown, with new streets, houses, shops, more amenities, electricity and the rest, and the oldest part of the town, "da Sooth End," is almost deserted owing to the shift of population farther to the south (to the Twagios quarter) and west, while the "Street" or "da Toon" proper has lost much of its central character, its main industries hardly have kept pace with this development.

CHAPTER XI

As you know, the herring fishing is Lerwick's main source of wealth. There is also a haddock-fishing, carried on mainly by Lerwick fishermen in small motor-boats during the winter and spring months. The average yearly number of barrels of herrings cured in Shetland, Decennial periods, is given in Andrew C. O'Dell's book, the *Historical Geography of the Shetland Islands*, as:

Years					*Barrels*
1821–30	.	.	.	.	2,906
1831–40	.	.	.	.	31,513
1841–50	.	.	.	.	7,443
1851–60	.	.	.	.	11,266
1861–70	.	.	.	.	5,689
1871–80	.	.	.	.	8,400

The same source gives interesting figures on the development of the herring fishing. In 1885, one of the "earlier peak years, when 370,238 barrels were cured, there was a native fleet of 320 boats, manned by nearly 2,000 Shetland fishermen, included in a total British fleet of 800 boats manned by 7,612 fishermen, besides 462 Dutch herring vessels fishing in Shetland waters with Lerwick Harbour as their main rendezvous."

The year 1893 witnessed a growth in the Shetland sail-boat fleet working the herring nets. Between this year and 1906, according to O'Dell, the Shetland sail-boat fleet reached "its maximum (between 300 and 400), and the use of steam simultaneously enabled English boats to come to Shetland. Before its advent only two English sail-boats had come. The result was the record year of 1905, when 1,783 sail-boats and steam drifters, manned by 21,201 fishermen, caught fish amounting to 1,024,044 barrels cured in the Shetland area, the whole catch being sold for over half a million pounds. There were 174 herring stations distributed through 27 districts, 46 in Baltasound,

LERWICK HARBOUR

J. Peterson

To face page 176

LOOKIN' DOON DA KLOSS   *Alfred Moore*

To face page 177

and 36 in Lerwick, and in Lerwick alone the shore workers totalled 2,483, of whom 1,985 were women gutters and packers."

In this same year 500 Dutch vessels fished in the Shetland sea.

In 1934 there were 293 boats fishing in Shetland waters, as quoted by O'Dell. These landed a catch of 153,519 crans, valued at £134,223. This catch filled 183,878 barrels. Most of the Shetland herring catch was sold in Germany and Poland.

The year 1935 saw an improvement, as 304 boats that season landed 203,960 crans, which were valued at £205,766. The number of barrels cured and exported was 246,450.

The 1936 season was a bit leaner, although more boats fished from Lerwick. These totalled 365, and their nets brought up from the deep 171,494 crans. The value was slightly higher than 1935, totalling £211,403. Barrels exported numbered 184,800. More boats came to the port in 1937, as 373 boats landed 144,185 crans; but the demand was very keen and the catch realised £223,023. Only 162,786 barrels were filled that season. An improvement set in again in 1938. The boats numbered 331, landing 171,369 crans, at a value of £225,245. The export of barrels of salt herring came to 191,160. The following year, 1939, was a disastrous year for the herring industry and for the port and trade of Lerwick.

Through the courtesy of Mr. D. Swanney, Fishery Officer, Lerwick, a fairly complete picture of the Herring and White Fishing in Shetland waters can be given here.

In 1940, 90 fishermen worked the nets, in 18 boats. They landed 334 crans, valued at £825. The fleet fell to 14 boats in 1941, with 68 men. The catch was 5,137 crans, valued at £14,082. In 1942, 208 men, in 40 boats, brought ashore 6,751 crans, realising £19,200. The fleet fell to 21 in 1943, with 100 men. The catch increased to 10,063 crans, with a value of £24,250. Twenty-four boats prosecuted the fishing in 1944, their crews totalling 124 men.

M

The catch fell to 9,953 crans, but the value increased to £28,509. In 1945, 220 men, in 35 boats, landed 12,194 crans, valued at £33,169. The fleet working from Lerwick in 1946 grew to 53 boats, almost all being Shetland boats, and they landed 63,001 crans, valued at £158,998.

The white fish landings from 1940 to 1945, inclusive, were: 1940, 28,419 cwts., valued £49,349; 1941, 21,975 cwts., valued £70,127; 1942, 20,757 cwts., valued £47,833; 1943, 22,786 cwts., valued £53,590; 1944, 26,032 cwts., valued £69,606; 1945, 40,789 cwts., valued £94,572.

The disposal of the 1946 herring catch was made up as: direct exports, cured herrings, Germany, 18,284½ barrels; Poland, 11,373 barrels; Klondyked (freshed) herrings, Germany, 23,134 crans. The herrings processed by the Herring Industry Board's factory at Lerwick amounted to 1,399 crans quick-freezed, and 232 crans kippered.

With the collapse of the salt herring markets in Germany, Russia and Poland, the Shetland herring fishing has reached a critical stage. As it will take time to regain these markets, other methods of processing are being tried. The commendable action of the Herring Industry Board, in erecting a quick-freezing and kippering plant at Lerwick, as well as taking over the guano factory at Hjeogan, Bressay, in the spring of 1946, has meant a lot to the industry. The Board's transport and marketing facilities, enabling fish to be carried fresh to markets in Britain, are also helping to tide over one of the industry's blackest periods.

The 53 boats operating from Lerwick during the 1946 season met in with good catches of prime quality fish almost every day of the season, with the result that the Shetland boats averaged well over £3,000.

The larger motor-boats averaged £4,000, the leading boat grossing the record sum of £7,000. The best of the smaller boats earned £2,600, and the only Shetland steam drifter, the *Maid of Thule*, grossed £6,800.

The quantity dealt with at the fish meal factory at

Hjeogan, Bressay, totalled 5,964 crans. These figures, supplied by the officials of the Fishery Board, appeared in the *Shetland News* for 17th October 1946. Other interesting facts from the report can be summarised here. The opening date was 4th June, conducted mainly from Lerwick and Scalloway. Some boats operated from Whalsay. In the first part of the season most of the fish were caught on the West Side. Dull weather was experienced, with fresh winds, and this seemed to favour fishing. There were no gales and the boats were never forced to remain ashore. A few crews met with disaster at the beginning of the season. On the 6th June, 100 nets, with buoys and ropes, were lost with the weight of herring in them. The value of this was estimated at £1,000. Seven firms were curing at Lerwick, and one each at Scalloway and Whalsay. Two kippering kilns were working at Scalloway, and one at Lerwick. Prices were: for local freshing, 88*s.* 8*d.* a cran; kippering, 80*s.*; curing and freshing (Klondyking), 55*s.*; Herring Board's price, 41*s.* 3*d.*; meal and oil factory, 17*s.* 6*d.* Many shots of between 100 and 200 crans were common throughout the season. The highest shot was 232 crans landed by the motor-boat *Humility* on 2nd July. On the 9th July the *Swan* came in with 170 crans, but she had given 30 nets to a Dutch drifter, which hailed 90 crans, so that the *Swan's* fleet had netted over 260 crans. There were only 151 gutters working this season, including 50 Irish youths. The pre-war figures were about 2,000 gutters. The number of coopers working was only 41. The most satisfactory feature of the season was that almost all the earnings remained inside Shetland.

Burra is perhaps the largest fishing community outside of Lerwick. A fleet of about 30 boats is manned by Burra men. Each boat has a crew of 4 or 5 men. Although most of the boats have changed over to seine-netting, the men occasionally still work the lines. Each man carries three "strings" of lines, a "string" measuring 60 fathoms. There are 600 hooks to a string, and 1,800 to a full line. On a great-line there are: cod-line, 360 hooks; halibut-

line, 216 hooks. It usually takes a woman 3 hours to bait
a line of 6 "strings," or 9 hours for a full line. Mussels
are chiefly used for bait, but in Burra "yoags," or horse-
mussels, are used. It takes 300 yoags to bait a full
line. Yoags cost 4s. 6d. per hundred. Generally the best
Italian hemp lines are used. In 1939–40 these cost 7s. 6d.
to 10s. a cut for haddock, and from 12s. 6d. to 20s. a cut
for halibut. To boats the cost of paraffin was 1s. 3d. a
gallon. Other gear, such as line-buoys, were 20s. each,
and electric dan lights 60s. each.

Although the weekly wage system is gaining in favour
with fishermen, the share system of dividing earnings is
still greatly in use. This system works out something like
the following. Suppose a boat to have earned £600 for the
season's fishing. Out of this has to be paid in the first place
the expenses connected with fitting out the boat for sea.
That is the "owner's account." Say it is £220. There is left
£380. That £380 is divided into two parts, each £190. The
owner gets one half, and the other is divided up among the
crew. If the crew is six men, the average will be £31 13s. 4d.
per man. But that is not to say that it is so divided. The
skipper, for instance, gets more than the "bush-rope boy."
Out of this average share the men have to pay certain
personal expenses, so that a man's final share will not
amount to a great deal.

Some of the men's personal requirements are probably
got from the boat-owner, who may have a ship chandler's
store as well. So that the owner-merchant's real return
from the boat is £220 plus £190 plus the amount paid
him by the men for oilskins and other things they require
during the season. From this it will be seen that if the boat
has an unsuccessful fishing, the men may finish the season
in debt to the owner. Of course some men are more
fortunate than others, as they may have "clubbed together" to form a co-operative concern to buy the boat; so
that the "owner's share" flows back to themselves instead
of to some owner-merchant, which means that the only
expenses are their oilskins, boots, and "grub," over and

above the oil, paint and other gear needed to make the
boat fit for sea.

As there have been no new boats built for the Shetland
fleet for some years, and with poor season following poor
season, practically ever since the Great War, the bulk of
the boats are in debt. From a questionnaire addressed to
the skippers of 31 motor-boats belonging to Burra, in the
winter of 1937, it was found that 26 boats were not clear of
debt. The average age of the boats was given as 34 years.
The total debt on 31 craft at the end of the 1937 season was
£5,393. The total estimated for reconditioning for the
1938 season was £1,800. The total debt due to gear was
£1,628, making a grand total of £8,821.*

An entirely new fleet of boats of the "dual-purpose"
type, new nets and other gear are urgently needed in
Shetland if its hardy fishermen are to reap the benefit of
its lucrative fishing-grounds, and thus help in stemming
the depopulation of the isles. Instead of the dwindling
fleet of about 120 or so boats of all classes at present
registered in Shetland, the fleet should number anything
from 250 to 300 or more boats and drifters, fitted with
modern motor engines and the latest scientific aids to
navigation and fish-detecting.

In spite of the "statistical black-out" there seems to be
a fair lot of statistics in this letter, and you are probably
weary of them by now, so what follows may help to dispel
the boredom of all these figures and show how the fish are
actually caught.

In a normal season thousands of men fish from Shetland,
the fleet of boats numbering almost four hundred. You
have seen John Grierson's fine film *Drifters*, so you'll have
an idea of the task the fishermen have. The men all have
the work shared out on board, each man to a certain task.

* *Shetland News*, 3rd February 1938.

Their hardest work is done at night and in the early hours, when most people are resting.

A drifter carries a "fleet" of sixty or seventy nets. Some large vessels carry a fleet of over one hundred nets. During some of the "crisis years" in the industry it was found necessary to curtail the use of great fleets of nets, to avoid having to "dump" herrings back into the sea. Another expedient was tried, of keeping half the fleet of vessels ashore one night, while the other half went to the grounds, and the following night sending out the vessels that had been ashore, and so on. They steam to the fishing-grounds, anything from fifteen to seventy or one hundred miles. Some nights dense shoals are encountered, nets often sinking with the load of fish. On other nights the shoals are "patchy," some vessels "hailin" good "shots," others getting a few baskets only, or returning "blank." Yet again some nights the boats "shoot" their nets only to find the shoals have moved to some other ground, either farther out, or closer inshore. Occasionally the shoals come right into the voes, when crofters get many hundreds of herring in a net or two stretched across the voe.

The drifters generally coal at the hulks the previous afternoon, or first thing on a Monday morning. The fishing week in northern ports usually begins on Monday morning, the fleet proceeding to the grounds each afternoon or evening while favourable weather conditions last. They finish the week on Saturday about noon, though with great landings fishermen and shore workers are kept strenuously at work often well into Sunday morning. The period Saturday noon to Sunday midnight is known as "da helly," or week-end, in Shetland. "Da helly" is the time of rest, recreation and meditation, when men from some of the country districts travel to their homes by car or bus.

The bunkers in, the men get water and provisions aboard, and set out for sea. Drifter after drifter scurries through the harbour, their funnels belching smoke, which, with certain winds, soon hides the houses of Lerwick under its pall. As the vessels clear the piers and jetties their mizzen sails are hoisted, acting as a steadying factor while at sea. Many fly the Red Ensign, or some "House flag." These, of course, are soon smoke-blackened and tattered. The funnels bear a variety of colours and designs—as stars, bands, large round spots, letters and the like—according to the predilection of their owners. Sometimes a single owner, but often a company, owns the vessels —as the "Bloomfield boats," the "Breech boats," "Westmacott's," and others. The Scottish drifters are generally "staid" and "quiet" looking, with dark-painted sides and funnels, although some of the modern Scottish vessels have brightly-coloured wheelhouses, at times adorned in front with the vessel's name in bold, floral-entwined lettering. The Scottish fleet, in their choice of names, betrays the serious-minded, religious folk of the fishing ports of the north-east coast. Names such as "Guide Me," "Faithful," "Constant Star," "Hope," "Providence," "Trust On," and "Hopeful," reflect the staid "dour" Scotsmen. The men from East Anglia, however, strike a more cheerful note with their "Cheerio Lads," "Ocean Angler," "Herring Ho," "King Herring," "Silver Spray," and "Jubilant." Their brightly contrasting funnels and touches of vivid colour about the superstructure, buoys and hull make for a cheery sight in Bressay Sound and along the harbour shore. The names of some of the Shetland boats, again, help to "date" them—as "Lord Roberts," "Kitchener," "Joey Brown," and the like.

The men have sea clothes and oilskins on board, the bedclothes in the crew's quarters below the galley, in the after part of the vessel. There is not much room to move about in these quarters, but it is near the engine-room and warm, if stuffy. The men, however, make the best of things, and as they are all well acquainted they get on without too much grumbling, except an occasional grouse about the weather and low prices.

Bad weather is frequent in the northern sea. It is then that one thinks the sea is a "dog's life." The drifter rolls and rocks, pitches and tosses like a mad thing. The men having got over seasickness long ago can of course stand any amount of rough weather. They are rigged in long sea-boots, oilskin "smookies" (jumpers or frocks) and sou'-westers.

For some time while the vessel is steaming to the grounds there is not a great deal to be done, unless to see that everything is ship-shape and "Bristol fashion." A sharp look-out is kept for herring-signs, as gulls and solans on the water, whales and porpoises. By nightfall the skipper thinks he has gone far enough. He orders the driver to slow down. The men peer over the sides, and see the herrings swimming not far below the surface. They look like a dark-green, silvery-streaked wall in the water. Often the surface appears "oily" when the shoals are about. This is due to minute organisms—plankton—on which the herring feed. With dense shoals herrings are sometimes seen near the surface, and as if jostling each other "out of the water." This is the time for each man to get down to his job. The nets are got up from the hold, the bank-board fixed between the hatchway and the top of the bulwark. Nets are hauled over this board. It keeps them from "hitching." A roller at the edge of the hatchway takes the strain off the nets as they are hauled up.

Two men take charge of the "shooting," as the casting of the nets is termed. One takes the corks, buoy-ropes or the "buff-strops," and the canvas buoys, the other takes charge of the nets. A third man looks to the "seizings" as the nets stream from the hold. He passes them to the mate, who fastens them to the thick bush-rope as it runs up over the roller or "jinny." The cook, usually a boy of from thirteen to sixteen years old, and often looking squeamish from sea-sickness, goes for'ard. His job is to tend the bush-rope, hence his name of "bush-rope boy." The rope is stowed away in a small rope-locker, or room, for'ard of the hold, on the starboard side. The boy, whether sick or well, has to look sharp and pay out the warp, for "shooting" nets is a rush job, all deck-hands, as

well as the skipper, tackling it in earnest. The seizings
are made fast to the bush-rope, one net after the other,
until all the "fleet" is "shot" over the side. The line
usually extends between two and three miles. A canvas
buoy is fixed to the corner of each net. It is quick work,
as the nets seem to leap up at one, flashing past in a twinkling. Practice makes perfect and the job is soon picked
up, all the knacks of how it is done, tying the knots securely
almost coming instinctively, so deftly do one's hands work.

The nets flop on the water, sinking below the surface
for about two fathoms. Buoy after buoy is thrown over-
board, the tide taking everything away past the vessel. By
the time all the nets are in the sea it is almost midnight,
time for a "spell" and a "blow." About twenty fathoms of
bush-rope separates the drifter from the first nets. This is
the "swing-rope." The bush-rope is made fast round the
capstan, the skipper swings the vessel's head to wind, and
she drifts with the tide.

The foremast, or main-mast, is lowered, the mizzen
sail secured, two white lights are hoisted, a warning that a
vessel is lying at nets. The direction of the nets is shown by
the lower light. With drifters seeming to cover the sea,
it is a fine sight in the dusk of a summer night. The
lines of nets with the hundreds of coloured buoys bobbing
in the swell, the dim light of the sky glowing on the sea.
Birds are flying near, or alighting on the sea near the nets,
where herrings may be seen "builin" or jumping out of
the water. Whales also are attracted, and they can be
seen rising and disappearing, only to break water again at
another spot. The crew go below for an hour or so's rest.
After a mug of tea they turn in, leaving a hand on watch.
Sometimes the skipper may take a notion to call the men
on deck to haul in the warp a bit to see if there are herrings
about. The rope is taken in to the first or second net, and
satisfied that there is a good "shot" in the making, they
let the line out again and go below.

It seems only a few moments ere the cry "Turn to,
lads!" is heard. The men tumble up on deck, perhaps to

see the sun peeping above the horizon. It may be a fine morning with just a trifle of swell and some "ask" or haze. It is a lovely sight watching the sun glittering on the waves and the imprisoned fish flashing in the meshes; but there is little time to admire the sunrise, as "hailin" starts with gusto. This is a hard, wet job. With stormy weather it is often fraught with danger. The bush-rope is hauled in, led through a block on the bulwarks not far from the capstan. It is put down into the rope-room, where the boy is crouched up to the knees in foul bilge water coiling down the heavy rope for dear life. One of the hands "casts off," loosening the nets from the warp. Two of the hands take the buoys and seizings and stow them in the "wings" of the hold. The nets are stowed on either side of the hold. Four other hands are down below in the hold shaking out the herrings. Big "shots" take a good few hours to haul on board. When the last net is on deck and the fish shaken free, the gear is stowed ship-shape, the skipper rings for "full speed ahead," and, setting a course for Lerwick, drives the drifter as fast as she'll go, so that the "ring" at the Fish Mart can be caught as early as possible. There is a better chance of getting the highest price when boats arrive early. The men take ashore "samples" of a few dozen herring, and these are scrutinised by buyers around the salesman's auction "ring." The crew's hardest work is, so far, over when the drifter is made fast at the curer's yard. Here they begin discharging, or "measuring," the catch. Two hands go below and scoop up the herring into baskets. A man stands on the pile of nets and pulls, or eases, the guy-ropes fastened to the derrick-rope which is fixed to an iron bar with hooks on either end. The hooks are clipped into the handles of the basket, which, full of slippery fish, swings upwards and shorewards through the air.

The skipper usually works the capstan-winch which hoists the loaded baskets, two men being on the stage loading them on to a trolley running eight or a dozen baskets at a time. The loaded trolley is run to the large wooden troughs where fisher girls are busy gutting the salt-sprinkled fish. "Measuring," or "cranning," takes some time, especially with big "shots," the men being covered with scales before finishing the job. Scales are everywhere: on the drifter's deck and wheelhouse, nets, stage and trolley. Decks are scrubbed down after all the herrings are landed, the crew again making ready for sea. With moderate landings most vessels finish for the week about noon on the Saturday, and in the afternoon nets are barked and spread ashore in parks.

CHAPTER XII

Looking down from the car on top of the 500-feet high hill, at the spot where the grinnd (gate) spanned the road, into the valley to the westward gave one a peculiar feeling. There was an "Alpine" touch about it, as the road up there "on the heights" was narrow and tortuous, and there seemed a sheer fall into the valley below. The road was a soft reddish-like clay, rutted where the few cars and lorries had passed. Here and there it was almost green with grass as there was no great amount of traffic going to the place. The wind was blowing fresh, with snow showers, from the north-east. On the top of the hill the wind pressed hard against the car as if trying to blow it off the road down to the broken bracken-strewn rocky land far below. Everything went well; the grinnd was opened and shut, a starved-looking moorit yow hardly noticing the car where she lay by the edge of the road. Soon the car was in over the hill and speeding down the incline into the valley. It lay, bleak and cold, with the firth a stretch of dirty grey-blue, white-crested water. The "white horses" were having a great time of it as the wind struck the firth. The daal "was a gey back-aboot hadd," and it did not look very inviting that kaald voar day. There seemed no sign of life in the place. The few sheep by the roadside looked weak and poor-amos (pitiful), after the lang hard winter. The daal and firth lay roughly south-west and north-east, the croft-lands and biggins mostly on the daal's western slope.

Turning the bend of the road above the most southerly croft, the first sign of life was seen in the reek rising from the lums of the croft biggins. The car passed a lad, bare-headed, with his sister; she wore a red beret. Farther along were three or four young women and girls hurrying by, keeping well into da side of da rodd as they became awaar a da car. These folk were on their way to da meeting in the schoolroom, at the head of the firth, the place which served the little toonship as kirk, polling booth, concert hall, library and the like. At the nort gavel of the old house of the deserted croft, on whose green-grown thatch roof some hens were pecking and scratching, two or three bairns were standing watching the car go north along the road. They were the bairns of the folk who lived in the most southerly croft, whose rigs and meadows adjoined the coarse outrun land separating the cultivated land from the peat moor. The bairns waved to the car's occupants and then began scampering about, jumping the stanks between the ley rigs of the old croft, their laughter and calls gey cheering to hear after the queerly dead-seeming aspect of the place as the cold Aaprile (April) wind came tearing in from the North Sea.

The pungent smell of the peat reek blown from the biggins was another reminder that life was still in the daal "at da back o' beyond." The ground seemed greyish-white, after a shower of snaa (snow). The firth was grey and cold. In the north was the making of another shower. The sky was heavy, not pleasant-looking at all. It was the first week of Aaprile, but here in the outlying hills the folk held by da aald style of reckoning, so it was still da munt a Merch with them. Forbye, some never bothered to "put on their clocks," holding rigorously by the aald time, or "Guid's time." As they said: "Aaprile widna come in till da twaalt," and "Simmermal Day" fell "on da 14th, or da 26th wi da aald style." This latter was the "Summer's Day," and it was said that the weather experienced that day betokened the wadder (weather) aa (all) simmer. It was maybe a notion, but here it seemed colder than in the town, about thirty miles to da south'ard. The high hills drew the wind, making of the daal a sort of tunnel, through which rushed the snaa-laden wind.

Outside it was cold and disagreeable, but the hospitality of the crofting folk inside the little two-roomed taekd house made up for it. They soon had tea made, setting down fresh butter, new-baked skonns, eggs and other fresh country fare. Before long the visitors were feeling warm again, as they sat by the open peat fire yarning with the folk. The talk centred on da wadder, sheep, kye, the hard winter "he had büne," prices of feeding stuffs, the prospects of the Voar, da War and the rest. The time soon passed. The folk did not heed the snow beating on the little window, nor da wind girnin ida door (the wind as if angry in the door). It came ever heavier showers as the evening came down, so there was nothing much ta geng furt for, unless to go with the guidman of the house to lend a hand in feeding the sheep he had in the laam'oose. The car had turned right away for the town as soon as the driver had taken some tea. He said he was wanting to win awa from "diss Guid-forsaken holl" as quickly as possible. After the sound of its motor died away over the hill the old sense of quiet again brooded over everything, broken only by the kye bröllin softly and the sound of the burn running to the firth.

The next day was as snell as ever, but the showers had eased. The sun shone through the clouds at times, and where it was sheltered from the wind there was a little warmth in it. The folk said there was a Voar feeling in it to-day, and when the reek was seen drifting in over the sooth hill from the place where they were burning the heather for the young lambs, the goodman said: "Faith, that's a proper Voar sign, I'm thinking!" A laevrik was singing overhead, and in the bare branches of the willow tree some sparrows and thrushes chirped cheekily. Down on the newly-turned rigs the black-headed peerie maas and some big swaabies were busy pecking for slugs and other insects. The crofter's dog let out a yelp and bounded down over the rigs, snapping and barking at the screaming birds. By the spray-ringed shore the seabirds kept up a continuous klaagin. They were never still a minute, but flitted here and there over the cliffs and out over the firth, apparently attracted by small fish. The shaalders scurried about, their sudden cries loud warning signals to the other fowls of intruders about. From the hills could be heard the Voar-fowl, the snipe or "heather-bleater."

Well, the place had seemed very deserted the day before, but now, with the sun trying to shine, the birds kicking up the merry devil, folk astir on croft and hill, and boats putting off to the firth and holms, the place took on an almost populous look—albeit the population did not exceed forty-five souls all told.

It was the Voar time that set folk astir. Already some rigs had been delled and the seed sown, but on the whole things this season were late, folk having a lot to do ere everything was finished to their satisfaction.

"Oregon pine" was the wood of which the crofter's new spade-heft was made, or at least so the postman childe said. He had been a seaman, had been "all round da world an back again twice ower," and no doubt kent a bit of "Oregon pine" when he saw it. After a bit crack with this visitor "from the outside world," asking him for tidings of "diss wearied waar," and if "da fokk wast ower" the hill had got clear of da 'flu yet, exchanging small talk on one thing and another, the crofting folk bade the postman "Cheero!" and went down over the dull green toonmal to the muckle rig they were gjaan ta dell (going to delve). The postman went on his road north through the daal with the mail, a big part of it being long official-looking envelopes, various Agricultural forms that had to be filled in and returned before a certain date. The toonmal was the green field before the house, or hamefield. Toon is the Norn word *tún*, or homestead. In summer, when there was plenty of girss, animals, maybe an ox or two, or a few lambs, would be teddird on da toonmals, but that day its grass was very faded and stunted-like, with a few hungry hens scraping and paekin over it.

The crofter paused to light his pipe, and, turning, let out an oath, for there, far above the house in what was known as the outrun pund, an almark yow had wriggled her way through the wire-fencing and was making down over the steep incline scarred by peerie stripes and pools, to the yaerd ahint da hoose, in quest of something a bit tastier than she had found in the open hill pasture. Some sheep are like that. Da kraetirs are for ever lyin hame-aboot da daeks, contrary-like, not seeming to care to geng away up into the hill grazing like other animals. Letting out a command that seemed to echo and re-echo in the daal, the man ordered his dog to "be awa eftir 'r, da bitch!" Cries of "Come in here, here, ahint 'ir, du fuil!" and "Come in afore 'ir!" and the like were sent echoing throughout the place. Folk on the farthest croft-rigs paused in their work of spreading manure, or delving, to look in his direction and then up towards the outrun lands, as they clearly heard the man's ringing tones. The dog needed no second bidding. He was itching for a scamper over da knowes and burns, away up there, after the contrary yow. He was off "like an arrow," bounding up through the toon, and through the fencing in a flash, barking loudly. The yow turned tail at the yard daek, and scurrying through the fencing regained the hill. The dog kept snapping and yelping at her, aye pausing to look back at his master, his tongue hanging out.

Soon he had the yow over the brow of the hill, away south by towards the Trowie knowe, and not only "dat contrary limmer," but seemingly all the sheep and lambs that had been grazing there. With the hillside cleared of animals—unless for a stolid, sad-eyed pony rubbing himself against a muckle stab—the dog, well content with himself, trotted leisurely down the slope, aye pausing to turn round and yelp warningly just in case the yows straggled back again.

Well, then, the folk reached the muckle rig be-nort da knowe which they intended to saa wi' taatties (sow with potatoes). Three of them were there ida Voar-rig, the crofter, his daughter, and another man. A bit at the foot had already been delved. Small haeps of dung had been wheeled on to the rig. These were placed in rows of four or five, about an equal distance apart. First of all the shaarn was spread as evenly as possible over the rig, which had been under oats the previous year. They had on rubber boots which kept their feet and legs dry and clear

ROOIN SHEEP

C. J. Williamson

To face page 192

PEAT-CUTTING

of the earth and shaarn. The muck spread, they began dellin. Standing in a line the delvers were shoulder to shoulder, the lass on the right. The crofter was on the left, as he had da fore-spade, and therefore set the pace at which they delved. The delvers kept an even pace, dellin from right to left; in this instance the rig ran east and west over a good part of the laich (lower) toon or croftland, so that they moved from south to north, and of course from da fit of da rig to da head, or top. As the land lay on an incline this meant that each year a certain amount of soil gathered, or over-spilled, at the foot to enlarge the rig and deepen the soil there, while as the head was reached the soil gradually grew shallower and the rocky channel became ever more clearly exposed. It seemed a wasteful way of working the land, but it was the way the folk there had worked for many generations. The lie of the land tended against ploughing, so they said; but that was maybe an excuse for a certain inertia and the clinging to olden methods. Each year some new earth was wheeled, or carried in kishies, on to the shail (shallow) parts of the rigs, but it never seemed to make much difference. The rain, too, carried much of the soil down with it.

Each furrow delved was a geng. The seed taatties, or da seed, were planted about a foot apart, as each geng was delld, so that the upturned and loosened earth from the next dellin was thrown over the seed in the previous furrow. The seed consists of taatties cut in halves with the cut side placed downwards. The dung was mixed with straw from the lambhouse (lambs' muck was said to be the best manure), and it was all mingled with the newly turned earth. The earth was delved to about four or six inches deep. The seed taatties were cut inside the house, and the young woman had carried them down to da rig in a kishie. She was expert at her job, and as she delved alongside the men until the end of each furrow was reached, and then hurried to plant the seed (with a bucket of seed in one hand and bending all the time, planting each bit of seed at an equal distance apart) while they went back to begin a new

N

furrow, the woman seemed to have more than her share of work. However, it was the way of the place, and "dey wir used to it," so it did not strike them as unusual. When a furrow was delved the woman would go for the pail which stood at the side of the rig (the dog lay there after his hill work, his eyes aye alert for the contrary sheep) and plant the seed on the newly loosened soil, then she would come back to her place in the furrow and take her spade and resume delving.

The crofter was on the outside, or left-hand side, of the geng, setting the pace. He was a good worker, so the three soon felt the sweat loosening as they "tore at wi' da spedds." He measured, with an expert eye (trained by over fifty years or so at the work), the size of the paet, or clod, as the piece of loosened soil is termed. This is loosened and turned over and broken up by all the folk dellin, working their spades in unison. The peat delved varies in size and breadth and depth according to the quality of the soil, but the paet that day remained fairly constant at from a foot to eighteen inches to two feet long, eight or twelve inches wide, and four or six deep. The delvers kept their spades about six or eight inches apart. It was about ten in the forenoon when they started dellin, then they went up to the house for dinner about one o'clock, leaving the spedds upright ida furroo. It was a little after twa o'clock when dellin was resumed. So the work went on, delving and planting until five. After this they had tea, and at 5.45 went doon ida voar-rig again, bending to their wark until the onset of da hümen about 8 o'clock. It kept mercifully dry all day, so by da hümen three quarters of that muckle rig had been blackened and saan.

The muck and wet mould clogged on the spades and on their rubber boots. Sometimes, when a particularly wet or boggy bit of soil was encountered, they would hear the earth grumblin as it gave a soughin sound as the spades were dug down to prise up the paet. The crofter said that loose dry blackish-grey soil was the easiest to dell.

First of all, the spade was held in both hands. The left

hand grasped the wooden heft, or handle, at or near the top, and the other hand grasped it about the middle. The spade was then set into the ground, held so that it inclined a bit backwards. Then each one of them brought up the right foot in unison, pressing down on the heel of his spade. This heel is a bit of wood, or iron, jutting out about two or three inches on the right side of the handle a little distance up from the iron.

This quick pressure forced the spades downwards, and the soil was cut. They pressed the spades down to a certain distance, which is usually gauged by the loose mould that comes up, almost hiding the irons of the spades. Then the spades were grasped firmly and the paet, or clod, prised loose; the paet was then lifted a fraction and turned up and right over, hiding the grass-covered and hardened top, so that the top side (or grassy side in the case of a rig sown to aets the year before) was hidden, the roots coming up to be shappit loose by the spades.

The spades all worked simultaneously. In this move-ment the three bent forward and downwards, so that the weight of the spades in their hands caused them to rest the under part of their right forearms on the right leg about mid-way between knee and hip.

After they overturned the paet of soil, they lifted their spades and struck and chopped and shulled the earth in order to break up da clod and still further loosen its top and spread the soil more evenly.

As they worked the folk kept conversing on this and that, aye pausing for "a blaa" and to straighten their backs and look aboot them. Most crofts were seeing similar scenes, as folk took advantage of the wonderful dry day. On the big croft north by (overlooking the firth), a man was plough-ing, a white mare hauling the "Oliver" along, the birds swarming over the rig and aye settling on the newly turned furrow as soon as the mare had passed. At the little croft south in the dale there seemed no sign of life. The folk's koo could be heard bröllin loudly as she rubbed herself along the fence. A woman on another croft was feeding hens, aye calling "Kit, kit!" as she scattered the maet to da hens who flew or scampered, squawking, to her. A woman on the croft near the burn-brig north past was kaain some geese up to the outrun lands. The crofter laughed, seeing this, then cursed: "Dat venoms o' gjaeslins ir a pest, I'm sure!" In the firth were two boats, with brown sails, bowling along out to sea. "Dey'll be o' a mind ta shoot lines ida Soond, yun childes," said the crofter, adding, as he spat in his luifs and grasped his spade, "I hoop dey hae some luck, dan we'll hae a bonn a fresh fysh frae Shaarlie fir supper!"

Although it was quiet in the dale, various sounds could be heard from time to time, the contrast seeming to heighten the sense of peaceful solitude. There could be heard the crying of the birds, the calling of sheep and kye, dogs barking, folks shouting; the soughing of the wind over the land, and the pluitin (mournful) surge at the shore. There were, of course, the various noises made by the folk working: loud breathing as they bent to the weight of the earth on the spades; speaking; frequent bursts of laughter; and at times the young woman sang. In a fine clear voice she sang some bits of old ballads, or again the latest hits heard over da wareliss (wireless). Then there was the sound of the iron blades cutting into the earth, feet pressing on the spade heels, and in wet patches a hissing or sighing noise; the sharp ringing of spade irons meeting stones in the soil; the clink of iron on stone, and occasionally the clang of spade striking spade.

And so the Voar day passed. It was hard, back-breaking work dellin the unkindly soil in the primitive way the folk had done for generations. Still, it was healthy work, among the fresh air and strong smell of shaarn, interesting work seeing the land being gradually blackened.

By da hümen the kye had been milked and fed, the young sheep that were going to be set on in the hill had come down from the outruns and were busy eating their supper of hay. The sun's afterglow struck the hills, and the dark umber was spangled with delicate violet, and for a few ghostly moments it seemed to quiver on the heights. On seeing this it was not difficult to grasp how the tales of trows and other eerie hill-folk had taken such a hold of the minds of the folk afore diss, in the days when things were not so complex and folk-imagery flourished. Then the afterglow faded and darkness came hurrying over land and sea. Over the hill, to the south-west, swung Orion, the three stars of da Lady's ellwaand, in his belt, bright in the frost-clear air. Over the eastern hill the moon came up, and in the firth the boats coming from the lines broke the silvery water. From the shore came the sound of sails rattling down, oars creaking, and men speaking as they snugged everything down for the night. The crofter's wish was gratified, as " Shaarlie's " ting a boat had got a good catch, and that night the folk had fresh haddocks boiled for supper.

CHAPTER XIII

CROFTING, of course, is governed by the weather. Most crofters watch the sky, sea and land, as well as the behaviour of animals and birds, for signs of change. One crofter used to watch his müddoo "doon ida laich toon." He said he knew by the way da curlie-doadies, kraataes, cockaloories and other flowers behaved, what like the weather was going to be. Nowadays the wireless forecasts are very useful, although it is a rare crofter who cannot make his own forecast by reading the sky for himself. Some of the old crofters never even bothered with clocks and watches. They had observed the sun's position in the sky at certain times, and the shadows it cast on certain parts of the hills and daals. "Whaan he's ower Joobidaal," as one man used to say, "he's twaal o'clock."

When it is heavy rainfall crofting work is almost at a standstill, although ditching, or taking up stanks, is often carried out in wet weather. At times with heavy snow some crofts are entirely cut off from the outside world. With strong gales there is the danger of hay and corn being sent flying "on the sea" if crops have not been properly snugged in hairst. During spells of bad weather hindering outside work, the crofter turns to and does some job or other inside the house or outhouses. There are a hundred and one things a man with "good haands" can do to keep things going and "hadd 'imsell oot a languor." With hard weather and little growing furt, the animals are generally kept inside, although both Shetland kye and sheep are remarkably hardy and able to fend for themselves. When animals are kept inside a lot of work has to be done by the folk, as carrying in water, corn, hay, kell, feeding-stuffs for the baess, as well as keeping the byres clean.

After heavy rain the corn may be laid flat on the ground, to be perhaps twisted and crushed out of all shape if, as often happens, the wind comes away with gale force.

This may happen when the ears of corn are beginning to be full of "maet." As the old rhyme has it:

> "Matjomass comes in wi' 'is flail,
> An' hits da aits apo da tail."

Sometimes badly laid and bruckit corn has to be cut by sickle, as the scythe is of little use.

Heavy rain lying in the level rigs often ruins the taatties.

When the burn swells with the heavy rain and comes rushing from the heights, it carries loose debris, and often sheep, with it to the sea, or throws its prey up on the burnside. In the spring some yows get weakened, especially after a heavy winter, and get swept off their feet by the torrent. Loose hay by the burnside, and even middling-sized kolls of hay, are often carried away. Even heavy planks of wood used as a brig are taken by the force of the burn. On low-lying meadows near the burn if the hay is allowed to lie any time, it "gengs doon," turns white and bleached, and becomes rotten.

During a long spell of hot dry weather things are nearly as bad. The ground dries up and gets caked and cracked. Cabbage plants, young corn shoots and grass get scorched and wither away. Most crofts depend for their domestic water supply on open wells fed by springs. With long spells of drought the wells dry away to nothing. Even the burn which in winter rushed and roared in fury dries away to a trickle, so that one can walk across its bed without wetting one's feet. At such times crofting folk have to watch every drop of water, for it may mean having to travel long distances to the nearest large well or loch.

Frost is another enemy of the crofter. It comes at unexpected times to "nip da taattie shows" and other vegetation. The mist-like dew, known as mill-dew, arising out of the heat, also harms the crops.

Some weather statistics may be of interest here, to show the conditions the crofter has to put up with. They are supplied by the Geophysical Observatory at Lerwick, and published in the *Shetland News* from time to time.

The year 1942 was the dullest since 1921, the average temperature for the year being 44·2 degrees, being ·3 degree below the average. The hottest days were the 8th of July and 27th August, each with 63 degrees. The 26th January was the coldest day, with 20 degrees, or 12 degrees of frost. The rainfall was not excessive. It came to 40·8 inches for the year, or 107 per cent. of the average, slightly more than normal. It was a very dull, sunless year. The aggregate amount of bright sunshine was 924·8 hours, 45 hours less than the previous lowest, recorded in 1937. The comparative statistics show that mid-winter temperatures in Shetland were not much lower than in mid-summer.

	June		*December*	
	Max.	Min.	Max.	Min.
19th,	50	38	47	45
20th,	53	44	45	41
21st,	54	47	46	42
22nd,	55	49	49	43

The month of December 1942 was wet and sunless, there being rain or snow on 27 days. The average temperature for the month was 41·5 degrees. The 9th was the warmest day with 52 degrees, the coldest being the 1st with 24 degrees. The rainfall was 5·51 inches, or 115 per cent. of the average, the wettest day being the 7th, with 1·65 inches. Gales were recorded on 10 days, fog on 2 days, and snow on 5 days. Sunshine aggregated 12·5 hours, this being about the average for the month.

During January 1943 the weather was not bad, but a lot of rain fell. The average temperature was 38·4 degrees, and the total rainfall was 4·16 inches. The 17th was the wettest day, with 9·56 of an inch. On 6 days there were gales, snow and sleet. The aggregate bright sunshine was 24½ hours. February saw a mixture of weather. It was a bit milder and sunnier than usual, but was wetter than the average. There were 146 hours of wind at gale force in a total of 15 days. The mean maximum temperature was 45·3 degrees. Rain fell on 24 days. Bright sunshine aggregated 46·1 hours, or 110 per cent. of the average, but only 18 per cent. of the possible. The 19th was the stormiest day, when there was a gust of 95 miles per hour, and three others of 94 miles per hour. The March weather was sunnier, milder and slightly drier than the average. Rain fell on 18 days, with one day of snow and six of gales. Thunder was experienced on two days, and there was fog on one day. On Monday, the 29th, there was a splendid display of aurora. On ten days gales occurred, the highest gust of 78 miles an hour being recorded on the 11th. The mean of the maximum temperature was 46·4 degrees, and the mean of the minimum 38·3 degrees. The rainfall of 2·96 inches was 93 per cent. of the average, the 13th being the wettest day. Bright sunshine aggregated 104 hours. April was mild, but wetter and with less sun than normal. The warmest day was the 21st, with 53 degrees, the coldest being the 7th, with 27 degrees. The rainfall came to 3·82 inches. There were 27 wet days, the rainiest being the 24th, with ·48 of an inch. On two days there was snow and sleet, and hail on five days. This wet, cold weather, with sleet and hail showers and keen northerly winds, told heavily on lambs. Many crofters reported severe losses, especially in the hilly country. The crofters had to be on the alert all the time looking to the sheep, often being on the bitter hills night after night. Many lambs were thereby saved. One crofter came on newly-born twin lambs lying in a pool with only their noses and eyes above the freezing water. He took them home, drying and warming them, and feeding them from a bottle. Those lambs which were dropped before the severe weather thrived fast. The rough weather hampered voar work, the 1943 voar being far behind in many districts. It was not possible to sow seed owing to the cold sodden nature of the soil until late in the month, although some crofters had sown as early as the end of March.

The May weather was much milder, but a lot of rain fell, with the wind at the north and north-west. The mean maximum temperature was 51·5 degrees and the minimum 42·5. Rainfall came to 3·21 inches, or 154 per cent. of the average. Rain fell on 22 days. Bright sunshine recorded aggregated 151·9 hours. On one day thunder and lightning was experienced. Peat-casting was in full swing in most districts during the second and third weeks of May, although some folk had made a start in the end of April. June was warm and dry, but with the sunshine below normal. The highest temperature recorded was 62 degrees and the lowest 38. Rainfall was 1·13 inches. Bright sunshine 114·8 hours. Wetter conditions prevailed during July, but it was very fine warm weather the whole month. It was bright and sunny, the weather experienced during the month being the best the islands have had for ten years. The mean temperature was 53·3 degrees. Tuesday, the 27th, was the warmest day, with 84 degrees. Friday, the 9th, was the coldest, with 43 degrees. The rainfall was 3·3 inches. There were 176·7 hours of bright sunshine. There was thunder and lightning on the night of the 31st. August also was an exceptionally fine month of weather, the hay harvest being cut, cured and stacked in fine condition and in record time.

The weather in 1944 and 1945 was very unsettled, the summers being noted for their excessive rain. Folk began saying it "was da waar 'at hedd da wite o' aa diss rain," what with so much gunfire, aerial activity, and "aa da rest." The year 1946, the first year of peace, was even worse, so the "gunfire" theory became deflated. After some days of fair enough weather in the beginning of spring, and again about the start of the peat-cutting season in late April, the summer came in with rain, unsettled conditions and "a hanging, dull sky." There was no warmness in the air, no "growth ida laand," and the crops

in August were still "far aback." Then September came
in with more rain and folk began to despair of having
any crops at all. With October, however, the rain eased,
and some fine, sunny, dry weather came as a godsend to
crofters, so that the crops were saved in the nick of time.
The taatties, however, were badly affected, some districts
experiencing something like a famine.

Of recent years crofters have been plagued by a pest in
the shape of a caterpillar infesting the cabbages and
taatties. On fine days many of these "butterflies" are
seen winging through the sunny air, flitting from plant to
plant. Bonny enough to look at, as they gleam in the
sunlight, these "butterflies" have done quite a lot of
damage to the crops. It is thought they were introduced
into the islands with cabbage plants imported by the
Naafi during the war, and distributed throughout the
islands. Large consignments of plants were flown north
by aeroplane, and as they were found very suitable for
Shetland soil many crofters took advantage of the favourable terms offered by the Naafi. In this way most of the
garrison troops were supplied by Shetland-grown cabbages,
and a certain amount was exported.

As will be seen, there is aye something to keep the crofter
and his family on the alert, and however "awkward-like"
and conservatively minded some crofters may seem, as a
class they are fairly mentally active.

Work on a croft, or small farm, is full of interest. There
are varied kinds of labour going on, with the different
seasons, as delving, or ploughing, sowing and harrowing
in Voar; peat-cutting and curing in late spring; weeding,
rooin sheep, tending kye in summer; mowing and hirdin
in hairst; taattie-ripin in late hairst and winter. This is
all skilled labour, however rough-and-ready it may seem
to town-dwellers. A crofter is usually "awkward-looking,"
at times covered with soil and aye seeming to have a smell
of manure about him. The "awkwardness" of course
comes from his heavy work on the soil. Generally speak-

ing, crofting folk are healthy, aye working furt ida fields among da fresh air. The work on most crofts, however, is of the drudgery type. Folk are aye "skutterin aboot da place at ee thing an annidder," from sunrise to darkness. Since most crofters are their own masters, to a certain extent, there are no fixed hours of work, no "overtime rates of pay," and no fixed wage rates. As a consequence crofters are unorganised, each man going on his own, and at times under-bidding some neighbour. Some farm-servants on the bigger holdings may work a twelve-hour day but get paid for only nine hours. With recent legislation, bringing farm labourers into line with other workers, conditions are improving; but as regards crofters in Shetland things are much the same as ever. Being his own boss he can "start when he likes" and knock-off when he likes, dependent always on da wadder. The animals, however, also govern his life, as he must be up early to tend the kye, in bad weather or good.

Crofting is above all a way of life, a tradition with roots in the udal past, when the udallers and bondis (freeholders and peasant farmers) broke out the garths, setters, leas and toons. Having to struggle against the elements, as well as man-made social and economic evils, crofting folk have developed hardihood, self-reliance and a habit of thrift. A certain cautiousness is also noticeable, too, and not a little "doubleness," as it were, inheritances from the long years of Scottish oppression when the Norn udallers were deprived of their lands and brutally subjected by the new overlords. So far "master of his own small holding," the crofter develops a healthy independence that makes for a querying of most things. This helps to stamp the crofter as a "conservative," and though out of necessity having to "conserve" or hain (save) upon everything won by his hard toil, he is by no means a diehard Tory. Shetland crofters never forget that famous landmark in history, the Crofters' Act of 1886, whereby smallholders won security of tenure and became nominally free agents. They remember with gratitude that it was a Liberal government that passed "da Act." As a consequence, Liberalism has been the political faith of most crofters, although some are now turning to Labour.

Having to struggle for everything that gengs ida mooth an apo da back, crofters are careful and thrifty people. No regular wages come into the house, as in the case of town-dwellers. It is a subsidence, but in some cases quite a good living is made, as in the case of the crofter who exported 1,500 dozen eggs, over and above the quantity used by his family, obtained from 92 pullets. In the majority of cases, however, things never get much beyond a bare minimum. And yet even with this minimum there is a certain satisfaction in feeling that one has defied the wind, rain and snow, subdued the barren soil, added something to it by one's sweat and toil and thereby gained a livelihood for one's family. Through constant striving and kempin with da laand there arises a certain attachment to it; something hard to explain, but a potent factor which fanciful theorists of "da sea-captain school" wishing to abolish da croft and set up "dream farms" instead would do well to consider.

The number of holdings in Shetland at 4th June 1946, as supplied by the Department of Agriculture for Scotland in August 1946, is given as follows:

No. of Holdings.
Above 1 and not exceeding 15 acres . . . 3,056
Above 15 and not exceeding 30 acres . . . 131
Above 30 acres 35

Making a total of 3,222

At 4th June 1938 the figures were:

No. of Holdings.
Above 1 and not exceeding 15 acres . . . 2,782
Above 15 and not exceeding 30 acres . . . 297
Above 30 acres 108

Making a total of 3,187
Or an increase over 1938 of 35 holdings.

About 2,000 crofts are in the 1-to-5 acre category, or, as used to be said, "da tree-acre an a koo" type.

The total acreage of crops and fallow (tillage) at 4th June 1946 was	8,116 acres
Total clover and rotation grasses	2,560 ,,
Total permanent grass	9,755 ,,
Total crops and grass	20,431 ,,
Rough grazings	323,483 ,,
Total crops, grass and rough grazings	343,914 ,,

Figures showing the extent of land settlement in Shetland from the same source are interesting, but tell of a certain slowness in tackling the problem.

Number of applications for new holdings and enlargements received and granted and farms subdivided during the period.

1st April 1912 to 30th June 1946

Applications Received.	*Period.*	*New Holdings.*	*Enlargements.*
	1.1.1938 to 31.12.1939	13	5
	1.1.1940 to 30.6.1946	3	—
Applications Granted.			
	1.4.1912 to 31.12.1938	114	231
	1.1.1939 to 30.6.1946	2	1
Farms Subdivided.		*No.*	*Area.*
	1.4.1912 to 31.12.1938	21 *	19,131 acres

Crofts vary in extent and fertility, but an average holding is roughly from 4 to 6 acres of arable land, used for tilling, with a certain acreage of coarse outrun land, and usually a share in the common hill skattald. Outrun may extend from 15 to 30 acres, and skattald rights vary with the nature and extent of hill grazings available. Only crofters have a right to share in the hill skattald grazings. Cottars have no land, therefore no sheep rights, unless tethering a lamb or two on the small patch of grassland near the cottage can be termed a right. It is this old skattald (from *skatt,* a tax, and *hald,* to hold; open ground for pasture)

* Including 5 holdings, with a total area of 203 acres, which have been continued as smallholdings without subdivision.

right that distinguishes Shetland crofters from those elsewhere. Many crofts, especially in the north, central and
western Mainland, and some of the isles, would be of
little use without the sheep-rights. The number of sheep
allowed on the skattald varies from place to place. In
some districts it is as low as 12, but in the north Mainland,
with its great spreading hills, from 50 to 70 head of sheep
can be kept on a crofter's mark. Each crofter has his own
distinguishing "mark," generally notches, holes, or rits,
cut in the animals' ears.

James S. Angus contributed a list of "Shetland Sheep
Marks" to the *Old-Lore Miscellany*, as follows:

Sheep Earmarks

Twa Hols,	
Aff at da rüt,	
Half ut ahint,	
Half ut afore,	Strae-draw,
Twa Ritts, or Rit an Tree laps,	Bit aff,
Ritt, or Ritt an Twa Laps,	Witter,
Half aff,	Rit i da Stü,
Krook, Shear, Shül,	Hol.

Recently other methods of marking, such as smearing
spots of paint or tying coloured threads on the fleeces, have
become more common.

A typical croft in the north Mainland is about 5 acres
arable and 25 acres outrun, with the right of keeping 65
head of sheep in the common skattald. The rent of such
a croft may be from £4 to £5, 10s. yearly, with a shilling
or two as rates, and an optional payment for "destroying
vermin," as crows, swaabies and similar birds of prey.
Anything from 15 to 30 rigs may be tilled on such a croft,
with a müddoo, and stanks between da rigs used for growing grass. The lie of the land, nature of the soil, incidence
of rocks and other things, determine whether tillage can
be done by spade or plough. Some crofts are easy to work,
others are of the kind described "as a ruckle a muckle
stanes an shail shannels, juist man-murder ta wirk!"

The croftland, or toon, is separated from the hill grazings by the rough stretch of outrun land, generally fenced in and used as a pund for grazing kye, ponies and sheep. The march-daeks separate the outrun from the hill grazings. With continual grazing on these outruns many have become very green, and some parts ploughed up and sown with grass soon become fertile infield land. Some crofters keep numerous sheep on their outruns, and it is very striking to notice the sharp dividing line between the dark rough hill and the green grass of the enclosed punds caused by this continual cropping by the sheep. Lambs and young sheep, or settnins, going to be "set on," or put into the hill, are kept on the croft during the late hairst, winter and early spring. They are kept in laam'ooses overnight, and fed with kell, hay, taatties. When the turn of the year comes and da green paek is once again in the land, the young animals are slipped into the hame hill in the forenoon and taken in again towards da hümen. In this way they are made familiar with the stretch of skattald near their owner's croft. They generally all tend to associate wi' dir ain klivgeng, and when hard weather comes, seek the familiar daeks, or lie hame-aboot. During the summer, of course, with the fine weather they go with the other flocks and are kaa'd far enough through the hills and lie ootadaeks. Some sheep stravaeg far enough, one crofter travelling "a roond twenty miles" into another parish ere he came on twa of his yows grazing among da unkan sheep. Others of the flock again do not seem to care to geng through the hills, but lie hameaboot, and seek to oag through the fences down into the toon to nose about among the growing crops. These almarks are often a pest, and have to be kept turned away by the dog. A three-cornered wooden affair known as da branks is often put on the necks of these almarks, so that they cannot get through the fences.

At the present time there are roughly 100,000 breeding sheep in Shetland, a big lot of them being of the pure island breed, said to have been introduced into Shetland by the first colonists from Norway. Like the native breeds of ponies and dogs, the sheep are small, active and hardy. Shetland has been long famous for the quality of the wool produced. It has indeed been a "golden fleece" land, albeit the crofting women not always getting their fair share of the gold. It is termed a "combing wool," and is very suitable for worsted. The best quality is soft and silky to the touch, and is termed "kindly" by the crofters. For warmth and comfort there is nothing to beat a swaary joopie next the skin. As there is no spinning mill in Shetland yet, the wool is spun into worsted yarn at mills in Scotland, and a good deal of adulteration, and even substitution, goes on in this way. Up to thirty years or less ago many women carried on their own spinning, by hand, on small spinny-wheels, of a Norwegian model. It was a rare house in Shetland that did not have a spinny or two, and some sets of kairds, as the most important items of "furniture." Kairdins, spinnings and makkins were common. In addition to getting the housewife's wool treated, ready for knitting or weaving, these events, when from a dozen to a score of young women sat busily working, formed lightsome social occasions during the winter and spring months. Hand-spinning is still carried on in the North Isles, while attempts recently have been made to instruct young girls in the art. The thread spun by the North Isles women is as fine as a silken thread, and when twined it is still delicate, but remarkably strong. This yarn is used for knitting fancy shawls, veils and scarves. The ordinary yarn is not so delicate, but is remarkably fine when compared with "coarse Scots worsted." It is knitted into shawls, jumpers, socks, spencers, gloves, and other garments. A stouter yarn is used for garments meant for hard wear, and for taattin Shetland rugs. These latter have a certain number of striking patterns in various colours worked into the fabric, such as flowers, especially the fern, the floral emblem of Shetland, stars, squares, rings and the like, thought to be of Norn origin. About 8 hanks, or roughly 800 "threads" of "lace yarn,"

o

can be spun from 1 lb. of wool. An average size Shetland fleece weighs about 2 lb., while sheep bred on the best pastures yield $2\frac{1}{4}$ or $2\frac{1}{2}$ lb.

The Shetland sheep are of various colours, the most common being white. Other colours are moorit, or moorred, ranging from a reddish-brown to fawn; black, including brown-black; grey, and shades of blue-grey; shaila; skroita. Other colours again are mirk-face, or white with brownish spots on the face. The mirk-face sheep are perhaps one of the oldest types and are very hardy. Catmuggit sheep are black on the under parts, with the upper parts, including the body, of another colour, as grey or moorit. Like the mirk-face the catmuggit are an old type. Burrit sheep have light under parts, with a black or moorit body; and blaegit have a lighter shade on the outer part of the wool fibre, not due to the action of sunlight. The sholmit sheep are of any colour save white, with a white flekk on face or head. Flekkit again have white flekks, or patches, on the body, and shaila sheep are a dark reddish-brown, iron-grey, the reddish-brown generally predominating. Skroita, or skrotti, is a sort of reddish-orange tinge, not very commonly met with in the flocks. These colour names are all Norn and very distinctive. When a flock of moorit sheep are troakin over a moor, or lying kroogin on the moorland near the peat-banks, they seem to blend with the surrounding countryside. The natural colours are used by the knitters, as making various patterns and designs in shawls, jumpers and the rest. The vivid colourings of the genuine Fair Isle goods, actually knitted in Fair Isle, are obtained from dyes manufactured from lichens growing on the rocks.

The most valuable wool is moorit. In October 1946 moorit was fetching 10s. 6d. a lb. Prices touched 12s. and 15s. during the 1914–18 war. White is at present selling at 7s. 6d. per lb., and grey at 7s. per lb. The perfect condition of Shetland wool has been the outcome of careful selection over many decades, as the sheep are akin to other native breeds. In 1790 there were about 1,000 "kindly-woolled sheep" out of about 100,000 head.   James Dickson, one of the Highland and Agricultural Society's judges, in his book, *The Breeding and Economy of Live Stock*, published in 1851, writes: "The sheep are not clipt, the fine wool being pulled off carefully by the hand, while the hair, termed 'scadder,' is left on the sheep, which wears off as the new wool grows. Some of the wool is so fine as almost to resemble silk, and none in the world is of such fine texture—the fineness of the yarns when shown being truly astonishing, and when manufactured into hosiery, is not to be equalled. . . . No question can, therefore, arise as to the propriety of keeping the present breed quite pure." A certain amount of crossing with Cheviots, Blackface, and perhaps with Spanish Merino, has occurred in some districts. Where this has been adhered to the pure Shetland breed has been greatly weakened.

There are, however, a fair number of pure-bred sheep in some districts, notably in the hilly north Mainland. Breeders anxious to preserve the pure bred have had some success with the Shetland Flock-Book Society, formed after the 1914–18 war. The spinners and knitters were the actual growers and wool-sorters, as the Shetland men have been mostly fishermen and seamen. Their wives and families were left to look after the flocks. In this way the selection has been largely in the hands of the knitters, and the breed profited by it. A peculiarity is the shedding of the fleece. The fleece loosens and is cast. If it is not taken off when this happens the wool is lost. All over the hills, sticking to heather knowes, edges of banks, barbed wire, lumps and threads of oo are to be seen during the shedding season. These lots of wool are termed laagets, and folk hentin them up often get quite a big lot of wool. The hentin-laagets, or hentilaagets, are "no man's property," or rather "all men's property," and no questions are asked as to their disposal. Sheep differ greatly in this shedding process. Some do not shed it so freely, and if it is not taken off at the proper time it gets raeffled, or "grown," with the new coat, and the sheep has to be shorn. Some sheep on wild inaccessible pastures go un-roo'd or shorn for three or four seasons, trailing their grown fleeces over the ground, a ragged and dirty sight. Not having been dipped for so long, vermin in the form of kedds, or kidds, oag over the fleeces. This shedding in itself has a big influence on the selection, for the reason that a breeder does not care to have the fleeces lost in this fashion when a little longer or a little rougher staple would safeguard the loss with a further profit in having a larger fleece. This tends against fineness. Improvements in dipping have lessened the loss by shedding during recent years.

Rooin is the term given to the removal of the fleece by hand while it is in process of being shed. It is not the same as plucking, but may seem so. Sheep of another breed would not be dealt with in this fashion, they would be clipped because they would not roo. Rooin avoids the cutting of the new fleece, which would be useless for spinning, and saves the longer pointed fibres which have the effect of protecting the fleece and skin from wet by running it off. Rooin is done at such periods as is consistent with saving the wool and getting it in a proper state for removal. The fleece is left on until the weather is satisfactory, and the animal can afford to have it removed without causing harm. When the flocks are kaa'd for rooin sometimes other tasks are carried out, as marking and libbin, or castrating. The summer kaain and rooin are the most important sheep tasks carried on, the summer wool being of the best quality. Another rooin is done in the late hairst, or winter.

The Voar is perhaps the busiest season of the year on a croft. The rigs have to be manured and delved, the seed sown and harrowed. In addition the crofting folk have to be vigilant day and night looking to the yows about to lamb. They must be out and about in all kinds of weather. They have to geng aboot da hills, perhaps for miles, searching out the weakened yows, succouring lambs and driving off the kraas, swaabie gulls and other birds of prey. These haunt the hills during lambing-time, seeking out the weak animals, sheep's laevins and the like. At lambing-time it often comes severe weather, with gales and snow. Sometimes the people take spades and dig away the snow to get sheep from the fanns. Flocks are rarely insured, so snaa-taen sheep are a big loss to crofters. Once with a very heavy snowfall in a north Mainland parish, the snaa fanns, or drifts, blew down off the high eastern hill, right over the top of a small hill, so that a sort of an arch was formed in the valley, under which folk could walk. Sheep under this heavy drift were snowed up for weeks. Some sheep lay under fifteen feet of snow. The sheep's breath had helped to melt the snow around them, so that when men came upon them very few had been smord, or choked. When looking for snaad-up sheep men bore down through the fanns all round the spot where they think the animals might be lying. Following this heavy snowfall, it was well into May before the last of the deep drifts disappeared from the hills. Another year snaa fanns lay in a slacky near a burn until July. A sheep lay under the snow for sixteen days that year. When the dogs came upon her one of her hooves had got frost-bitten, and it fell off. The yow lived, however, and had lambs after that. Another yow was nineteen days under da fanns.

After the lambing-time and most of the seed has been sown, the peat-cutting season comes on. The moorlands are in the hills and daals, sometimes at a good distance from the crofts, although in some places peat-moor is found quite close to the arable land, and at places actually inside the toon. Crofters usually set on certain days for peat-cutting, staying at the banks from morning till dayset if the weather is favourable. Peat-castin is done by means of a spade-shaped implement known as a tushkar, or tusker as the south Mainland folk pronounce it. A tushkar is about three and a half feet long in da wooden heft, and is rounded and smoothed. At the foot of the heft an iron feather about seven inches long is fixed. This is fixed at an angle, and the lower edge of the feather is sharp, enabling it to slice through the wet, tough moor. The tushkar is held in both hands, thrust down through the moor, then forward, then back, and the lump of peat is loosened and cast up on the top of the bank to dry. The peats are laid on their sides, in the shape of daeks, with spaces between each paet to allow for the passage of the wind. Lying like this, to a height of three or four feet, the daeks dry in a few weeks, and then da paets are raised, or set up on end, in little roogs of three, four or five peats. Left like this for a time, they are later roogd in small heaps, the wettest paets being laid on top. The fuel when dry is either stacked in the hill, or wheeled or carried to the crofts, to be there biggd into large stacks. A crofter may get about a dozen fair-sized stacks with a good paet season, half of which he may leave in the hill, the rest being taken home to the croft. Like most other crofting jobs, the womenfolk lend a hand in the paet-wark; raisin, especially, being done mostly by women. When a whole family gets down to the job of castin and curing paets a large quantity of fuel is "mined" at the banks. Banks vary in length and depth, some being as deep as four or five paet, or more, a paet averaging $1\frac{1}{2}$ feet in length. A bank measuring 130 feet in length, 3 feet in width, and with a depth of twa paets, or 3 feet, has been reckoned, on a rough count, to produce about 4,160 paets.

CHAPTER XIV

WHILE on the subject of da Voar, and Voar-wark, the following may be of interest, as showing something of various tasks about a typical croft in the north, as well as a few impressions of the surroundings.

For da muckle taattie rig, as described in a previous letter, the crofter hurled about 160 barrow-loads of muck on to it, three loads dumped at an equal distance apart being termed a raa, or row. The rig lay in da laich, or lower, toon, and was partly visible from the croft biggin.

When the folk were inside for their meals, they left the spades standing upright in da furroo. The peerie maas came paekin over the newly turned earth, and some yows came nosing among the withered stalks of the old taattie shows, looking for small taatties bared by the rain. The seed taatties were fetched from da müldie-hoose, or taattie-hoose ida yaerd, into the biggin, where they were cut in two. Folk commenced dellin da rig after breakfast time, about 10.30 a.m., and finished for the night at 8 p.m. It came a still, clear moonlight night, with a touch of frost in it. The moon was shining "as clear as a bell" high in the south-east, and the stars were bright and twinkling. A horse-gowk, or snippikk (snipe) ida hill was "haddin 'im a wark," with its peculiar eerie on-carry. The tree staarns in Orion's belt lay low over the western hill, and the whole daal was still and quiet and gey oorie like, so that notions of trows came to folk, for all the signs of civilisation ida biggin, such as da wireless-set and da Lucas electric "fixin" that lit up all the biggins with a fine clear light. It seemed as though the ghostly blue-grey lights on the dark frost-held hills and rigs, on the burn and the quiet voe, were dancing, and over at da aald doon hooses it looked forlorn and weysome. Not a soul was about, the only things moving being a staig in the upper toon and some yows in the outrun. As the crofter closed the byre door, he stood a little watching da staarns an da müne. His red cow gave a low mowing as she munched at the hay, and the black ox seemed restless as it stamped on the packed, straw-littered floor near its mother, a black flekkit whaig. The fine weather did not hold for long, as it came wind soon after midnight, and rain laid on. The wind gowled and girned, oorie-like over the thatched roof, as it soughed down off the hills. The burn at the foot of da toon kept up a loud din. It came a dry dull day, with flaans of north-west wind off the hills. Folk left off working ida rig when da van was seen coming over the road at about 2.30 p.m. The crofter bought some feeding-stuff, such as bran, oil-cake and meal. The oil-cake was poured into a sack, and satisfying himself it was da correct weight, the man paid the vanman and then bought some loffs, saasir-maet and other goods. Grumbling that "da roond pownd is needed noo fur whit ye got fur eight shillings afore da waar," the crofter waved a "Cheerio!" to the vanman, slung his kishie over his shoulder, took the sack of oil-cake in both hands and went doon da toons again. Soon after four men and two women were trying ta grip a horse that had been lying about the place for weeks. After two or three attempts, during which the horse, with other ponies, jumped the fencing between the crofts, laying some of the crofter's stabs in bruck and snapping the straining-post in the njeuk of the north pund, the horse was eventually lured into a quarry hole and tied up. Later on it was led off up the road by a woman with a grey shawl wuppid aboot 'ir head. Another woman was trying to entice a pony to her by holding out some straw and crying "Shookie, shookie!"

The wind went around to the south'ard. It was dry and not so cold, and when bursts of sunshine bored through the clouds it felt warm. The folk were dellin in a smaller rig, after the four o'clock's tea. This rig had had 15 barrow-loads of lamb's muck wheeled down on to it. It was going to be set with two kishies of seed. One kishie of seed taatties is estimated to grow about 10 kishies of taatties. In da muckle rig 12 kishies of seed were set. This was reckoned to produce 120 kishies in late hairst, when ripin' (gathering) would begin. Scots oats were 8*s*. 6*d*. a bushel, and one bushel of seed oats would be sown in one of the smaller long-shaped rigs. The crofter said that the folk in the croft at the western side of the Ness never got da sun from Hallowmas to the 15th of February. He said da folk afore diss saa'd bere in some of da best rigs, but it was hardly ever grown ida nort noo. He said his mother had told him da hill at Fjaellness used to be covered with heather. "Hit wiss black wi' hedder, shü taald me," but now it was all green, without a staak a hedder to be seen. This was caused by the sheep that had been set on there. They routed the heather, and made the grass come bonny and thick. In the fine summer days the laand of Fjaellness was reflected green in the still voe, but lang ago it was as if the voe were blood-red with the reflection of the heather.

The Saetter Stane oot at da Ness was an aald kraig-stane, the crofter said. He had draan many a piltikk oot dere, and wi' da ebbs, doon ida saandy stretches at the head of da voe dey had draan aafil a spoots. "Rivin'" or tearing lambs' muck was a tough job. It was said to be the best manure, and it certainly has a strong enough smell. At the bottom of the hard-packed earth and dung layers, or flakes, the floor of da laam'oose was black-coloured, like tar. When he was cleaning the lambhouse the crofter had to work stooped, owing to the low walls and roof. The folk of the croft had about 24 peerie aald Shetland hens. They were mostly white, but some were flukkrit, the cock being black. They had a dozen djukes, four being "Indian runners." Speaking of the horses, the crofter pointed to their dung on the grassy toonmals. He said: "It'll be midsummer afore ye kood tedder a koo dere!" He meant that the dung kept back growth in the earth, it "was dat coorse!" He had had ta shull the dung away frae da face o' da stack during the snowy period, as the horses sheltered in the lee of the stack, eating the straw off da laam'oose ruif.

Oat seed must be winnowed first, said the crofter, before ye geng ta saa hit. The folk came to da south side of the house, near da yaerd-daek, to winnow da coarn. It was in the forenoon, and the crofter shook his head as he looked about him. It was going to be "nae wind ava," he said. "Na, feth we, we'll gjit nae koarn winnood wi' diss," nodded his wife. However, the man thought he'd try it, so they all gathered be-sooth da house, on a green knowe. They had a flakki, made from aald mael-bags, spread out on da green. The oats were poured from a sack in a heap on to the flakki. The crofter and his wife kept taking up handfuls of aits. Then as da ears fell, the anns (chaff) blew away to the lee side of da flakki. It was fitful gusts from the south-west, and the crofter aye paused, annoyed when the wind seemed to fall away for good. Then the winnd'd ears were put into another sack and carried doon ta da rig. The hens came squawking, scampering, flying over da toons, to da knowe, paekin and scratching, and paekin at da sack of aits. The crofter's lass "skirrd!" the hens away, and sent the dog after them, but they aye returned and kept scraping and paekin among the laevins on da girss. An old white yow kept nosing around. She belonged to the crofter's aunt, and he was aye sending the dog after the yow. When the folk went away, the yow came to eat the bits of straw, chaff and other leavings. A steady wind, not too strong, said the crofter, is the best for winnowin da koarn. All the corn having been winnowed, the crofter took a kishie-foo, and went down into the rig to saa it. "Is it a flood yit?" he asked, looking towards the voe. "I tink he is," said his wife, "bit whit odds makks it?" she asked, laughing. "Da aald fokk aye held be it," said the crofter. Then satisfying himself on this point, he held the kishie before him, with his arm under the kishie-baand, and began to "shew" da corn. He shew it sparsely from top to bottom of the rig, then shew a second time, with his right hand lightly scattering the grains. Then his wife got the harrow under way, and dragged it along. A length of kyaarr (coir) ropp was fastened to da harroo. The harrow was roughly oblong shaped, with seven or eight spikes, each about 7 inches in length, in each side of the harrow. It was made of thick wooden bars. The coir baands were over the woman's shoulders, then with her hands held back, gripping the ropes, she leaned forward and went over the ground two or three times until the seed was hidden and the ground looked fairly even. The roots and grass and other bruck taken up by the spikes lay at the sides of the rig. The sowing and harrowing of this rig took up about an hour. It was a hard task the woman had, dragging along the harrow. It was a ticklish job, too, as care had to be taken that the spikes did not go too far down into the soil. In the forenoon the crofter sowed three kishies of oats in the south part of the rig.

Discussing his fodder, the crofter said he had had two "fairly good desses of hay" and five fair-sized skroos o' koarn in the yard. Now, about the middle of Aaprile "wi' da new style," he said it had almost all gone but for a little hay and one sort of a skroo. This skroo was wuppit aboot with bits of bags, torn blankets, old coats and the like, but still "da venom's fools," or hens, would come and play the merry mischief with it all, rivin out da strae, strewing it about the place. The dog was kept busy chasing the hens, but they aye came back to resume their tearing.

The following day it was showery, with heavy raags of rain, and up to about noon the wind was south-westerly. It fell away to gusts off the hills in the afternoon. At night it was dry and cold, with "da snippik" having a great night of it wailing in the hills. A lot of rain fell in the early morning and the burns ran in spate. Next morning the crofter went to muck his nort laam'oose. It held six lambs and seven gjimmers. He carried down twenty-three kishies of muck to da nort rig. The folk were hard at it all day, dellin and sowing. In the late afternoon a woman was seen going north the road carrying a sackful of lubba, or coarse grass, which grows on mossy ground. She had been plucking da lubba in a place known as da

Flossy knowes. The crofter straightened himself, looked towards the road, and waved a hand in greeting. The woman waved back, and trudged along, her fingers active at her knitting. The crofter spat and looked towards the big croft north past, where a lad was ploughing. "Dat's a sign a Voar!" he said, pointing, as the birds followed the plough, calling shrilly. The geese from the neighbouring croft came south over the rigs, and the man sent his dog after them. That morning "da stibble ditches were staandin in a loch a water," but with the wind the land dried again. The crofter's wife went out of da rig to da byre about noon to let the kye out to the outrun. They browsed there until about eight o'clock. The kye from a croft north past were driven south into the hill. A lot of kraas were flying about, two came and perched on da corn rig, and the dog let out a yelp and bounded after them. Calling hoarsely, the sinister birds rose up and flew off towards the western hill. The crofter said he had reaped 74 kishies of neeps from one rig the previous hairst. He said 95 sack-bags of hay were got off da müddoo in the lower toon of his neighbour's croft two years previously. The following year, however, the hay all "good ta dirt, as da man koodna gjit at hit; hit aa good doon, yunder whaar hits lyin sae white laek yun . . . ida white müddoo . . . hit wiss a dead loss."

At about eight o'clock on Saturday night it was showery, but not too cold. One of the neighbour women was "only gjaa'n ta'stack, ida sooth hill!" The crofter laughed, and shook his head: "Yah, her! Diss is juist her time a night!" A shaila yow belonging to one of the south toons was taken by the burn on Saturday morning. It was carried right down to the saandy ayre near the shore, where the maas and corbies came to paek at her carcase. This same crofter had had a lot of sheep lost in the same way.

"Da Stripes" was the name of a boggy stretch of land in the high outrun. Here on Saturday night, as the crofter was looking for some of da lambs which had not come in from da hill, he saw two maas going about the damp, grassy patches. They were paekin aboot something, and he wondered what it might be. Maybe it was da aald moorit yow that had gone to the hill from the pund. She'd maybe not been able to get across da Stripes, and got stuck ida saft ground. And yet, he said, da yow didn't seem ta be dat puir amos after aa. After a little he took his staff, and with da dog set out up over da pund ta finn oot whit da maas were hunting for at da Stripes.

He said there had been plenty of sillikks in da voe the previous hairst. They were aff at da eela ee night whin wan o' yun Heinkels flew by! They had got sillikks six nights running, in a new boat belonging to one of the north daal crofters. The boat lay drawn up in a noost behind the house which stood a little way up from the sea edge. The crofter said sadly, his ain aald boat was aa donn. She was lying, with three others, rotting in their noosts. Speaking of the sheep and of how they knew the lie of the laand and the change of seasons, he said: "Wance da sheep begin ta finn da green paek dir nae haddin dem; dir nae keepin dem in eence dir awaar a da paek." His wife was sitting makkin 'ir sock. She held up the knitting, and nodded: "Yea, dat's true. Da sheep begin ta geng ta da tapmist pairt a da hills wance comin on ta Mey." The man nodded and laughed: "Yiss, an Mey'll shüne be here! Dan we'se gjit Mey sillikks!"

The maas flitted over da rigs on Sunday forenoon. It was raining early in the morning, so the crofter said da fools wid be eftir da wirms comin oot eftir da rain. A flock of starlings flew south by, over da lower rigs, about noon. About 1.30 p.m., one of the young crofters from the nort toon was going north alang da banks with his dog. He would be "lookin fur casualties, I waarn," laughed the crofter. Some sheep fall over the banksis, or geng doon ida ebb, eftir waar, and never have power to get up again. Then the young fellow went up over one of the old ley toons, then back again and down into the ebb. About half-past two a man came in a car, and went out along da eastern shore of the voe, in long waders and wielding a trout-waand. He went as far out as the rocks below the Ness toon. The wind was blowing out the voe, with some white caps in it, and it was cold, with the wind right in the angler's face. The voe was blue, but near the shore and ayre it looked green coloured. Then the angler went out a bit along da western shore, aye castin his flies, but seemed to have little luck. A great muckle stane, an earth-fast stane as the crofter called it, lay on the ground at the back of one of the crofts. It was about six feet high, covered in parts with dark green lichen. It had a name, said the crofter, but for the moment he couldn't recall it. Maybe it was da Goarstie, or something like that, and it was one of the old march-stanes, used as boundary lines. "Da Ootrie," he said, was the name of one earth-fast stane in one of the nort toon's rigs.

Pointing out the infield and ootfield lands, he pointed up to the western fences. There's "fine broon earth" up yunder ida rigs abüne and at each side of da aald hoose, he said. It was da best infield laand, and that used to be all the laand that was wrought at one time by da aald fokk afore diss.

One day, he said, when they were kaain sheep at da eastern hill, he came on a nest. It was a dunter's nest, and there were eggs in it. A boy with him found another nest. They took the eggs home, but dey were sittin. A third crofter found another nest with eggs, so "they aye minded on that day's kaain, wi' finnin aa yun nests!" When da first days of May came in, he said, dey'd finn plenty of maas' eggs aff ida isles.

CHAPTER XV

As has been said, crofting gives a subsistence living, sometimes fairly good, at others a bare minimum. Fixed hours and regular wages are almost meaningless terms to most crofting folk. For long periods hardly any money is seen in some crofting households, unless for "da bit o' pension" the old folk draw, or the half-pay of some seafaring member of the family. Barter is still common, the crofter's wife exchanging eggs, wool, knitted goods, taatties, kell, for bread, meal, groceries, clothes, feeding-stuffs, sheep dip, at the travelling shop, a motor-van from the nearest shop.

Even remnants of "trucking" are in evidence in backward places, the knitter seeing no money for the woollen goods she sells to the merchant. Instead she gets so much goods for the article. A practice existed up to recent times whereby the merchant deducted a certain sum, usually 3*d*., off each shilling of the value of the knitted garment. The first real break in this unjust system came when the Scottish Co-operative Wholesale Society opened its branch in Lerwick, and gave knitters full value for the garments sold. This giving "a shilling for a shilling" helped greatly in breaking down these relics of feudalism and a time when working folk had to submit to the "masters" without a murmur.

With the success of the S.H.K.A., founded in the summer of 1943, this and other injurious practices should get short shrift. Already over 4,000 members have rallied to the association, which is now a registered producers' Co-operative Society. Its turnover in 1943 was £10,000, and in 1944 about £45,000. Its plans for the better production and marketing of the famous hand-knitted hosiery are well advanced. It also aims at a spinning-mill inside Shetland.

Women in Shetland became aware of their power, and of the extent to which they had been ruthlessly exploited by the merchants, by the increased demand for knitted goods that followed the opening of the Co-operative store in 1938. Then with the war an ever-increasing demand set in. Knitters began to get double, even treble, prices for their skilled handicraft. The increased demand following the war led to a number of mushroom firms springing up, and the actual stating of prices to be paid in numerous advertisements in the local papers.

This demand, and the introduction of a system of having to give up clothing coupons when buying woollen yarn, or getting wool spun at the mills, gave rise to much discontent. Out of the agitation, the women resolved upon organising themselves. This event, which took place in the summer of the fourth year of the war, was rightly hailed as a Shetland landmark, as knitters had always been the most downtrodden and backward section of the Shetland working class. Mr. Prophet Smith, a seaman, and Seamen's Union official, was largely instrumental in getting the association on its feet. It later received help from the Scottish Agricultural Organisation Society.

The only time crofters in some places see any "great" sum of money is about a roup time, when they go to the district cattle sale with kye and sheep and other stock and produce. At times they hire lorries and go to the Market Green at Lerwick with "twa sheep" (a drove) to sell by auction. Of course, nowadays crofters get subsidies from the Government for sheep and cattle and increased acreage cultivated, as well as being encouraged to gather seaweed, shoot skarfs and engage in various "new industries." In addition, the Scottish Wool Growers give favourable prices for wool, and the Crofters' Supply Agency arranges for the supply and distribution of artificial manures, seed taatties, seed corn, lime, arranges for tractors to be hired, and other services. With it all, however, crofting by its very nature is not a steady income-bringing occupation. In some places crofters sell sheep and wool to the nearest big merchant, but roups and displenishing sales are the main marketing places for selling and buying live stock and croft produce.

YOUNG SHETLANDERS

C. J. Williamson

KNITTER   *C. J. Williamson*

To face page 225

As most crofters never bother to keep books, it is difficult getting facts and figures giving a truthful account of the "economics of crofting." When asked about this, one man shrugged and smiled: "Economics of crofting? Hit's aa economics if du axes me! Man, dir naethin in croftin' ava!" While this may be somewhat exaggerated, it conveys part of the truth. There seems so little "coming into" the house that most folk never think of "keeping a tally" on things. And yet, in the case of not a few croft biggins, quite tidy sums lie for long enough "ida kjist njeuk," if not in the Lerwick banks.

Incomplete data supplied in 1939 by a crofter with 4 acres of arable and 28 acres of pastoral land, with a share in the common skattald grazings, situated in the north-west Mainland, may be of interest here.

The rent was £4, 2s., and the holder, in drawing up a "balance sheet," gave his liabilities as standing at £84, 7s. His assets included:

	£	s.	d.
40 Sheep & lambs, at an average value of 10s. each	£20	0	0
3 tons taatties, at £7 a ton	21	0	0
Oat crop, £4; Hay crop, £1	5	0	0
14 hens at 3s.	2	2	0
Improvements on buildings	50	0	0
Making total assets	£98	2	0
With liabilities deducted	84	7	0
Leaves assets valued at	£13	15	0

In his "Profit and Loss Account," among the items on the "Dr" side were:

	£	s.	d.
Labour expenses in spring	£7	15	0
Feeding stuffs	8	0	0
Manures	1	0	0
Tar for buildings	1	0	0
Harvest costs and expenses	6	0	0
Rent	4	2	0
Peat fuel, transport and general expenses	3	0	0
Total "Dr."	£30	17	0

P

Items on the "Cr" side were:

	£	s	d
1 ton of taatties	£7	0	0
Wool sold	3	0	0
Eggs for season, 6 months . . .	3	12	0
Potatoes used for home consumption, for 6 months	4	10	0
Total "Cr."	£18	2	0

The total income from the croft was given as £18, 2s., and total expenditure £39, 7s.

Another croft of 4 acres arable and 7 acres pastoral, with right to the skattald, paid £4, 8s. rent. The crofter kept 1 horse, valued at £15; 2 cows, valued at £20; 48 sheep at an average price of 10s. each, amounting to £24; and a dozen hens, valued at £1, 16s. In a statement of income he gave "milk average (maximum) 3 pints daily, at 3d.; wool, 56 lbs., at 1s. 9d.; eggs, 1 dozen per week, average per annum at 1s. per dozen; and taatties used, 7 lbs. per day, at 5d. per day." His expenditure was given as "general upkeep, and expenses about 2s. 8d. per week; rent at 1s. 6d.; and rates at 1d. per week."

A case of some interest on the question of local unemployment benefit claims was determined in the summer of 1938, and the report as given in the *Shetland Times*, for 23rd July 1938, can be given here for the light it throws on a matter that vitally affected Shetland crofters "in the bad old days of the slump."

The applicant was a road foreman and also the tenant of a small croft, "for which he paid an annual rental of £3, 10s.; his unemployment insurance contributions were insufficient to entitle him to unemployment benefit, but he was paid off last winter. He was refused benefit, on account of the possession of his croft, by the local referees at Lerwick. Their decision was confirmed by the referees at Aberdeen. Leave to appeal to the umpire was at first refused, but the matter was reopened, and the umpire heard the case and issued a decision in favour of the claimant. It was pointed out on the man's behalf that the claimant was not prevented by his croft from following his usual employment on the roads. His record at work showed that he had never had to take time off to work the croft, and also it was shown that the income from the croft did not exceed £1 a week, the limit which a claimant for unemployment benefit was allowed to earn in spare-time work. The umpire's decision was in the following terms: 'On the facts before me, my decision is that the claim for benefit is allowed. That the claimant could ordinarily have followed his occupation as a crofter in addition to and outside the ordinary working hours of his usual employment as road foreman is clear from the fact that he has done so in various times throughout the year and on a full-time basis when work on the croft is most required. He has been able to do so because of the assistance given on the croft by members of his family. The net annual rental is stated to be £3, 10s., and, according to the evidence before me, the net profit from the croft is within the statutory limit specified in section 35 (5) of the Act.' "

In the hairst some few years ago, crofters at a displenishing sale bought the following animals and crop at the prices stated. White lambs, 11s. 6d., 6s. 1d. and 5s. 10d. each; moorit lambs, 4s. 3d. each; black yows at 14s. each; and white gjimmers at 11s. each. A two-year-old white yow sold at 12s., as did a white ram. A three-year-old cow changed hands at £8, 5s., and a calf at £1, 10s. Hay sold at 2s. a koll, and corn at 3s. 3d., 3s. and 2s. 6d. a thrave. One dozen hens fetched 5s., and 6 ducks 6s. A strae'n kishie sold for 2s. 6d., a spinny-wheel for 1s., and a pair of kairds for 6d.

At the cattle sales in Aberdeen in the last week of August 1943 Shetland cross stirks sold at £15, and from £7, 15s. to £11, 17s. 6d.; Shetland cows, calved, sold to £9, 2s. 6d., and cross Shetland yow and wedder lambs sold at £2, 15s. 6d. Other Cheviot cross lambs from Shetland sold at 33s. 3d. and 37s. 6d. At the Market Green,

Lerwick, in the first week of September 1943, small lambs fetched 12*s.* 6*d.* and 15*s.* In October 1946, at the Aberdeen sales, cross Shetland lambs realised 28*s.* each. Shetland cattle, of the smaller type, sold well, stots selling to £25, 17*s.* 6*d.*, heifers to £25, 7*s.* 6*d.*; cow in calf, £15, 2*s.* 6*d.*; cow calved, £16, 7*s.* 6*d.*; farrow cow, £10, 15*s.*; and calves, £8, 2*s.* 6*d.* Cheviot lambs fetched from £2, 6*s.* 6*d.* to £1, 10*s.*

A Shetland cow is distinguished from other breeds by its smallness. It is a hardy animal with short, sturdy legs, finely made head and inward-turning horns. It weighs from three to six hundredweights. The principal colours are black, white, black-and-white flekkit, and dun-coloured. The eesit coloured kye of some of the outlying isles are thought to be sprung from an old native breed. The eesit kye were said to be "da Finns' kye," and "da trows' kye." Shetland kye thrive on the coarse grass on the crofts and outruns. They are outside practically every day of the year. They fend for themselves in the hills, and by the shore where the seaweed gathers. With the tide out da kye geng doon ida ebb, seeking out tasty morsels from the heaps of waar and tangls (seaweed) lying exposed. Cattle often stand for long enough ida ebb, eating waar.

There are about 9,000 head of kye in Shetland, almost all of the native breed. The Shetland cow is more economical to keep, as imported cattle cannot stand the climate so well. They require more feeding-stuff to make them yield a profitable milk supply. Shetland cattle are remarkably free from disease. In 1945, 2,500 kye were inspected, and not one case of T.B. was discovered. They are regular milkers, some kye, without any extra feeding, having been known to yield about 4½ gallons of milk a day. A fair yield runs from 2 to 3 gallons daily. A Shetland yearling was worth about £5 in 1936. The beef of the Shetland cattle, like the mutton of the native sheep, has a flavour peculiarly its own.

The main part of the grazings of a typical croft is

generally composed of fields, or toonmals, covered with grass. The kye and calves are tethered on these flower-strewn homefields, or along da stanks between the cultivated rigs when these are not kept for maain for hay. Here they find plenty of sustenance when they are kept on da toon. They are also tethered on ley rigs, and sometimes a cow is led along the grassy edges at the roadside. At times a koo tethered by the roadside troaks across the road and holds up the traffic while she gets a few mouthfuls from "da idder side." Some Shetland names for kye are Sholmie, Riggie, Riddie, Kjullie, Flekkie, Blackie, or Swartie and Essie.

An old "cow-call verse" ran something as follows:

> "Komma, komma, haestie, komma
> So saal du no' gjit a scoldin;
> Fal-al-da-ral-da-ree-doe kjoara!
> Nippirt Naanie, an aald Langspraalie,
> Still komm ower, me Sjalma,
> Fal-al-da-ral-da-ree-doe kjoara!"

The price offered in August 1943 by an Edinburgh merchant for pure white Shetland wool to members of the Shetland Flock Book Society was only 4s. a lb. The Scottish Wool Growers, Ltd., offered wool producers in the islands, who export their own clip direct to the Mainland, 3s. 6d. per lb. for white, 3s. for black and grey, and 3s. 9d. for moorit. The fleece of a sheep weighs about 2 lbs., although some weigh 2½ lbs., and even 3 lbs. A knitter will make an ordinary size jumper from 2 lbs. of wool. It usually takes a week of fairly exacting work to get a jumper "knitted to any sense," though some can complete one in four days. Prices for jumpers and other garments vary, but during the war as high as £2 was paid for a jumper with "Fair Isle" strip design in colours. During the slump days of 1938–39 knitters thought themselves lucky if they got 7s. 6d. for a well-knitted jumper of latest design. In October 1946 all-over Fair Isle jumpers reached £4, 15s. and £5; gloves, 12s. 6d. to 14s. per pair; berets, 12s.; and open-work jumpers, £3, 10s.

That other native of Shetland, the pony, is of hardy stock. Some crofters still have one or two ponies, for doing various jobs about the place, although the tendency has always been for farmers to breed ponies for export. They used to be sold to coal owners for work in the mines, but this trade has fallen off in face of mechanical hauling appliances now coming into use underground.

In the first year of the century something like five thousand ponies were grazing on the Shetland hills. A writer in the magazine *Scotland* gives interesting facts about the "Sheltie." "The Shetland pony," he writes, "has been known to live and thrive on land so poor that even the red deer or blackfaced sheep could not subsist there for a single season. He is protected by a thick and long coat of hair which is unpenetrable by even the severest weather, and a strange provision of nature is that the foals during the first winter of their lives grow even a longer and warmer coat than that of the more matured ponies.

"I have seen these youngsters, when shedding their coats in early June, with big rolls of the matted hair hanging from their bodies like wool from a blackfaced sheep. This covering of hair is not the only protection which these ponies have, as a long and thick mane of hair covers their head and neck, while a long bushy tail shelters their hind quarters. Thus clad the little Sheltie is ready to face any weather, and it is only when deep snow covers the ground that he ever gives it a thought, and even then he is able to fend for himself, as by scraping the snow with his little fore feet he can get at sufficient grass to keep him going. It is commonly thought that the ponies of Shetland were individually made small by the severity of the conditions under which they lived, that they were and are dwarfs stinted by starvation. But this is not the case, as ponies reared in southern climates and on the richest of pastures show no tendency whatever to increase in size." *

* "He can Face any Weather: The Breed of the Sheltie," by J. M. Macdonald, in *Scotland*, Spring, 1938.

Some crofters are expert hand-loom weavers, and with an increased demand for Shetland tweed of recent years, it is thought that a revival of weaving may take place. During the war as high as £5 a week was earned by some crofters from weaving, without interfering very much with the work on their holdings. Recently a Shetland Hand-loom Weavers' Association was formed, on the lines of the S.H.K.A., but its development has been held up by the slow supply of new looms.

CHAPTER XVI

INTEREST in Labour and Socialist ideas took shape in Shetland as early as the eighties of last century; but before this the educational work of Arthur Anderson, and his successful challenging of the Tories when he stood as Liberal candidate for Orkney and Shetland, had a big influence among Shetlanders. "Polling took place on 1st September 1847. The combined electorate of both groups of islands would not have exceeded 450, and in Shetland there were only two polling booths, one at Lerwick, and the other at Burravoe, in the island of Yell. When the result was declared, it was found that Anderson had been elected by a majority of 26, the actual figures being—Anderson, 209; Dundas, 183." *

For the first time "ordinary" Shetland folk dared to think and speak in a different way than their "masters" of the land and the ministers of the kirk. The times were seeing great changes. The new industrialism was spreading, even to the most remote places, and with this new life came new ideas. The semi-feudal rule of the landmasters could not stand up to the ideas of Liberalism and Free Trade. Their power gradually declined, until in 1886, with the passing of the Crofters' Act, they had to stand down in face of the inevitable.

The people were now free agents, with security of tenure on the land, and with this went the banishing of fear. Alongside this went some little encouragement to improve and develop their crofts. Shetlanders never forget that by his setting up of the Shetland Fishery Company at the west side—with inducements to men to fish as free agents and to be able to sell their catches in a free market—Anderson had been one of the first to challenge the power and privileges of the landmasters. The Crofters' Act gave to the Shetland working folk self-

* *Arthur Anderson : A Founder of the P. & O. Company*, by John Nicolson.

"

respect, and with self-respect came the desire for a fuller and better life than had been the lot of their forefathers.

It was as if a great burden had been lifted from their shoulders, and so when, in 1889, "da Commission" came north to hear evidence from every toonship in the islands, the people were not afraid of "speaking their minds." It was the most important topic of conversation in every home—"da Commission," and what "So-and-so" had "said," and how much arrears this man and that had to his name. It was in the nature of a revolution, this loosening of tongues in a people who, up till then, had seemingly been "dumb" indeed. When folk read the reports of the harsh treatment and semi-serfdom they had had to endure, indignation was rife. The evidence of the Commission, following on the evidence of the Truck Commission of 1872, and that of the Napier Commission some years before the passing of "the Act," are revelations of the harshness of the rule of the landmasters.

The *Shetland News* gave very full reports of each day's sitting of the Commission. In its issue for 19th October 1889 we read: "Ollaberry, 8th Oct. A division of the Commission . . . drove down to Ollaberry on Monday, and opened a sitting in the church to-day. A cattle sale was going on in the forenoon, so the sitting was begun at one o'clock, when all those attending the sale adjourned to the church to watch the proceedings of the Commissioners. . . ." In the same issue there appeared: ". . . Ollaberry, Thursday. Robert Anderson, Tome, North Roe, being asked to take the oath, said—I would speak the truth before God and the Court, but I object to the formality of oaths, as the Lord of Lords and King of Kings says 'swear not at all.' While I honour this Court and obey all the instructions of man, I obey Him as final Judge. One might commit perjury, but one looking on Him as a final Judge would speak the truth. . . ." He went on: ". . . He had stated them (the arrears) as £13 in application, as that was the last statement he got from the local manager before he put in his application. He held the arrears to be

£7, 13s. 8d., and he would produce accounts to prove it. . . ." With regard to improvements, witness's own statement was read: "Laying out on a different plan and changing the aspect of almost the whole croft—involving new drains, cutting through hard layers of stone," etc. The circumstances affecting the value of the holding Anderson gave as: "Water from a considerable watershed, town of Stowie, flooding, little descent, difficult drainage, a ponderous rock, little dip, resists good tools, mildew burns potatoes and stint corn in a few hours. Worst in district for potato disease."

Gilbert Stout, of Lunnasting, gave some interesting revelations as to the conditions the haaf men had had to put up with in the first part of the century, when men had to be helped out of the boats on getting ashore, they were so weak from hunger. The "Laird of Fogrigarth," at the west side, produced interesting data on how much meal he ground at the mill, and another man in Northmavine spoke vigorously of how he hoped the "day would not be far distant when they had liberty in the far north," and said the masters did not like him, they did not like a seafaring man who spoke his mind. Others gave interesting evidence, in spirited tones, all making for highly stimulating reading in the local papers.

Then with the Educational Act and the building of schools in every parish came enlightenment, wider opportunities and all the benefits of the "laer" folk had had to forgo. Education, opportunity, became now the birthrights of every child.

It was little wonder that, in such an atmosphere, Liberal ideas took good root. The *Shetland Times* became the popular paper with Shetland folk, as it was first in the field, and espoused the cause of Liberalism and progress. It soon became widely read in the islands, those not in a position to subscribe getting a loan of da neebor man's copy. In this way copies were read until they fell sinndry.

Radical ideas, too, came to Shetland with seafaring and other men. *Reynolds' News* and similar papers were brought home by men who had been away sailing. Journals with progressive ideas also came to the islands from Shetlanders in the colonies and in North America. News of the fight of the crofters of the Highlands and Western Isles was discussed, the work of the Highland Land League was followed with interest, and the activities of the Democratic Federation and the agitation of men like William Morris and H. M. Hyndman kindled feelings of admiration in remote Shetland crofts.

In 1893–94 a lawyer, W. G. Lennox, attempted to organise a Crofters' Defence League in Shetland, "with the object of creating ultimately a peasant-proprietor class. The aims of the League, which was largely trade union in organisation and principle, were (in return for 2s. a year subscription and 2s. 6d. entrance fee): (1) To insure against expensive litigation; (2) to act against petty tyranny of the landlords; and (3) to advance money to pay rates and thus add 600–700 names to the Voters' Roll." *

In the late nineties the progressive movement took shape. The Lerwick Working Men's Association was founded by about six working men. They held meetings in a room in the large building at the north end of the street, now owned by Messrs J. & J. Tods, Ltd. The Association did good work in the sphere of local politics and education for some years. In the first years of the century the Lerwick Branch of the Social Democratic Federation was founded, largely through the initiative of "Left-wing" members of the Association, such as James Robertson, J. J. Haldane Burgess, Frank H. Pottinger and others. Among the supporters of the new branch was J. J. Haldane Burgess, the author and poet. He was an enthusiastic Socialist in those early days, and remained steadfastly so till his death in January 1927. He followed the news of the Russian Revolution with intense fervour, the story of the struggles of the Union of Socialist Soviet

* *The Historical Geography of the Shetland Islands*, by Andrew C. O'Dell, pp. 55–56.

Republics and its leaders, Lenin and the Bolsheviks, filling the scholar with admiration.

The S.D.F. branch soon gained adherents in the town and throughout the islands. *Justice* and the pamphlets of Bebel, Marx, Harry Quelch, Keir Hardie, Robert Blatchford and other pioneer Socialists were in circulation in the town and read in fishing-boat and croft.

Blatchford's *Clarion*, his *Merrie England*, and the cheap reprints of progressive and rationalist literature issued by the R.P.A., had a big circulation in Shetland. The branch began agitating for better housing conditions, and in the Town Council elections of the early years of the century its working men candidates ran on a Socialist and Labour platform. This was regarded with great astonishment by some of the local "ruling class." They could not see why "ordinary" workers should need to bother themselves with politics, either local or national. Those same people scoffed at the idea of building new houses, in airy surroundings, for working-class families.

One of the Branch's members, the late David Sutherland, watchmaker, served on the County Council for some time. He was responsible for the famous motion pledging the Council to nationalise the land. This resolution was passed without any opposition. Willie Stewart wrote a column-length article on this decision in the *Clarion*.

The Lerwick Branch persisted in its work. It gained more adherents and was successful in getting candidates elected to the local Council and School Board. Before long, the S.D.F. (later the S.D.P., and still later B.S.P.) was a power in Lerwick's political, cultural and social life. It had groups in some of the crofting districts, and early in its career some members developed very "Left" leanings, and got the *Weekly People* and other Socialist Labour Party literature from New York. They tried to get *The Socialist* into the Reading Room, but one of the "Right-wing" members kept a wary eye going and prevented this. Notable national speakers, as Quelch, Jack Williams, Kennedy, John MacLean and others, came north, packed meetings being held on the Esplanade and at the Market Cross. The local Debating Society became pretty much a "branch" of the Socialist branch, so effectively had members "bored from within."

In *Justice*, 7th August 1909, under the feature headline "The Movement," a report from the branch is worth reprinting: "Lerwick.—During the past six weeks we have conducted Sunday evening meetings with comrade Joseph F. Duncan (I.L.P.). The meetings were well attended, but owing to the comparative failure of the herring fishing the collections and sales of literature were not up to our usual standard. We also had the assistance, on 25th July, of comrades J. R. Leslie, organiser, Shop Assistants' Union, and George Williamson, Secretary of the Zetland Socialist Society, Leith, both natives of Lerwick. Leslie gave a very interesting address on 'Vested Interests versus Public Interests.' He spoke ably, and his remarks were well received by the crowd. Williamson then moved, in a short and clever speech, a resolution of protest against the hospitality being offered by the King and the Government to the Czar of Russia. Comrade Duncan seconded, and when Comrade Pottinger (chairman) put the resolution not a single voice or hand was raised in support of either the Government or the Czar. The meeting was one of the largest and most successful we have yet held. The sales of literature amounted to £1, 5s., and the collection to 11s. Dr. Dessin, of Bradford, arrived last Tuesday for a week's visit.—M. L. MANSON."

Trade Union branches were organised by members, whose propaganda, educational and social activities were widespread and finely organised. Even the town's message boys were not immune from the spirit of the times. Dissatisfied with their paltry wages and long hours, they organised themselves and went out on "strike" shortly before the Great War.

When the S.D.P. became the British Socialist Party, not the least virile branch was the "Lerwick Branch." All this progressive activity naturally annoyed some of the landed and merchant class and their hangers-on. Even the Liberal *Times* got a little scared, and in its famous feature "Current Topics" not a few words were penned "agin' da Soshilists!" Some of the younger members organised a Cycling and Rambling Club, going to the country at the week-ends and on holidays, enjoying themselves in the open air and at the same time spreading some Socialist propaganda. They had a tent at the Sands of Sound, near Lerwick, camping out during the summer months. Here, on a flag-staff, they flew their "banner"— red background with golden edges, and in the centre grew the "tree of production" with branches labelled "distribution," "exchange," and so on, all of which they had dedicated themselves to "nationalise" for the common good when they had persuaded a majority of their fellow wage-slaves of the desirability of voting a majority of Labour men into the House of Commons. The "Current Topics" man, on one of his walks, chanced to see the banner flapping in the breeze that blew off the voe of Sound. Straight away he wrote a piece that week on the "Red Flag" unfurled in the peaceful north.

During the years leading up to the war of 1914–18, the Branch's activities increased in scope and influence. Its members in the various local government bodies did splendid work in the face of opposition from vested interests. Their devoted self-sacrifice to the cause of the people was rewarded in part by the Council's adoption of a new housing scheme, work on which began soon after the war. The local press was often not free from hostility towards the work of the Branch and Socialists in local bodies, although on the whole it gave much prominence to letters on progressive subjects; letters and reports that were eagerly read and discussed in every Shetland home.

With the war, and most of its members away on active service, the Branch declined, and little progressive political activity took place in Shetland till a year or two after the armistice. The progressive movement again re-formed, inspired by the revolutionary ferment that followed the

Russian Revolution. The Economics Club, a non-party Socialist group, was founded in March 1921, carrying on fine educational work for over four years. The "old Branch" had long discussed the founding of a Shetland Socialist paper, but nothing had ever come of it. It was left to the Economics Club to realise this "dream of the earlier Socialists," when, in 1922–23, it published six numbers of a Socialist educational journal. This was named *The Shetlander (For Shetland Workers)*, and it met with a warm welcome all over Shetland. It carried for an editorial "banner" the famous statement by Marx and Engels: "In every historical epoch the prevailing mode of economic production and exchange and the social organisation necessarily following from it form the basis on which is built up, and from which alone can be explained, the political and intellectual history of that epoch." The paper met with a good response locally, and among Shetlanders in the Colonies, something like a hundred or so subscriptions coming from New Zealand. The club and its paper strengthened the Socialist movement in the north, and when, in 1924, the Lerwick Labour Party was founded, Economics Club members took a leading part in its activities.

The party carried on work on the lines of the "old Branch," at one municipal election running six candidates, five of whom were elected. The party continued active till about 1928. For a year or so no organised Socialist movement existed in Shetland, although groups of individual Socialists and Communists continued propaganda and educational work. Then in 1934, when unemployment was assuming big proportions, the Lerwick Workmen's Club was founded, acting as a social and recreational centre for workers. Although not directly interested in politics, the Club came to be regarded as the centre of the Labour movement. Its social work filled a gap in the town's life for some years. A year or so later the Shetland Book Club took up the work of education for Socialism, rallying progressive trends and striving for some broader movement. This emerged in 1937 with the founding of the Shetland Labour Party. This party had contacts all over the islands. In the 1938 local election four of its candidates were returned after a keenly contested fight. It adopted a minister, Mr. MacKinnon, as prospective Parliamentary Labour Candidate for Orkney and Shetland. After numerous successful meetings, with support growing daily, the candidate withdrew. A Shetlander, in the person of Councillor J. J. Robertson, of Edinburgh, was then adopted as prospective Parliamentary Labour candidate for the islands.

With a loud-speaker van, full of Socialist literature, Mr. Robertson conducted many fine meetings all over Shetland, winning popularity by reason of his Shetland birth and upbringing, and his forceful, challenging appeal to his kinsfolk to be done with the Tories and return a son of the working people to be their spokesman. His meeting in Hamnavoe, Burra, in the winter of 1937, was crowded out, folk braving the bad weather to come and hear "one of themselves" speaking on the need for drastic changes in social and political life.

In February 1939 there took place a strike of bricklayers and labourers working on the housing scheme at Lochside, Lerwick. The bricklayers struck work to help the labourers obtain Union wages and conditions. Inspired by some active-minded young bricklayers from Glasgow (whose organising activity and stirring speeches at the strike meetings on the Esplanade and in the Union rooms at Harbour Street are still remembered with gratitude in the homes of many Lerwick workers) the strike was successful and labourers returned to work under better conditions. Some of the brickies were victimised and "laid off," but all came out again and they were reinstated.

Unemployment was high in Shetland in 1938–39. The workless combined together in a branch of the National Unemployed Workers' Movement, which focussed people's attention on the seriousness of the problem. Helped by its national headquarters and the activity of members, the

C. J. Williamson

WEAVER (HAND LOOM)

To face page 240

To face page 241

NET MENDERS

branch got some anomalies put right and did a great deal of valuable educational work. By its work it showed the workless they still had certain rights in society, and that by organisation they had the power to remedy grievances.

During the summer of 1939, about the same time as Councillor Robertson was holding his meetings, the N.U.W.M. arranged inspiring meetings on the Esplanade and in the Town Hall, the principal speaker, Bob Cooney, having been Political Commissar in the British Battalion of the International Brigade in Spain. With the outbreak of war the Prospective Parliamentary candidate resigned, the Labour Party and other progressive movements practically ceasing to exist. Trade unionism, however, grew considerably, and the remarkable success of the Shetland Hand Knitters' Association is a good augury for the future.

The Shetland Labour Party was re-formed in December 1943, and since then it has grown remarkably. It has branches in Bressay, Yell and Sandwick, with groups of active members in Cunningsburgh, Sandsting and Northmavine. At the General Election in July 1945, the Party realised an ambition of generations of progressive Shetlanders when it was able to put forward a Labour candidate to contest the Parliamentary seat of Shetland and Orkney. Despite lack of time and opportunity to hold many meetings, besides the fact that the Tories had a strong pull in Churchill and his war-time leadership, as well as having four reactionary newspapers against him, Prophet Smith, the candidate, polled 5,208 votes, only a little over a thousand less than the Tory, whose supporters were mainly subsidy-bought farmers and their employees.

The S.L.P. contested a number of seats at the County Council election in December 1945, and was successful in winning four seats.

Q

CHAPTER XVII

The dialect spoken in Shetland is a distinctive one. It is made up of what is left of the old Norn speech, intermingled with Scots, English, and some German and Dutch words and idiomatic peculiarities.

It is not possible to give a very satisfying account of such an important subject as folk-speech in a letter. Much of interest would be found in Jakobsen's *Old Shetland Dialect and Place-Names of Shetland*, as well as his big *Etymological Dictionary of the Norn Language in Shetland*; George Stewart's *Shetland Fireside Tales*; Inkster's *Mansie's Röd*; Burgess's *Rasmie's Büddie*, and *Rasmie's Smaa Murr*; and James Angus's *Glossary of the Shetland Dialect*.

The speech of the Norse "western island" colonies, of Iceland, Faroe, Shetland, Orkney and the Western Isles, was at first the speech of the colonists and settlers who left Norway for the new lands "west over the sea."

As time went on, the people of each place developed a form of speech peculiar to themselves, but of course related to each other and with a common origin.

Icelandic is probably a classic form of Norse, the fountain-head of the old Norse literature. It has not suffered the same inroad of alien words and influences as Shetland and Orkney. Faroese, too, has not undergone such a big dilution with outside elements. The Shetland crews of the cod smacks, working the Faroe banks, had no difficulty in conversing with Faroe folk when they were ashore in Tórshavn, Traangisvaag, and other ports. Icelandic and Faroese are therefore the nearest to Old Norse, although very many Old Norse forms seem peculiar to Shetland. Orkney Norn, on account of Orkney's proximity to Scotland, probably has suffered the most from admixture with Scottish speech. Shetland, again, probably has a purer form of Norn than Orkney. In the Shetlandic there are a few Dutch, German and

Danish words, brought to the north by fishermen, traders, shipwrecked men and the like. There are still elderly people with a very pure Norn Shetlandic, differing from the speech of the younger generation. Some young people, living in the town, knowing very little of crofting and sea life often find it difficult at first to understand the older country folk. There is, for all that, a great deal of folk-speech used in the town, and with Shetland Norn taught in the school and encouraged on every occasion no great time would elapse before the youngest again knew the glories of their mother-tongue.

In outlying places, as Fair Isle, Foula, North Unst, Fetlar, Papa, and some parts of Yell and the Mainland, the structure, idiom and accent are basically Norn, the Fair Isle accent and idiom being almost Norwegian in form. The Whalsay speech is also very pure, especially in the use of vowels.

Jakob Jakobsen, the famous philologist, came to Shetland in 1893 to begin the first of his researches into the remains of the Norn language. As a Faroese he had met in with Shetlanders, particularly fishermen, who had sailed to Faroe. This was his first contact with the Shetland dialect. He found it akin to his own beloved Faroese, and soon came to have a strong attachment to Shetlandic. He had no difficulty in understanding the Shetland men, and Shetlanders conversed with ease with the scholar when he made his journeys from croft to croft throughout Shetland. His interest was aroused, and after leaving Tórshavn for Copenhagen University, he took up the study of the languages of the various northern islands. On coming to Britain he read Edmondston's *Shetland Glossary*, and Stewart's *Fireside Tales*. This was before he came to Shetland, and on arriving there he saw right away that a large field lay waiting him. He travelled all over Shetland, meeting in with scholarly men in each district, as Laurence Williamson, Robert Jamieson, Robert Cogle, and conversing with the crofters and fishermen and their women folk inside their houses, outside on their crofts and also in the fishermen's boats. His work was successful in rescuing over 10,000 Norn words, many "fragments" of Norn rhymes, legends and sayings, as well as hundreds of place-names. He again paid a visit to the north in 1894–95 and completed his tremendous labours. Returning to Copenhagen he published his main work, *An Etymological Dictionary of the Norn Language in Shetland*, a work as yet not sufficiently known by the people who should have hailed it with acclamation—the Shetlanders.

James Inkster, James Angus, J. J. Haldane Burgess and other Shetland writers and poets also did much valuable dialect studies. Inkster's *Mansie's Röd* has often been styled a classic of the dialect. Laurence Williamson made a lifelong study of the dialect, much of his work being unselfishly placed at Jakobsen's disposal. Mr. John Stewart, M.A., and Mr. Walter J. Robertson, both of Whalsay, are among two of the younger Shetlanders who have given the subject of the dialect their attention. Plans are afoot to prepare a *Wordbook of the Shetland Dialect* and other books on the dialect and place-names.

Some people are of the opinion the dialect is decaying. They say it has outlived its usefulness. The Shetlandic, however, is a part of every Shetlander, his mother tongue, and it should not be looked down upon, but used as often as possible by Shetlanders when conversing with Shetlanders. A big share in this "despising attitude" of some towards their own homely speech is due to the educational system. This is drawn up by an administration in Scotland and carried out largely by Scottish officials and teachers who think standard English is good enough to use in schools. This neglect of Shetlandic, Shetland history and culture has played a large part in glossing over Shetland patriotism. Many young Shetlanders grow up half ignorant of their own fine cultural heritage. When a sufficient number of Shetlanders really become "Shetland-conscious" perhaps some attempt will be made to make use of the best of Shetlandic in Shetland schools, at least for a part of the school-day. Until then those interested in all things Shetlandic should organise themselves to foster and cherish and develop everything essentially Shetlandic that is worth retaining and handing on to future generations of Shetlanders.

A marked peculiarity of Shetlandic is the method of modifying the "th" sound at the beginning of some words, as "that," "Thy," "them," "thee," into a "d" sound, as "dat," "Dy," "dem," "dee." "Peerie" is a word unique to Shetland and Orkney. It means "small," or "little." "Du" is the personal pronoun Thou, or you, and is used in the same form as in German. Almost every district in Shetland has its own variation in words and their meanings, while the pronunciation of some words varies from district to district.

In the North Isles of Yell, Unst and Fetlar there are significant vowel sounds, as the Shetlandic words *snaa* (snow), *caald* (cold), *taald* (told), *twa* (two), *kail* (cabbage), *pael* (pail), become in the North Isles speech *snaw*, *cauld*, *tauld*, *twaw*, *keel*, *peel*. Whalsay, again, has a distinctive vowel usage not met with elsewhere in Shetland. Whalsay folk say *tain* (ten), *maen* (men), *saed* (said), *spaed* (spade), *byrn* (bairn, child), *tye* (tea); when people from the Mainland usually say *tenn*, *men*, *sedd*, *spedd*, *bairn* and *tay*.

The dialect is used extensively "hame aboot," that is, in the family circle, and when speaking with acquaintances. Standard English, or "talking proper," is adopted when speaking to strangers, or "superiors," as an older generation of islanders would have termed them, such as the laird, minister, schoolmaster or certain officials—and on other important occasions. The slow, soft-spoken rhythmic northern speech, with its Quaker-like forms of expression and Scandinavian accent help to distinguish it from other dialects. It strikes a stranger as "foreign" sounding, just as Lerwick gives the impression of having something "Continental" looking about it. The fundamental structure, accent and idiom are Northern, making it expressive and musical. The folk-speech lends itself to tale-spinning and poetry, while used with all the natural gusto of the country folk it can be an effective medium for wholesome humour. Owing to its make-up the dialect is a bit difficult to write, as there is no recognised standard form, each writer having a way of his own, usually adhering to the "phonetical" method, writing words as near as possible to their local pronunciation without using too many phonetic symbols. Recent dialect literature seems to have taken this phonetic form; but research at present in progress with the aim of preparing a "Wordbook" of the dialect based on lists compiled by numerous interested people may also help to formulate something of a standard system, at least for literary purposes. As perhaps can be expected, the homely "kailyard" and humorous burlesque type of literature are strongly represented in the written dialect material of the islands. In Shetlandic often a single word or two or three words, used with a certain emphasis and at times gestures, is all that is needed to convey the meaning of a sentence containing a number of words in English. By variations in emphasis, intonation and gestures used in any *aff-lay* of speech a Shetlander of the older generation can be very expressive, conveying quite a lot of meaning by playing upon the vowel-sounds and other features of the dialect. For instance, by the ways in which the following are pronounced or used quite a lot of expression and meaning can be conveyed. *Shu*! (She!); *Shu, shu*! (She, she!); *Na* (No); *Yah*, or *Yea* (Yes); *Du* (You, Thou); *Du, du*! (You, you!); *Dee* (Thee); *Dem* (Them); *Hit* (It); *Never spaek*! (Don't mention it!); *Weel*! (Well!); *Weel, weel*! (Well, well!); *Aye*; *So*!; *Dat, dat*! (That, that!); *I hear dee*! (I hear you!); *So, so, dan*! (So, so, then!); *Guid faa dee*! (May good (or fortune) befall you!); *Hye tung*! (Hold your tongue! or Do you really mean to tell me!); *Na, bairns*! (No, children! Generally used in very astonished tones as if something is hard to believe); *Tellna me*! (You needn't tell that to me! Used in a way as if to convey what one is hearing comes as no surprise); *Faantin ida önderpaet*! (Very hungry after having cut all the upper runs of peats and now working at cutting the "under-peat" or lowest run of moor, and therefore worth a square meal); *Whit* (or *whaat*) *says du?* (What do you say? or Can it really be true?); *Dat fir onnything!* (That for any-thing! or It's hard to believe!); *Fir such'n a story!* (As sur-prise and bewilderment at the startling "story" or news one hears); *I never ken!* (in the North Isles, *I never keen!*); (I don't know! used in a non-committal often "philo-sophical" manner); *He's yung Yülyit!* (It's early in the even-ing yet! or There's no great hurry for you to go yet!); *Twa* (Two of anything. This word "twa" in Shetlandic can stand for two things or half-a-score, or any unspecified quantity, as "Twa sheep ida hill" may mean literally "two only," or a flock of twenty or thirty "head"; "Twa paets," either "two peats," or a kishie-fu' (basket-full) of peats, and so on); *Ill-helt!* ("Ill health!" a malediction); *Deil folloo dee!* (The Devil follow you! a malediction); *Da black sheeld sit annunder dee!* (The Devil sit under you! a malediction); *Geng du!* (Go you! or You can go, no one's caring!); *Mirk an müneless* (Dark and dreary, sad, sorrow-ful, dark, as when there's no moon); *Wanliss* (Oneless; having not one friend, homeless); *Da face a da fremmd* (The faces of strangers; not having one's own friends to greet one); *Paece be wi' dee!* (Peace be with you! A benediction, a survival from pre-Reformation days); *Cuist oot* (To cast out, or disagree); *Cuist oot an flett* (To disagree, and argue, or scold, angrily); *Twa'r tree* (Two or three, used in much the same way as "Twa," meaning "a few," "some," and the like).

The Shetlandic pronunciation of the letters of the alphabet is something as follows:—

A—ah; B—bay; C—say; D—day; E—ae; F—eff; G—jee; H—eetch; I—aye; J—jye (at the beginning of many words J is pronounced like Y, as *Jarl* is *Yarl*); K—kay (many words in Shetlandic with a "C" (say) beginning can also be written with a "K" beginning); L—ell (in certain parts of Shetland, as at the west side, the "L" sound is pronounced very deep and pure); M—emm;

N—enn; O—oh; P—pay; Q—k'you; R—err; S—ess;
T—tay; U—you; V—vay; W—double-you; X—ex; Y—
wye; Z—tzid. Besides these there are other peculiar vowel
sounds, chief of which are: Ø—eu; Ö—as in "road," or
"rode"; U—ui; AU, or AW, as in "saw." Sometimes
"W" and "Q" sounds are interchanged at the beginning
of some words, as *Whaam*, or valley, is sometimes pronounced *Quam*. The "K" sound at the beginning of many
words, as *knife*, *knee*, is pronounced in Shetlandic as
k'nife, *k'nee*. Older Shetlanders would never say "nife,"
"nee," as in English. Other expressive Shetlandic forms
are "GJ," as in *Gjain'* or "going," the Shetlandic "J"
pronounced as "Y." Younger folk, however, tend to
say *Gain'*, dropping out, or slurring, the expressive
northern "Y" sound. *Skjimp*, the Shetlandic word for
"sarcasm," is sometimes pronounced as *skimp*. The older
pronunciation was to sound the first three letters as
"*Sk'y*imp," but younger people have a tendency of slurring the "y" sound. Older people always say *gjimmer*, "a
female sheep in her second year," where younger people
say *gimmer*.

To make a comparison of Shetlandic and Norwegian, as
you suggest, would take up too much space, as there are
many hundreds of similarities, but a few remarks may be
helpful. The Norwegian examples given here are from
Hugo's Simplified System, in *Norwegian Simplified*, and
some words from *Gyldendals Ordbøker*, the 1941 edition
published by Blackwell, Oxford.

In Shetlandic, to pull slowly on oars to keep the boat's
head on her course is to *aandoo*. The Norwegian to lie or
rest on the oars is *andøve*.

Shetlandic.	Norwegian.	English.
Dee	*De*	*You*
Dere	*Der*	*There*
Hame, or *Hemm*, or *Heim*	*Hjemme*	*Home*
Tirsty	*Tørst*	*Thirsty*
Stöl, or *Creepie*	*Stol*	*Stool*
Yae, or *Yah*	*Ja* (pron. *Yah*)	*Yes*

Shetlandic.	Norwegian.	English.
Na	*Nei*	*No*
Whaar (North Isles, *Whaur*)	*Hvor*	*Where*
Bord	*Bord*	*Table*
Göd, or *guid*	*God*	*Good*
Mornin	*Morgen*	*Morning*
Hoose, or *Hús*	*Hus*	*House*
Mann	*Mann*	*Man, husband*
Stör, or *stoor*	*Stor*	*Large, big*
Lang	*Lang*	*Long*
Dat's hit	*Det er*	*That's it*
Koffd, or *kaufd*	*Kjøpt*	*Bought*
Funn	*Funnet*	*Found*
Finn		*To find*
Skreev	*Skrevet*	*Written*
Faider, or *Fadder*	*Far*	*Father*
Midder	*Mor*	*Mother*
Bridder	*Bror*	*Brother*
Breeder		*Brethren*
Sisster	*Soster*	*Sister*
I'	*i*	*In*
Ida		*In the*
Apo, or *apon*	*Pa* (pron. *paw*)	*Upon, on*
Til, or *ta*	*Til*	*To*
Frae, fra, fae	*Fra*	*From*
Under	*Under* (pron. *ooner*)	*Under*

In the islands to "write" is to *skreev*; and in Norway the word "written" is *skrevet*. The Norwegians say *kjøpt* for "bought." A Shetlander of an older generation would say *koffd*. A Shetlander says he has *funn* (found) something, while a Norwegian says *funnet*.

Du is wylkomm would be something like the older Shetlander's way of saying "You're welcome." In Norway it is *De er velkommen*. Here a "knife" is *k'nife*, and in Norway it is *kniv*. In both cases the "k" is pronounced. A *fyrstikk* is a "match" in Norway, whereas in the islands the old word *taandstikk* (North Isles, *taundstikk*) is still used. *Bloom*, as a flower, is used in Shetland when describing anyone with a brightly-coloured face. In Norway *blomst* means "flower." *Hvis* is "whose" in Norway. Here we say *whaas*, as in "*Whaas boat is yun?*" ("Whose boat is that," or "Whose boat is it?") *Dirs* is "theirs" in Shetland, and in Norway "theirs" is *deres*. In Shetland they say *frae,* or *fra* and sometimes *fae* for "from," when Norwegians say *fra*. *Til* is "to" in Shetland and Norway alike. *Whaat?* or *whit?* in Shetland means "what." In Norway they say *hva? Spaeks du Engleesh?* is how a Shetlander would say "Do you speak English?" A Norwegian says *Snakker De engelsk? Forstår De meg?* is Norwegian for "Do you understand me?" In Shetland they used to say *Førstas du me?* A "child" in Shetland is *bairn*, and in Norway *barn*. *Whaar ir?* (North Isles, *Whaur eer?*) is the Shetland way of saying "Where are?" In Norway this is *hvor er? Hvor kommer De fra?* or *hvorfra kommer De?* is Norwegian for "Where do you come from?" In Shetlandic this would be *Whaar* (North Isles, *Whaur*) *comes du frae?* In Norwegian *spørre* means to "ask," and in Shetlandic the word is *spørr* or *spuir*.

Some of the phrases, sayings and differences of usage are valuable items of the Shetland dialect. A pithy Shetlandic saying *Ta ride ipo a sweerie horse* means, "To arrive late." Another, *A sweerie dug is shun appered*, is "An unwilling (or lazy) person is easily put off." Saying farewell to a guest one says, *Blissin' be wi' ye!* The other responds, *An' so be wi' ye*, or *An' so be dat!* This is said to be a survival from Catholic days. The priest at the end of Mass says: *Dominus vobis cum!* ("God be with you!"), and the congregation responds, *Et cum spiritu tuo!* ("And with your spirit!") This is similar to "An' so be wi' dee!" Other phrases used in the islands are *Guid be aboot me!* and *Guid saefe dee!* The first is generally said in surprised tones, the second when someone choked. *Guid sit i' da haands* (North Isles, *haunds*) *dat* . . . is a thanks-offering for some gift, or receipt of good news. *Whin* (or *Whan*) *Guid's time comes* is an allusion to the allotted span of life. A phrase very common in Eshaness, Northmavine, is : *Mosst michty blyde ta see dee, böy!* This is : "Most mighty glad to see you, boy!" *Gjittin dee kail* (North Isles, *keel*) *troo* (in some parts *trow*) *da reek!* is an expressive Shetlandic phrase meaning someone is in for a most fearful scolding. *A peerie start* is a "short period of time." *Waap* is a word meaning to "throw" out (or in), an older form is *oot-waap* (or *in-waap*, or *doon-waap*). *Oot-wale'ins* means anything that's left in a heap, or anywhere, after the best of it has been *wale'd* or selected. The German word for "elect" or "vote" is *wäle*.

"*So, dey wir nae mair a yun sam, bit didna shu geng ida kjist-njeuk ben, an purrl fir twa störs shu hedd wuppit ida njeuk a ir sylk hanky, an dan, feth, ee wan a ir wid be plaesd fir shu kam an ledd dem i' me luif!*"

This put into English would read something like: "So, there was nothing more of that; but she went into the ben-room and searched in the chest-corner for some coins she had tied in the corner of a silk handkerchief, and then, faith, she wouldn't be pleased until she came and laid them in my palm!"

"*Hit wis bün him a boannie day, wi' da sun sheenin da lovvlie, an wi' da waarm* (North Isles, *waurm*) *pirr frae da wast doon aff a da Björgs. We wir awa sooth-be it da paets, raisin. Hit was aafil lovvlie wadder, yah, odious praetty, an dey wir a braa* (North Isles, *braw*) *lokk a fokk ida hill. Dey wir a aald* (North Isles, *auld*) *wife dere wi'r kishie.* (In some districts, *keeshie.*) *Shu wis koosin up peerie roogs a paets, da bruckit klodds, mould* (in some districts, *moold*) *an a'* (North Isles, *aw*). *Da stack wis kovvrd wi' faels* (North Isles, *feels*) *an dey wir sum yows dere ruitin among da lowse faels. Da aald body hedd biggid da stack at da bank da year afore, shu taald* (North Isles, *tauld*) *wis* (West Side, *is*). *Da burds wir singin ida lift. Hit wis lightsome hearin apo dem. Dey wir haarly* (North Isles, *haurly*) *onny burn wi' da drout he wis bün. Dey wir sum moorit tings a yows awa aest ower on da moor* (or *mör*) *da laams* (West Side, *lamms*) *wis yaarmin* (North Isles, *yaurmin*) *an friskin aboot dir midders. Da peerie yalloo flooirs wis growin a' wye, aafil* (North Isles, *awfil*) *boannie ta see among da heddir-kows. Da maas* (North Isles, *maws*) *wis aye fleein aboot near da banks whaar da fokk wis sitting takkin an aer* (Whalsay, *ire*) *a tay* (Whalsay, *tye*). *Da blue reek frae da lowin taands* (North

Isles, *taunds*) *lay ida daal* (North Isles, *dawl*), *haarly movvin a pjaa fir da wind wis naethin.*"

The above is something as follows: "It had been a bonnie day, with the sun shining lovely, and with the warm breath of wind from the west down off the Björgs (hills). We were away south at the peats, raising (setting up wet peats on their ends to dry). It was very lovely weather, yes, very pretty, and there was a lot of folk (or people) in the hill. There was an old woman there with her kishie (straw-basket). She was building up (or throwing up) small heaps of peats, the small broken clods, loose moor and all. The peat-stack was covered with bits (usually rough squares) of dried turf, and there were some yows (ewes) there eating and scraping among the loose bits of turf lying about. The old wife had built the stack at the bank (run of peat-moor) the previous year, she told us. The birds were singing in the sky. It was lightsome (cheery) hearing them. There was hardly any burn running, with the time of drought it had been. There were some moorit (moor-red, a sort of brownish-red) things of ewes away east over on the moor, the lambs were bleating and frolicking around their mothers. The small yellow flowers (celandine) were growing everywhere, very bonnie to see among the heather-clumps. The seagulls were always flying about near the banks where the people were sitting drinking some tea. The blue smoke from the burning brands (peats) lay in the valley, hardly moving a breath for the wind was nothing to speak of."

The best-known Shetland authors are J. J. Haldane Burgess and George Stewart. Others who have written stories and poems are L. J. Nicolson, Robert Sinclair, Basil R. Anderson, James S. Angus, James Inkster, T. P. Ollason, John Nicolson, W. A. S. Burgess and W. Fordyce Clark. With the exception of John Nicolson and W. Fordyce Clark, still alive and writing, all those authors belonged to the period from about 1870 to 1930.

Robert Sinclair, an Aithsting man, wrote *Da Tief i' da*

Neean, a story based on a folk-tradition of an outlaw who lived in a large cave at Neean's Neap, a cliff at West Burrafirth. This was serialised in the *Shetland Times* in 1879. The story reveals Sinclair as a considerable writer, and its wealth of Shetlandic words and terms makes it a valuable piece of writing. Indeed, it attracted Jakobsen when he began his researches, and in his *Fragments of Norn* he reprints an incantation from the story. It seems strange that such a story, whatever faults in construction it may have, with its authentic local colour, words and traditions, should not have been reprinted right away in book form.

Two years before, in 1877, George Stewart published his *Shetland Fireside Tales* in Edinburgh. It had a ready sale, on account of its true-to-life story and the wealth of folk-lore, legends, poetry, traditions it contains. The dialect in the *Tales* is well handled, and contains many words and turns of speech peculiar to Dunrossness, Stewart's native parish.

The *Fireside Tales* contain perhaps the most complete narrative of many aspects of Shetland crofting and fishing life and work, with descriptions of the people's amusements, songs, tales, superstitions and beliefs ever written. The book helped to whet Jakobsen's desire to make a thorough study of the island Norn. The ballads in the *Tales* are Stewart's own work, but they are based on the old ballad form and are fine examples of such poems as were popular among Shetlanders before the days of newspapers and wireless. The ballad, or "fugitive" rhyme, was the "broadsheet" or newspaper of the time. Every event seeming to have any significance in the eyes of the people—as a shipwreck, storm, haaf incident, peculiar custom, noted people, heavy snowfall, appearance of big schools of whales, a house on fire, and the rest—was made the subject of a "rhyme" or "ballant," the "makkar" or rhymester usually wandering from house to house reciting his "story." As most folk had retentive memories, the ballads and tales were "minded upon" and recited around the firesides during the long evenings, or outside at some work where a lot of folk were gathered, as on a fish beach, in a haaf lodge, at a sheep-kru. In this way the material was handed on, often with additions and alterations as people added or adapted to suit their fancy. Stewart's ballads were among the first of the local "rhymesters'" (and each neighbourhood had its rhymester) work to be written down and presented in a literary form. Most of the work of those strolling makkars and "sagamen" has been lost, or survives only as mere fragments in the memories of old folk. A rhymester from Lunnasting, in the north-eastern Mainland, was Sinclair Irvine. Soon after the wreck of the S.S. *Pacific*, of Liverpool, on an island near Whalsay in 1871, Irvine "made" the ballad the *Pacific of Liverpool*. He composed other rhymes, as *Da Foy, Bonnie Hoose o' Vidlin, Kirstie Wattie*, and others.

Laurence J. Nicolson's work is all in the form of songs and poems, most of which have been collected and published in the book *Songs of Thule*. Some of his poems, as *A Lullaby* and *Da Last Noost*, have been set to music. Nicolson won the proud title of the "Bard of Thule," being acknowledged by his countrymen as their "Poet Laureate."

After his death his place in the realm of Shetland letters was taken by Haldane Burgess. Burgess's poems and stories became well known far outside of Shetland. He was equally at home in the dialect and in English, his dialect poems, as *Scranna, Benkled Tinnie*, and others being hailed as among the best of their kind. His best-known book of poems is *Rasmie's Büddie*. This contains the long poem *Scranna*, a description of "Rasmie," a typical islander, having a severe tussle with "da Black sheeld," or the Devil. It is full of the quiet, humorous, philosophical way of facing up to problems, characteristic of the Shetland crofting and seafaring folk.

After trying everything he can think about to overcome Rasmie's spirit and lead him to the darkness of despair, the evil one is finally vanquished. The strength of the stoical northern spirit triumphs, and although the wind moans "oorily ower da stubbly rigs" and "duns" eerily in the chimney, Rasmie sits calmly contemplating the rout of his enemy, who gathers his tail about him and slinks hurriedly "oot ower da yard-daek o' Scranna."

Burgess's best-known stories are *Tang: a Shetland Story*; *The Viking Path: a Tale of the White Christ*; *Some Shetland Folk*; *Shetland Sketches*; *The Treasure of Don Andreas*, and *Rasmie's Smaa Murr*. A scholar of northern literature, history and languages, Haldane Burgess was well known in scholarly circles in Scandinavian countries. His article *Yule in Shetland*, written in the *Laandsmaall*, and published in the magazine *Norsk Jöl*, attracted a great deal of attention as the work of an outstanding scholar. The Bergen and Oslo newspapers reported his death in January 1927, with regret, one having a long editorial tribute to his learning, literary and cultural work. Burgess was Shetland's "Poet Laureate" from the death of L. J. Nicolson, and his *Up-Helly-Aa Song* has been called Shetland's "National Anthem."

Basil Ramsay Anderson, a young man from Unst, wrote a number of fine poems in the dialect, the best of which are *Comin' frae da Hill*, and *Auld Maunsie's Crü*. This last poem is generally held to be one of the best poems ever written in the Shetlandic. It, together with *Comin' frae da Hill*, gives vivid glimpses of many phases of life and work in the crofting districts, in well-written verses revealing the born poet and a master of the dialect. After Anderson's death his poems and some letters were collected by Jessie M. E. Saxby and Gilbert Goudie and published in the book with the peculiar title *Broken Lights*. Anderson left home as a boy to take up a situation in Edinburgh, where he met in with George Stewart, L. J. Nicolson, Gilbert Goudie and other northern poets and writers. His premature death robbed Shetland of one of her finest writers.

James Inkster wrote the book *Mansie's Röd*, revealing a great knowledge of the dialect combined with rare literary skill. The dialect of "da Röd" is widely held to be one of the best examples of written Shetlandic to be published. T. P. Ollason brought out his sketches and stories, mostly of Lerwick life, in *Mareel* and *Spindrift*. James Angus, a ship's carpenter, proved to be a worthy rival to Nicolson, Burgess and Anderson in the field of Shetland poetry and the equal of Inkster in his handling of the folk-speech. Angus's *Glossary of the Shetland Dialect* is a fine study of the folk-speech, and his *Echoes from Klingrahool* is one of the best Shetland books. W. A. S. Burgess, Haldane Burgess's brother, wrote numerous sketches, the best of which were published in *Hinniwirs*. John Nicolson's best-known works are *Arthur Anderson: A Founder of the P. & O. Company*; *Shetlan' Hamespun*; *Folk-Tales and Legends of Shetland*, and *Restin' Chair Yarns*.

Writers of a younger generation are William Sandison, whose *A Shetland Merchant's Day-Book in 1762* is a finely written piece of original historical research all too rarely met with in northern literature. John Peterson wrote *Roads and Ditches* and *Streets and Starlight*. D. H. Sandison, Hugh Sutherland, Stella Smith and Tom Henderson are other young writers and poets of promise. Other younger writers are grouped in the movement associated with the Shetland poetical circle and the proposed Shetlandic Wordbook.

To the questions whether the dialect can be used for serious creative work, or whether Shetland writers should concentrate on English as their best medium, and will there be a re-awakening of the creative Shetland spirit leading to the making of poems and stories and plays of more than ephemeral value, answers are hard to find.

That the dialect is a splendid medium of expression and should be fostered is seen from Stewart's, Sinclair's, Anderson's, Angus's, and Burgess's writings, as well as the work of the younger writers. The profound economic, social and political stirrings of modern times are bound to have an effect on creative thought in the islands as elsewhere. Shetland in the past has produced notable writers, and there is little doubt that while there are people living, working and thinking in Shetland, there will also be seen a reflection of all this striving in the field of literature. In the main this will depend on the willingness and ability of the islanders in setting their economic and political life in order, co-operating with the general progressive movements in the British mainland as well as in the Scandinavian countries.

R

CHAPTER XVIII

THE query "What could be done to bring about a higher standard of living in the islands?" is important, and some of your suggestions are interesting.

As society is at present constituted, nothing much need be looked for by the mass of the ordinary people. The small landed and moneyed class is well enough off. Unless for minor readjustments here and there, its members do not seek to alter things. While it can be said that nothing short of a fundamental change in society, namely, from capitalism and decay to Socialism and life, will bring back prosperity and happiness to the Shetland islanders, at the same time, given a progressive government, such as we now have, a programme could be drawn up and enforced which would lead to an all-round social and cultural advance.

The Labour Government is going to help the outlying communities, like Shetland, and it is up to the Shetland people to co-operate with the people's government to get things done.

In the past, the natural resources of the islands have sustained almost double the present population without any organised methods being applied. With planning and the aid of all the marvels of science, the natural resources of land and sea could be made to expand rapidly. Shetland could be a well-off community, with industries and commerce developing daily, forming the basis of a cultured life for 50,000 or even 100,000 people. Shetlanders abroad, seeing prosperity coming to their old homeland, would have heart to satisfy their longing to come back to the islands, bringing with them experience and initiative, finding scope under the new conditions prevailing. If the moneyed interests seemed hostile to the innovations, the government would not let the selfish interests of a handful stand in the way of a better life for the many.

The programme adopted by the Shetland Labour Party in 1944, for the development of the crofting and fishing industries, as outlined in the pamphlet *Crofting and Fishing*, is in line with the spirit of the times. If adopted by the Shetland people and applied, this plan would soon raise the economic and cultural level in the islands.

With the permission of the Shetland Labour Party, this programme is included here as the final letter in this series.

The programme is in two parts, the first one dealing with Agriculture. It begins with general remarks. While recognising that in Shetland, as elsewhere, a full solution of agricultural and other problems is contingent upon the adoption of the policy of National Ownership of the Land, the Shetland Labour Party believe that the short-term programme here outlined, in conjunction with the rest of Labour's plan for Shetland, can ensure a reasonable measure of prosperity and decent living conditions in rural Shetland, and thus arrest the depopulation which threatens the future of the Islands.

It has been estimated that a minimum holding of 12 acres arable is necessary for full subsistence. In Shetland there are, according to the latest statistics, 3464 holdings of under 50 acres, including outrun and hill pasture, and these have an average of about $5\frac{1}{2}$ acres arable. It is *not* the policy of the Shetland Labour Party to make all holdings "economic," in the sense of "able to provide subsistence," as this would inevitably and disastrously lead to further rural depopulation. Consequently, we urge that where a holding becomes vacant, it shall not be given as an enlargement of holding, if there is any other applicant prepared to reside in the house and work the land. To ensure that a suitable tenant is secured, the control of setting of vacant crofts should be vested in the County Agricultural Committee, and these crofts should be set at the rent paid by the former tenant, compensation, if any, to be assessed by the Committee. Wherever enlargement of holdings can be granted without infringing this principle, they should be made, and any new holdings created should be designed to provide full subsistence.

Wherever there is cultivable land at present used for stock raising, and where a demand exists for new holdings or enlargements of existing holdings, this land should be bought by the Department of Agriculture and broken up into holdings of not less than 30 acres, including 10 to 12 acres arable, or given as enlargements to bring existing holdings up to this standard. Surveying, allocation and supervision of this land should be undertaken by the County Agricultural Committee.

A first perquisite for the introduction of scientific tilling and improvement of soil fertility is the adoption of closed drainage for all arable land. Surveying and planning should be in the hands of the Agricultural Committee, work to be carried out by or on behalf of the tenant, who should receive a grant of 75 per cent. of the cost, including labour costs.

Maximum soil fertility should be obtained by schemes for proper rotation of crops, balanced manurial schemes, plus adequate liming, to be prepared and supervised by the Agricultural Committee. A much greater degree of mechanisation is necessary if Shetland agriculture is to be advantageously developed. For this purpose, tractor ploughs, cultivators and reapers would be acquired by the Shetland Rural Development Society. Regional grouping of crofts and allocation of these implements will be the affair of the Agricultural Committee and its district sub-committees. Mid-season cultivation and other essential farm work obviously will be handicapped, unless there are a certain number of horses available in each district. It would be the affair of the Committee to see to this, and to work out a scheme whereby either horses are owned by the Society and left in the care of certain tenants who are suitably recompensed, or it is made advantageous to certain crofters to own and maintain a horse or horses for district use. All problems of local allocation would be decided by the district sub-committees.

Existing scattalds should be enlarged wherever possible by the inclusion of outlying islands and presently enclosed sheep runs unsuitable for breaking up into smallholdings.

A more equitable division of hill scattalds and removal of local anomalies in scattald rights are necessary, and would necessitate a review of all decisions of the Scottish Land Court on the point.

Planned schemes of drainage should be introduced where practicable, particularly to eliminate and reclaim dangerous bogs. Where practicable and profitable, schemes for the eradication of rank heather, application of lime and manure, and, in certain areas, re-seeding with hardy, hill grasses, should be embarked upon. The Agricultural Committee, in conjunction with the Department of Agriculture, should conduct experiments, such as are at present being carried out in the Western Isles and elsewhere, in the conversion of suitable tracks of peat into arable land with a view to establishing new smallholdings. Further proposals are included under the next heading.

CATTLE.—Three main types of cattle are required in Shetland: dairy cattle for the dairy farms, a dual-purpose type for the average croft, and the "Shetland" type for certain areas where the grazing is of poor quality. Sires of milk-producing strain, of a beef-producing strain, of dual-purpose types, and of the "Shetland" type should all be recognised and allocated in the best possible manner to meet local requirements. All sires should be of a recognised standard or pedigree. Tuberculin-testing should be made compulsory for all cattle in the Islands and for all imported cattle.

SHEEP.—Two types of sheep are required in Shetland: (a) the pure Shetland breed whose wool is essential to the major local industry, and (*b*) cross Shetland sheep which can be maintained on better pasture. To maintain the quality of Shetland wool, it is essential that the pure Shetland sheep be segregated and maintained on the pastures unsuitable for the hardier breeds. This would make possible the improvement of the existing breeds under scientific supervision. Pure-bred tups of the most suitable popular breeds should be available for those crofters desiring to specialise in mutton production, and these tups should be held and controlled at recognised centres.

Poultry farming, with breeding and feeding on scientific lines, should be developed to the largest possible extent in Shetland.

Market gardening should be encouraged and developed so as to supply the bulk of local requirements of vegetables during the greater part of the year.

A Shetland Rural Development Society should be constituted on co-operative lines, registered under the Provident and Industrial Societies Acts as a Limited Company, and affiliated to the Scottish Agricultural Organisation Society. It would act as a protective and marketing organisation for crofters and others engaged in agriculture in Shetland. Capital necessary to secure the achievement of its aims would be raised by every land-holder becoming a shareholder in the Society. A Committee of Management would be elected at an annual general meeting of shareholders, and would hold office for one year.

The Society would be responsible for the bulk purchase of all agricultural requirements, and the organisation of the sale of all agricultural produce and stock, including dairy produce, through local co-operative dairies. It would own and maintain transport for collection and distribution of members' goods. It would be the business of the Society to inaugurate and organise rural industries, such as Handloom Weaving, and to co-operate with the Shetland Hand Knitters' Association and such other rural industries as may be organised.

Instead of the present system of Regional College Control, a Central Advisory Scientific Committee under the Department of Agriculture for Scotland should maintain representatives qualified to act as scientific advisers to County Agricultural Committees. In Shetland, members of this Committee would be appointed by the Executive Committee of the Shetland Rural Development Society, and it would function through district sub-committees. Duties of the Agricultural Committee are detailed under the appropriate headings.

With regard to the vitally important question of Agricultural Education, the views of the Shetland Labour Party are summarised in the following recommendations:

(1) That the responsibility for Agricultural Education shall be in the hands of a specialist member of the Education Committee staff.

(2) That the teaching of Agriculture shall be extended in the County, and that Centres be established in suitable districts where pupils from surrounding areas may be taught the principles of agriculture.

(3) That a model smallholding shall be established under the direction of the Education Committee where pupils may gain a practical knowledge of their subject.

(4) That Young Farmers or Smallholders' Clubs shall be formed in each district.

(5) That the County Agricultural Committee and the Department representatives shall be empowered to give every possible assistance in the carrying out of these schemes.

All secondary roads should be upgraded to trunk road standard, and further provision of branch roads made to each holding. All inhabited islands should be provided with adequate piers and ferry services. Telephone communication should be extended to ensure that all outlying districts are provided with a public call-box.

A general survey of all present rural houses and steadings should be made to decide which are capable of improvement and which need to be replaced. In replacing houses, it should be ensured that the type of house is suited to the climate and location, and includes, so far as possible, all modern conveniences.

These recommendations apply equally to crofter and cottar houses. The Shetland Labour Party most strongly deprecate and will oppose the erection of any large number of cottar houses in rural areas unless (*a*) some local industry or occupation has been established, as in Whalsay and Burra, to provide a means of livelihood for the occupants, and (*b*) crofters' houses in the district have been brought up to the same standard. Unless these conditions are observed, the consequence of any such policy would be to aggravate the drift from the land, and the ultimate result would be further rural depopulation and waste of public money.

While welcoming the steps proposed by the Youth Advisory Council to provide cultural, social and recreational amenities in rural districts, we would urge the executive bodies to bear strongly in mind the needs of the adult community. The provision of these amenities and facilities and the implementing of the proposals in this report are complementary; without the former, all measures to ensure rural prosperity would fail to prevent some degree of rural depopulation; without the latter, there may soon be few left to whom these amenities could be provided.

The Party's Fishing Industry programme is equally comprehensive and far-reaching. It reads: While holding that nothing short of national ownership of the fishing industry can bring it back to full prosperity, the Shetland Labour Party believe that the adoption of the immediate programme herewith outlined can do much to revive the industry and increase the population and the real wealth of the Islands generally.

We propose that the present three-mile limit, within which trawling is prohibited, be extended to twelve miles. For this purpose Shetland should be, contained within a diamond, the twelve miles to be drawn from the four points—Unst, Foula, Skerries, and Fair Isle.

In order to provide adequate protection against poaching, three fast motor vessels should be stationed in Shetland at suitable ports; this protection to be reinforced, if necessary, by an air patrol.

As an additional deterrent, the penalty for infringing the fishing limit should be: for the first offence (*a*) confiscation of gear and catch, (*b*) a fine of £500, payable by the owners of the trawler, (*c*) suspension of the master's ticket for one year. For the second offence the penalties would be the same, but the master's ticket would be cancelled.

In view of the increasing scope afforded to the large line and seine-net fishing boats by a twelve-mile trawling limit, crofters' home fishing grounds—to be delimited by a commission representing crofters, fishermen and the Fishery Board—should be protected against any form of seine-netting.

We would urge that both the Shetland white fishing and the herring industry should be organised as a Producers' Co-operative, and receive an initial subsidy from the Government. A Development Board should be set up to organise the industry on co-operative lines and to obtain, with Government assistance, suitable dual-purpose type fishing vessels, which could be used for both white and herring fishing.

The Producers' Co-operative would work in harmony with large co-operative concerns, such as the Scottish

Co-operative Wholesale Society, in order that the whole catch could be marketed to the best advantage at a guaranteed price, and conveyed direct to the retail markets in the south by fast sea and air transport.

The Development Board and Co-operative should also explore the possibilities of reviving the Shetland dried salt fish industry, as there is likely to be a big post-war market for this commodity. Shetland took a leading place in this industry during the nineteenth century, and there seems no reason why it should not regain its old place in the markets for dried fish.

As outlined in our Agricultural programme, piers should be provided at convenient ports throughout the Islands for the needs of boats and the industry generally.

In Orkney the lobster fishing has greatly expanded during recent years. It is bringing in a large income to Orkney fishermen, and as there are numerous lobster grounds around the Shetland coast the industry should get every encouragement here. It could be developed by the Producers' Co-operative, by the provision of suitable craft and gear, and the securing of an advantageous market.

The Shetland Herring Fishing Industry has always been a great source of wealth; but in the past Shetlanders have not reaped the benefit from their toil at the nets. This can and should be altered. Steps should be taken to re-organise the industry on co-operative lines, preferably as already suggested, as part of a general Shetland Fishermen's Co-operative, since, with the dual-purpose boat, the same crews would generally also engage in the white fishing. As an interim measure, a system of loans to fishermen would need to be set on foot. This would enable fishermen to clear their boats of debt, help in the building of new boats of the most modern type, and in every way help men to surmount any difficulty that might arise.

There seems no reason to doubt that if the matter is

energetically taken up by the Government, extensive markets for salt-cured herring can be obtained in the Union of Socialist Soviet Republics and in the liberated countries. The British herring industry should have an unequalled chance to recapture Continental markets. A Development Board should be formed to reap these advantages. For this purpose we propose that the export and foreign marketing of salt-cured herring be undertaken solely and directly by a central Government authority set up for the purpose. This body would purchase all the salt-cured herring meant for export at an agreed price, fixing a fair profit for the curer and a reasonable minimum price to the fishermen. Among the numerous advantages of this would be the elimination of middlemen's oncost and of restrictive monopolist practices. In brief, it is proposed that, as an immediate step in the reorganising of the herring industry, foreign marketing would be nationalised, as has been done by the New Zealand Government in the case of agriculture produce with such marked success.

Kippering, freshing, canning and other treatment of herring could be greatly expanded and new markets secured if the finished product were served up to the consumer in a clean, attractive form. A great demand for kippers and red herring would ensue if the fish were properly graded and wrapped in grease-proof, sanitary containers. Fresh herring should also be hygienically treated, thus enlarging the market in this country. These matters would form another of the Co-operative Association's ventures, in addition to canning and brine-freezing of herring in establishments in Lerwick and Scalloway.

It is widely held that the spotting of herring shoals from the air was a very beneficial measure, as it saved fuel and time in steaming in search of fish. We urge that this aerial spotting be continued and developed by the use of aeroplanes based on Shetland.

As an essential part of this programme, the erection of

an ice and cold-storage plant, fish-meal and guano factory, and a box and barrel factory, should be gone on with. These plants and factories, with subsidiary concerns, should be located near the town and be owned and run by the Fishermen's Co-operative.

Provision should be made by the Co-operative for the building of suitable sheds for baiting lines, storing gear, mending nets and lines, etc., as near as possible to the fishermen's houses.

The reorganisation of the Shetland fishing industry on co-operative lines should make possible the payment of a guaranteed minimum wage as a first charge on the profits, and the instituting of a comprehensive insurance scheme to provide pensions for men disabled at sea and for dependants of men lost. It would also make provision for payment of wages to men kept ashore by prolonged bad weather or other causes where they are not covered by unemployment insurance.

We believe Shetland to be the best possible base for White Sea trawlers, owing to its geographical position. It is the most northerly base which could be established in Britain, and one with excellent harbour accommodation. Facilities for the rapid transhipment of catches to carriers which would take the fish to mainland ports could very soon be provided in Shetland's many fine havens. Considerable steaming would be saved to the trawlers. This again would enable them to stay longer on the fishing grounds. Social conditions in the Islands would be improved and the population tend to rise if Shetland men saw some alternative means of earning a living other than "sailing" in the ships of the Merchant Navy.

An all-the-year-round trawling industry, centred on Shetland, would provide this alternative, and many of Shetland's three thousand merchant seamen, if offered this assured means of earning a livelihood near their homes, would give it a trial.

It is not suggested that this trawling should be done in the Shetland haaf, nor in the North Sea, but in the far northern waters. Trawling in itself is not harmful if properly controlled. Naturally enough, with the depredations caused by illegal trawling around our shores, a deep-rooted prejudice against trawling is universal in Shetland. This, however, is breaking down. Fishermen here are more ready to work with nets and trawls. Seine-netting is more popular. Shetlanders, if they want to move with the times and take advantage of any scheme that is likely to benefit the Islands, should seriously consider this aspect of things.

A Shetland Co-operative trawling concern should be set up to control this new industry. It would be a people's enterprise, clear of big vested interests in the trawling, shipbuilding and associated concerns. The fleet should number, say, one hundred trawlers to begin with. This number of vessels should be transferred from the fleet of large fast trawlers on Government service, on generous loan terms to give the venture a good start. Fast sea and air transports would be able to ply between Lerwick and the markets on the mainland, carrying the catches. These vessels would carry back coal, oil, and other requirements. A Fishery Development Board would be necessary to get this scheme going, this Board to negotiate a long-term loan, etc., in the initial stages.

Immediate harbour improvements should begin with the building of a continuous quay from the north end of the Fish Mart to the point of Victoria Pier. The quay should be of solid concrete face and provided with at least two mobile electric cranes. Any scheme to lengthen and widen Victoria Pier is calculated to benefit one shipping company only. A plan of much bolder dimensions must be provided in the interests of the whole people. The contention that such a quay as we propose would be exposed to weather does not bear much weight, as only very rarely does a south-easterly wind set in sufficient sea to make things disagreeable for any large craft berthed alongside.

The principle of one pier in Lerwick stands condemned. One pier gets cluttered up with ships all round it, and generally these all belong to one concern. What is needed is a long quay face that can berth six or eight ships of sizable tonnage in a line. This would give a chance to the S.C.W.S. ships, or ships of any other company, to run to Shetland. With the adoption of the scheme, wharfage would be provided for the shipment of all herring, etc., from the quay. Somewhere in the north harbour a proper coaling berth should be built so that trawlers and drifters could coal with steamers alongside. A proper dock in the north harbour for line-fishing boats is long overdue. The Harbour Trust should obtain powers to buy out, or take over, one or other of the existing docks, and enlarge and improve it for the use of line-men.

A bigger breakwater is required in the south harbour. This should extend from the Deuk's Neb, at the South End, to Victoria Pier, the present breakwater to be demolished. The Fish Mart should be demolished. This would leave plenty of space for loading and discharging facilities. Slipways and dry-docking facilities at convenient places along the north harbour shore should be built. A shipbuilding yard will become necessary, and should be built either at Gremista or on the Bressay side. Engineering shops, electric plant, repair workshops, coal depots, oil storage facilities, a ropery and net factory, saw-mill and other enterprises will be required to service the new fishing and shipping industries. All these should belong to a Shetland People's Co-operative Society.

INDEX